The City of Man

NEW FRENCH THOUGHT

SERIES EDITORS
Thomas Pavel and Mark Lilla

TITLES IN THE SERIES

Mark Lilla, ed., *New French Thought: Political Philosophy*

Gilles Lipovetsky, *The Empire of Fashion: Dressing Modern Democracy*

Pierre Manent, *An Intellectual History of Liberalism*

Jacques Bouveresse, *Wittgenstein Reads Freud: The Myth of the Unconscious*

Blandine Kriegel, *The State and the Rule of Law*

Alain Renault, *The Era of the Individual: A Contribution to a History of Subjectivity*

Marcel Gauchet, *The Disenchantment of the World: A Political History of Religion*

Pierre Manent, *The City of Man*

Marcel Gauchet and Gladys Swain, *Madness and Democracy: The Modern Psychiatric Universe*

Pierre Rosanvallon, *The New Social Question: Rethinking the Welfare State*

Jean-Marie Schaeffer, *Art of the Modern Age: Philosophy of Art from Kant to Heidegger*

Pierre Manent

The City of Man

Translated by Marc A. LePain

With a Foreword by Jean Bethke Elshtain

 NEW FRENCH THOUGHT

PRINCETON UNIVERSITY PRESS · PRINCETON, NEW JERSEY

Copyright © 1998 by Princeton University Press
Published by Princeton University Press, 41 William Street,
Princeton, New Jersey 08540
In the United Kingdom: Princeton University Press, Chichester, West Sussex

Translated from the French edition of Pierre Manent, *La cité de l'homme*
(©Librairie Arthème Fayard, 1994)

Fourth printing, and first paperback printing, 2000
Paperback ISBN 0-691-05025-2

The Library of Congress has cataloged the cloth edition of this book as follows

---

Manent, Pierre.
[Cité de l'homme. English]
The city of man / Pierre Manent ; translated by Marc A. LePain ;
with a foreword by Jean Bethke Elshtain.
p. cm. — (New French Thought)
Includes bibliographical references and index.
ISBN 0-691-01144-3 (cloth : alk. paper)
1. Philosophical anthropology. 2. Civilization—Philosophy.
I. Title. II. Series.
BD450.M267713 1998
128—dc21 97-42953

Published with the assistance of the French Ministry of Culture

This book has been composed in Adobe Bauer Bodoni

The paper used in this publication meets the minimum requirements of
ANSI/NISO Z39.48-1992 (R1997) (*Permanence of Paper*)

http://pup.princeton.edu

Printed in the United States of America

10 9 8 7 6 5

ISBN-13: 978-0-691-05025-6 (pbk.)

Contents

THIS CHALLENGING WORK defies current categories. It belongs to no school. But it displays in abundance Pierre Manent's gifts as an interpreter of the Western philosophical and political tradition. Or, perhaps, one should say "traditions." For, as Manent demonstrates, the Western tradition is a many-sided affair. He is primarily concerned with what might be called a history of the present, a present that is always a presence: that which is before us; that which has been deeded to us; that which we remember and that which we forget but forget in a way that carries forward what we believe we have left behind. Thus, today's modern man "flees the law given to him by nature, by God, or that he gave himself yesterday and that today weighs on him like the law of another. He seeks the law he gives himself and without which he would be but the plaything of nature, of God, or of his own past. The law he seeks ceaselessly and continually becomes the law he flees. In flight and in pursuit, with the difference of the two laws always before him, modern man proceeds in this way to the continual creation of what he calls History."

We are, then, burdened in ways we cannot acknowledge. For acknowledgment would be tantamount to admitting that we are neither so free nor so sovereign as we claim; indeed, as we require, given that we are modern men and women. And one of the chief aims of modernity was to unburden us. What were we to be released from? From our own natures, for one thing. Manent claims that at present we are "obsessed with man and everywhere today people talk about man." But we simultaneously deny that there is any such thing as a *nature* to that creature we call man or the person. A prime characteristic of "modern man," who is without a nature, is his or her "self-consciousness." But conscious of what? Not of a nature: that we have abandoned. So, beginning with the seventeenth century in England and France, Manent's story goes, we played out a tug of war between the ancient world of virtue and the modern world of commerce and liberty. Commerce and liberty won.

Montesquieu is key here—and Manent is a gifted reader of Montesquieu—for the "primary intent of *The Spirit of the Laws* is . . . to weaken decisively the authority of the Ancients, of the idea of the 'best regime,' the idea of virtue, in order to replace it with the authority of the present moment, of the modern experience, summed up in the notions of 'commerce' and 'liberty.'" This new regime, this Age of Enlightenment, is most often remembered as the apogee of both "Reason" and "Nature." Provocatively, Manent insists that the "Age of Enlightenment deals a decisive deathblow" to both. For "its active principle, its sovereign notion, is neither Reason nor Nature, but the present moment.'" Having climbed aboard that merry-go-round, we cannot get off. The present can only be justified in terms of itself. But the moment we proffer justification, that moment itself is past; hence, delegitimation lurks in the wings. So we reaffirm our sovereignty and proclaim the moment of the definitive present all over again. This can never stop. For were we to pause, catch our breaths, and begin once again to remember what we have forgotten, we would no longer be modern. We would be borne back into the past in some way. We would be forced to abandon the modern anthem and to recall ancient themes.

This is not so obscure as it may here sound and as the reader will discover as he or she works through this complex and erudite text. There are many riches to discover and to uncover along the way. Take, for example, Manent's discussion of virtue. He argues that virtue "was one of those ideas of political and moral philosophy that assured communication between Greek and Roman philosophy on the one hand and Christianity on the other." The two traditions differed on virtue, of course, but they held some notion of virtue or the virtues in common and could at least engage one another. But once the language of virtue is lost, or transformed radically to refer not to the general or to what is "in common" but to a principle of singularity and particularity exclusively, communication-across-virtue, so to speak, becomes difficult if not impossible. The danger and seduction of incommensurability looms.

The vast changes on the level of thought assayed by Manent have institutional embodiments or moments. The city-state was the home of classical and republican virtue and it gives way before the onslaught of modern sovereignty. The city as the locus of civic life is denuded. Similarly, Luther's reforms "disarmed religion in the face of temporal power." Henceforth the two kingdoms would be driven apart in a way that made it more difficult for some alternative power to challenge the emergent and triumphant power of centralizing monarchies and sovereignties. Virtue itself falls into bad odor as just a way to talk about and to extol "unnatural obedience to a repressive rule"—here Montesquieu. The emergence of the modern state, then, with the extraordinary presuppositions of sovereign power, necessity, and willing that accompany it, is unthinkable "and could not come about apart from the polemical relation it has simultaneously with the Greek city and civic life on the one hand and the church and Christian religion on the other." Here I wish Manent had spent a bit more time on the titanic struggle between the symbolism of the two Romes—the imperial city and the site of what he calls "the invisible empire," with its vicar, the *servus servorum Dei*, the servant of the servants of God. But he promises us at the end of this volume that he will turn in future to a study of the "separation of the two Romes." For now we must rest content with the fact that he at least recognizes that there are portentous issues here imbedded, issues ignored systematically, for the most part, in modern political theory.

Manent evaluates the gulf that separates ancient and modern in a second way. He argues that classical political thought—and this includes the Middle Ages—took its bearing "from the *viewpoint of the actor*, the citizen or statesman," but modern man and woman, as constructed from the viewpoints of sociology and economics, respectively, embraces "the *viewpoint of the spectator*." This is presumed to be the more "scientific" approach, and it is one that "accords no real initiative whatever to the agent or agents, but considers their actions or their works as the necessary effect of necessary causes." Another paradox, then. We proclaim our sovereignty as a form of restless presentism. But we embrace modes of analysis, indeed entire *Weltanschauungen*, that reduce us to entities caught like flies in the spider's web of social and economic forces. Our epistemology dictates, on one level, the radical particularity of each and every entity. But our "scientific procedure" grinds these particularities into mere "cases of general laws." Thus we have laws of history and laws of economic life and sociological laws and all the rest. But what is lost is politics and action. The human agent is ignored or depleted. Politics becomes mere foam on the surging tides of historic and social necessity.

Manent's discussion of sociological viewpoints and economic systems helps us to understand why he claims Reason, too, has been abandoned in modernity. For reason "must be eliminated by real human actions and concentrated in the scrutinizing gaze of the scholarly spectator. Thus the tissue of implicit common deliberation connecting every man to the men he seeks to understand has been torn." Yet another mini-sovereignty, so to speak, is created: that of the sovereign "spectator's viewpoint," a viewpoint "constitutive of social science." There is no rock-ribbed notion of humanity, no set of stubborn givens or a palpable there-ness to stay the scholar's hand. Humanity is just another "unknown 'X' subject to be determined by an indefinite number of sociological determinants" leaving the observer "sovereignly free to choose the point from which he will 'observe' this determination of the unknown by the sociological determinant."

What a contrast this is to seeing the human person as a political animal! You don't have to embrace the classical position *tout court* and to hold that a "man is truly a man only inasmuch as he is a citizen," to see what Sheldon Wolin years ago called the "sublimation of the political" at work in the triumph of functionalist sociology and econometrics. Politics loses any distinguishable and distinctive subject matter. So we get yet another fateful separation. The state is separated from society and church. Then the state is divided into a separation of powers. Churches become sects. Society is fragmented into "an indefinite number of 'groups.' From now on life will be lived in the 'age of separations.'" But Manent's analysis shows that this age of separations is also an age of agglomerations. There may be constitutional separation of powers on the level of the state but the state grows ever more powerful as power drains from the peripheries to the center. Society may be composed of many groups but society ingests politics, and politics—tending to that which we hold in common—oozes into a general sociological morass. We can no longer think politically.

At the same time, having abandoned a human nature, we move into the realm of speculation about universal psychological motivations or desires or needs. One answer we have come up with, an answer Manent associates with Adam Smith and the creation of *homo oeconomicus*, is that we are driven to better our condition, to restlessly, ceaselessly, "improve" ourselves. So, increasingly, society appears to us as "Economy writ large because it acts as a system of utility, labor, and value. In such a necessarily homogeneous system, where only equal values can be exchanged, there is no place for the power that necessarily introduces difference and inequality, first of all among the haves and have nots. Commercial society nurtures and contains the immanent utopia of a powerless society, a depoliticized city." In the very midst of this radical depoliticization, we are called upon to affirm ourselves. But just what self are we to affirm? If you push the sociological subject or economic man very far, you find yourself pushing on thin air, pushing into a kind of vacuum. As Gertrude Stein might say, there is no there there.

The great creators of liberal political thought, Hobbes and Locke first and foremost, enter the picture at this point but not as rescuers; rather, as thinkers who put the finishing touches on the potrait of Manent's "modern man." For Manent, each, in his own way, reaffirms and deepens the "general philosophical proposition that man as man is the arbitrary creator of his laws and moral notions"—even, remember, as this same creature is subject to meta-laws of sociological, economic, and historic necessity. After all, the "genesis of the legitimate political order from the starting point of the solitary individual obeys a strict necessity" of its own. Rights, our trimphant form of discourse in modernity, are on pretty shaky ground, argues Manent, unless there is some ontological terrain on which to locate these rights. But that is precisely what the philosophers of "modern man" cannot allow. You cannot simultaneously destroy ontological perspectives and then try to drive a pylon deep enough into ground you have excavated in order to sustain commitments to a regime of rights. Isn't that exactly what we have done or are trying to do, Manent in effect asks?

So we content ourselves with a tautology. "Man is the being that defines himself by the fact of having rights." This is pretty thin, Manent insists, for with an "unprecedented liberation of man," we have also freed this modern person from that which alone could secure his freedom and make sturdy her liberty: we have made the modern person a creature "now impenetrable to Being." Thus "severed from being, the notion of human rights by itself lacks ontological density." So we embrace that which we will be unable to sustain over time given what we have rejected. This, Manent concludes, is our dilemma. But we refuse to recognize it as such because to do so would be to challenge the presuppositions of our own sovereignty and the sovereignty of the forces at work in, around, and through us. That his penultimate chapter bears the title, at once menacing and exulting, "The Triumph of the Will," comes as no surprise at this juncture in his work. A rich discussion examining the difference between willing and authentic choosing caps off this rich and difficult work—difficult not because Manent writes in an obscure manner—he does not—but because if we take him seriously we are forced to confront presuppositions we prefer to cherish. In "giving birth" to ourselves, we have abandoned that which alone can nurture and sustain us. This is Pierre Manent's mordant message.

Jean Bethke Elshtain

The City of Man

To the memory of Allan Bloom

A combination and a form indeed,
Where every god did seem to set his seal,
To give the world assurance of a man.

The Question of Man

O profondeurs! faut-il encore l'appeler l'homme?

VICTOR HUGO, *La Légende des siècles*

I

WHAT DO WE REALLY MEAN when we use the word *man* today? Whom are we speaking of when we defend human rights or engage in the human sciences? Not only do we lack a clear answer to this question, we do not even know how to go about asking it. Our speech is obsessed with man and sings his praises without inquiring who he is. A few perhaps hope to unlock the mystery, but how?

The guidance once provided by ancient authorities is no longer available. Of course, people rejoice that the democratic regime leaves man free to think about himself as he wishes and they even respect religion's claim to teach man his destiny. But they see that philosophy itself, in its most forceful or influential forms, basically has turned its back on the question. Man commands humanity's attention everywhere today, yet never perhaps since the time of Homer has the question embodied in the word *man* been so little explored.

A situation such as this offers fertile ground for two temptations, one rash, the other cowardly. We would be foolish to be taken in by the apparent simplicity of the question about man and with inflated confidence in our abilities to know. But we would not be any less misled in being intimidated by a subject so close to us that we turn back simply to the history of ideas. Addressing the question in the here and now may leave us prey to arbitrary prevailing opinions and the current state of knowledge, but placing our confidence in history only leads to endless investigation and constitutes refusal to face the question honestly. Since recourse and indifference to history are equally fatal, the right path is indeed straight and narrow.

Perhaps this first step is closed to us because it is already behind us. The fact is that with the word *man* goes the obligatory Homeric epithet *modern*. We would like to suppress the epithet, thinking we would go straight to the heart of the matter, but that would be wrong. *Modern man*, the sovereign acknowledged by history, the true King of kings and everyone's good friend, is our first guide to self-knowledge. We need first of all to ask what *modern man* is.

This suggestion puts us on our guard, however. We already are aware that in asking what modern man is, we have cut ourselves off from the prior question, what man is. How are we able to inquire into what we presuppose? Moreover, the first question loses its significance. But if man is man by the fact of being modern, then the question what man is no longer arises or no longer interests us. At least we would know what modern man is. Yet even that is not certain since we would always be in doubt as to whether modern man is in fact man. Common sense, of course, at this point rears its head, saying, "I know very well I am a man!"

Common sense always knows very well what it knows, including what a man is. Unfortunately, that has not stopped it from thinking or acting as if it believed that a "new man" was being constructed precisely when inhumanity reigned over a quarter of humanity. In the life of the mind it is not enough to pinch oneself in order to stay awake. The truth is that we have before us two questions that condition and cancel one another. One could say that it is necessary, and impossible, that being a man and being a modern man are one and the same thing.

II

Modern philosophy is founded on this impossibility. Its assertion of a radical difference between man and modern man distinguishes it from prior philosophy and perhaps from philosophy *tout court* that takes man as its horizon. For modern philosophy, modern man, who has grown out of the "immaturity" for which he himself was responsible,[1] defines himself by self-consciousness. The gap between man and modern man, between the absence and the presence of self-consciousness, is so great that it is strictly speaking impossible for modern philosophy to use the same word. In the past man defined himself as rational animal, according to his specific difference in terms of genus and species, but modern man determines himself in an altogether different way.[2] Man was commonly spoken of as "being this" or "being that" or simply "being," but modern man cannot be said "to be," with or without qualification. Modern philosophy rejected the words and phrases that were meaningful in classical philosophy and that are still used in everyday speech. It went so far as to reject explicitly the word *man* itself and to speak instead of self-consciousness, mind, the will to power, *pour-soi*, or *Dasein*. The modern philosophers had to invent a new vocabulary and rework and reinterpret the old one, since the tradi-

tional language of being, substance, genus and species failed to articulate
the difference.

III

In recent centuries everything has come to be qualified as "modern." Agriculture, art, devotion, industry, society—all have been given the epithet
that designates, and more often than not celebrates, the glorious difference
between modern and premodern life. Yet what do chair styles, mechanized
harvesting, and free mores have in common? To conclude that the adjective has lost all meaning, one would have to banish the obscure but irresistible feeling that makes us use the adjective and to understand it as
designating a necessary and even a central part of our experience. The fact
is that we know with certainty, or rather we sense instinctively and as it
were infallibly, what it is to be modern.

There is no one among us—not even the most reactionary and implaca-
ble enemy of the modern world—who does not experience the feeling or
consciousness of being modern and perceive it as a blessing. It may be seen
as a mixed blessing and the feeling we have of it can be more or less sweet
or bitter, but the feeling never leaves us. We feel superior to those who
came before us. This is not because we consider ourselves more intelligent
or more virtuous or in general more capable than they. We sincerely admire their abilities and virtues and willingly acknowledge our inferiority
as we stand before the Parthenon and Chartres cathedral. Yet even this
humbling experience does not erase the consciousness and secret delight of
our superiority as moderns. What more do we know, what more are we
than the men of Athens or Chartres? Only that we are modern and that we
know it.

We are modern, which means that we are "historical." The men of
Athens or Chartres may be greater or more creative and have greater aesthetic or religious sensibility, but they lack the feeling and consciousness
of being historical and of living in history which is proper to us and that
makes us moderns. Once a man has this feeling—and we all have it—he is
marked by it forever and he will always be glorious, however modest he
may be. The consciousness of being historical is the central and perhaps
also the strangest aspect of the modern experience. Modern philosophy is
convinced that the experience of history is the most profound and decisive
experience.[3]

In the pages that follow I shall study the paths modern philosophy took
to arrive at this conclusion. I shall examine more generally how the consciousness of being modern has modified the consciousness of being man
and whether it has increased or obscured our understanding of man. My

concern will be first to describe and then to evaluate the main aspects of the human phenomenon according to the modern difference. I shall consider in turn three elements each of modern self-consciousness and modern self-affirmation. The only validity such an account can have lies in its fidelity to the phenomenon itself. It belongs to the reader to attest to its validity and to judge for himself.

PART ONE

The Self-Consciousness

of Modern Man

CHAPTER 1

The Authority of History

THE INQUIRY we are about to engage in does not allow us to select our starting point. It does not leave us free to frame our "hypotheses" or to choose our "values." Only a historical inquiry in the most basic sense of the term can lead us to identify the moment and the context in which the historical point of view and the consciousness of being modern first came to light and were articulated. It will perhaps be said that before we take up this quest for an origin we must first work out the criteria for defining modernity, a project which is itself conditioned and determined by our "hypotheses" and "values." Such is not the case, however. To become modern is to become conscious of being modern and we are seeking the point at which this self-consciousness is formulated in explicit terms. Natural reason itself is both necessary and sufficient to identify this point, but methodological prostheses would only serve to compound our natural clumsiness. Moreover, there is little to fear by way of a challenge here. What we are seeking is precisely a massive historical fact, in the form of a general sentiment that is all the more interesting and revealing in that it is more general, less questionable and, as it were, unanimous. Who does not know and see and sense that being modern and being aware of being modern begin in the seventeenth century in England and France?

That it begins in France is clear enough. The quarrel of the Ancients and the Moderns emerges in France near the end of the seventeenth century. But however "modern" and "innovative" the administration of Louis XIV, the long reign of the great king clearly does not belong to "modernity." Joubert wisely set 1715 as the end of the ancient world, and we can indeed see ourselves as moderns in the years immediately following the death of Louis XIV. The Regency at last makes us feel at home, not so much because mores were free but because in a more general way we can see that at that moment in history the French, and the Europeans along with them left behind the ancient world once and for all. Not only do we who have the advantage of hindsight know this, but the more alert men of the time did as well. This capital fact makes itself felt, for example, in the swaggering tone of Voltaire. As early as 1721 Montesquieu published *The Persian Letters*, the book that signals with the greatest finesse the departure from the ancient world and the entrance into the new, and which is set just before and after the death of Louis XIV. But it is not until 1748 that Montesquieu develops fully the forms and nuances of the new consciousness. *The Spirit of the Laws* is the first major philosophical work to take becoming modern and living in history as its theme.

II

The movement of *The Spirit of the Laws* unfolds between the two poles of Ancient and Modern. The one is the ancient world of republican "virtue," the other is the England of "commerce" and "liberty." Between the ancient and the modern there is the present of the French monarchy. Besides what has been, what is, and what is emerging, there is also the ever possible threat of despotism. Thus Montesquieu exhausts all the modalities of being. His is a philosophical ambition, to grasp all the forms of the human world.

The composition itself of *The Spirit of the Laws* indicates that the Ancient-Modern polarity is the world's wellspring. When he speaks *ex officio* as a political author bringing "new ideas," even new ideas "without a mother,"[1] Montesquieu distinguishes three types of regimes: republic, monarchy, despotism. However, the English regime has no place in this seemingly exhaustive classification. In the early books, England is visible only from afar. To be sure, what is said in book 6 about the organization of the judiciary suggests that contemporary England is more akin to a republic than to a monarchy; in book 5, chapter 19, Montesquieu speaks without naming it of "a nation where the republic hides under the form of monarchy." But all this remains indecisive as England remains hidden beneath a veil. The regime of the happy isle, neither truly republican nor even less monarchical, seems to call for a modification of the initial tripartite classification. Yet Montesquieu does nothing of the sort. The man who knows exactly what he thinks and where he wants to lead us seems to regard England as would an observer who stands intrigued and disarmed before a radically new and incomprehensible phenomenon.

Having at hand only an unrevised classification and in despair over what to do, he takes refuge in the distinction one can always appeal to between appearance and reality. Why does a philosopher construct such an original classification of political regimes from which he omits the one regime he prefers and which he sees as the regime of the future?

Some will attribute this strange procedure to Montesquieu's ineptness. Many will hold that, whatever the reason, this is a detail that ought not to hold up so broad an inquiry as ours. The first are really too bold to impute to Montesquieu an error which they themselves would not have committed. The second forget that our sensibility has been blunted by a habit of more than two centuries where the "tradition of novelty" has held sway unchallenged and that perhaps Montesquieu himself cannot give us much help to take stock of what is needed to confront and to understand the appearance of a genuinely new phenomenon in the human world, if such a thing is possible.

Let us then observe how suddenly England emerges and unfolds in book II in this critical passage at the end of chapter 5:

> There is also one nation in the world whose constitution has political liberty for its direct purpose. We are going to examine the principles on which this nation founds political liberty. If these principles are good, liberty will appear there as in a mirror.
>
> Not much trouble need be taken to discover political liberty in the constitution. If it can be seen where it is, if it has been found, why seek it?

These singular statements yield their meaning once they are placed next to the closing lines of the following chapter, the most famous chapter in *The Spirit of the Laws* and one of the most memorable texts in all political literature:

> Harrington, in his *Oceana*, has also examined the furthest point of liberty to which the constitution of a state can be carried. But of him it can be said that he sought this liberty only after misunderstanding it, and that he built Chalcedon with the coast of Byzantium, before his eyes.

Why did Montesquieu frame this fundamental chapter with two references to Harrington that echo one another? Why does he fault the English writer for not "finding" English liberty? After all, when *Oceana* was published in 1656, it was not "before his eyes." On this score we need to bear in mind that Harrington sought to follow the ways of "ancient prudence"[2] that were continued, as he saw it, by Machiavelli. Montesquieu thus frames his presentations of the new regime with a heightened double-barreled critique of that last great representative of what is usually called "classical republicanism." The principles of ancient prudence, even as perfected by Machiavelli, conceal from view what is there "before his eyes" and prevent him from grasping what is new.

It remains to consider the striking terms of Montesquieu's critique, which can be summed up in the opposition between "seeking" and "finding." For the first time in the history of philosophy, a philosopher invites us to cease "seeking." Is this because we have found what we are seeking? So it seems, or else the critique of Harrington would lose its force. But in an inverse way this critique is in no way plausible: how can one not see that what was sought has been found? We must conclude that Harrington's error resides rather in the fact that he was seeking when he should have found and that, consequently, nothing guarantees that what he was seeking was what he ought to have found. Let us apply this lesson to our own situation. We Moderns have found, or ought to have found, what we were not seeking, what neither the Ancients nor those who, like Harrington, want to imitate or even surpass them, were seeking. By opposing "seeking" and "finding," Montesquieu does something altogether different than to distinguish a problem from its solution. He opposes two attitudes, two approaches: one, "seeking," is the search for a principle or foundation that resides in the nature of things or man; the other, "finding," consists in turning to good account what fate brings our way and what, it appears, could not have been. "What fate brings"—I use this vague and outmoded expression deliberately. One might want to say "brought by history," but that would be to decide the question. By his profound play on "seeking" and "finding," Montesquieu constructs for the reader "before his eyes" neither Byzantium nor Chalcedon, but the modern idea of history.

III

Near the end of chapter 6 we learn that the blueprint for the English regime comes from the Germans: "This fine system was found in the forests."[3] If we place this statement next to other passages in *The Spirit of the Laws*, we will be tempted to conclude that English liberty continues or reproduces the liberty of "the state of nature," man's prepolitical state, and that the English regime cannot be understood within the classification of regimes precisely because it is not properly speaking a political regime. But such statements are dangerously abstract and might even appear profound. We need to stay closer to the surface. In the forests, even the German forests, whatever some may say, no one thinks about or "seeks" the best regime, be it the one that offers the most liberty or requires the most virtue. But at times, without any effort or merit on our part, the foot stumbles upon a treasure, which is what happened in Europe. In other words, the solution to the political problem in no way follows from the rational and deliberate quest of the best regime that haunted Harrington. Events in Europe were wiser than the wisest of the ancient philosophers and Machiavelli himself. Too many Europeans still continue to "seek" with their sights turned to the past or toward heaven above. They have only to open their eyes and look before them, in the effectual and present reality, to find the good they need and desire and to take hold of liberty.

Harrington saw in Machiavelli the great modern successor, the "learned disciple" of the "old prudence." That was not the aim of Machiavelli himself when he defined his project in these biting terms:

> (But) since my intent is to write something useful to whoever understands it, it has appeared to me more fitting to go directly to the effectual truth of the thing than to the imagination of it. And many have imagined republics and principalities that have never been seen or known to exist in truth.[4]

Machiavelli would not have been less severe than Montesquieu with regard to Harrington, whom he would have numbered among the *molti* who seek imagined republics. But while Montesquieu takes up and plumbs the principle of Machiavelli's critique against those who construct an imaginary "best regime," he places the accent elsewhere and even inverts the critique from an active to a passive stance. Machiavelli sought "to go directly to the effectual truth of the thing " [*andare drieto alla verità effettuale della cosa*] in order to reveal the salutary necessity of evil. This is again, in a different but still discernible tempo, a "seeking" and even a "quest for the truth." For Montesquieu there is no need to "go directly" [*andare drieto*] to the salutary things; it is better to allow them to appear and then to recognize them and finally to let them produce their wholesome effects. At the time he is writing, those effects are already unfolding, at least in England. The "effectual truth" [*verità effettuale*] is a new kind of reality that the ancient philosophers, along with Harrington and Machiavelli, were not able to find—it is a "historical fact."

IV

The primary intent of *The Spirit of the Laws* is thus to weaken decisively the authority of the Ancients, of the idea of the "best regime," the idea of virtue, in order to replace it with the authority of the present moment, of the modern experience, summed up in the notions of "commerce" and "liberty." Therein lies the principal difficulty of this enterprise.

To justify substituting one authority for another, the two authorities first must be compared. However, since this is a matter of authorities, there can be no comparison strictly speaking. A comparison presupposes identical or similar criteria. To work out a rigorous comparison of incompatible or at least disparate criteria at the base of the impudent authorities of the Ancient and the New would be to abolish from the outset or, more precisely, to refuse to recognize the authority of the modern experience as such. It would be in effect to appeal to a universal criterion or principle beyond both the New and the Ancient and rooted in Nature, in any event on a basis that overlooks or that encompasses history. The idea of the best regime would in that very way be reestablished or rather maintained. In brief, Montesquieu has to persuade his reader of the superiority of the Moderns and of modern liberty over ancient virtue, without being able to make a comparison between the two regimes or the two criteria. He has to compare and conclude regarding superiority while eliminating or invalidating the very notions of comparison and superiority. This difficulty more than anything else explains the extreme complexity of *The Spirit of the Laws*. In particular, it explains why the English regime has no place in the classification of political regimes that is presented as exhaustive. The English regime brings with it its own criterion, the new criterion of liberty. Consequently, if it is indeed the regime of the greatest liberty, it can be said strictly speaking to be the "best."

Montesquieu's apparent ineptness reveals the complexity of the steps reason must pass through to find its way in a human world that can no longer be brought under one unifying principle, as Nature was for Aristotle and the European tradition that followed him. The fruitful unity and all-encompassing power of this principle was expressed and unfolded in the exhaustive classification of political regimes, an essential tool of classical political philosophy which brings back the diversity of human political experience to the unity of a principle. But Montesquieu, by letting it be seen that the English regime cannot be integrated even into the radically new classification he devised, asserts "before our eyes" that the realm of politics can no longer be exhaustively and thus adequately covered by any classification of regimes whatever. He could not make us sense more subtly or profoundly the upheaval the novel English regime was beginning to work in human affairs. Nothing less than the rule of reason was being overturned. In the midst of new satisfactions one discovers an unprecedented impotence. The unity the human world is always striving to weave and to articulate is now struck with uncertainty. If every classification of political regimes henceforth is essentially deficient, one must conclude that reason can no longer provide a reasonable account of the human problem as a political problem. The venerable definition of man as "political animal" and "rational animal" is implicitly bankrupted.

This new regime of reason has been called the Age of Enlightenment, a glorious phrase that reverberates with the words *Reason* and *Nature*. In reality, however, the Age of Enlightenment deals a decisive deathblow to both. Its active principle, its sovereign notion, is neither Reason nor Nature, but the "present moment." The authority of the New is still too recent, too new to be precise, to have found an appropriate and commonly accepted conceptual expression, and so it enlists in its service the remarkable words Reason and Nature. These words can now be easily appropriated, separately or preferably together, since they have lost their place as principles in the world of the emerging new authority. They no longer guarantee the syntheses of the human world since they are incapable of giving an account of both the ancient world and the new authority, which is also the authority of the New embodied in the agglomeration of events and effects that is "England." Reason itself cannot give an account of the New since, in the Enlightenment's polemic against prejudice, it puts itself on an equal plane with the New and merges with it. Nature, Reason, and the New together constitute an essentially flimsy world that has never before appeared in human history and that is neither anchored in the One nor attracted to it. Hence the eighteenth century's incomparable charm, in our eyes as in its own.

This state of grace did not last. The French Revolution sought to reinstate the unifying principle with an arrogance, an energy, and a cruelty honed by the displacement that preceded it and that was so mild by comparison. Thinkers, too, both before the revolution and with a heightened sense of necessity and urgency after it, sensed this fundamental weakness of the Enlightenment and undertook to overcome it in the realm of speculation. Reason once again had to be made coextensive with the human world, which had triumphantly and delightfully emancipated itself from it under the forms of the New or as an effect of it. Thought accordingly rose to one of its highest moments in the heroic labors and inebriation of German idealism, whose achievements overshadow and color our perception of the preceding epoch. That is why it is so important to have an exact understanding of Montesquieu, who gave the most exact description and the most faithful phenomenology of the Enlightenment. As we have noted, Montesquieu takes as his theme the important fact which he is the first to examine seriously, that reason cannot give a reasonable account of the New. Reason cannot bring together under any unifying principle this agglomeration of events and effects condensed in the new world which is England. In fact, it can only view it with warm approbation. Without being able to give a rational account of what satisfies it, Enlightenment reason believes more things than it actually understands. As faith seeks understanding, *fides quaerens intellectum*, one has to ask whether modern reason has ever overcome this contradiction.

V

Montesquieu does not confine himself to noting the inadequacy of traditional reason that, bound somehow with nature in a common principle, pretended to restore unity to the world. He forges new approaches aimed at reestablishing at least some kind of equality between the new reason and new world. This endeavor presupposes a critique of the ancient notion of unity and its foundation that will not simply assert but explain how inept ancient thought is and so close off any noxious return of the old. We shall observe an instance of the new approaches in Montesquieu's critical analysis of virtue, the idea that lies at the heart of the traditional understanding of man, Christian as well as Greek.

Our natural starting point may be found in these two sentences: "The political men of Greece who lived under popular government recognized no other force to sustain it than virtue. Those of today speak to us only of manufacturing, commerce, finance, wealth, and even luxury."[5] This sounds like an implicit critique of the moderns. Here, at the start of his undertaking, Montesquieu identifies with his most likely and most honorable reader, the good citizen bred on good authors who is astonished and troubled at how much current popular views differ from traditional principles. But in truth these sentences actually already contain the radical critique of the convention they appear to take up and confirm.

Nothing is manifestly false in this brief sketch, but it tacitly abolishes what constituted the proper meaning and significance of virtue in the eyes of "the political men of Greece." Those men "lived under popular government." Granted this is the case, since just about all the Greeks of interest to posterity lived in Athens, at least as long as they opted not to go into exile or were not compelled to do so. They recognized that no other power but virtue sustained the body politic. Again, this is the case, if we allow that simplifying things entails exaggeration, but that in no way means that they saw in virtue the principle of popular government.[6] On the contrary, we know that there were forceful critics of democracy who found that it deliberately and insolently refused to give virtue its proper place.[7] The Greek "democrats" appealed to liberty rather than virtue.[8] What was for "the political men of Greece" the principle of the critique of democracy becomes in Montesquieu's formulation the wellspring of its functioning. No doubt Montesquieu's approach reeks of bad faith, however hidden it is. He allows himself such bad faith because it is indispensable to his enterprise at a critical stage in order to weaken or even do away with the attraction the venerable notion of virtue can still hold for the contemporary reader.

Virtue was one of those ideas of political and moral philosophy that assured communication between Greek and Roman philosophy on the one hand and Christianity on the other. The two traditions differed in what they considered the virtues to be and how they ranked them, but they at least held in common that human life is called to find its fulfillment and happiness in the exercise of the virtues or of virtue simply. This notion sums up the practical universal principle of both Greek philosophy and the Christian religion: all men, from one end of the world to the other, are equally called to live according to virtue, that is, to perfect and fulfill their nature as much as they can, despite great inequalities in their capacities, be they natural qualities or supernatural graces, to attain such an end. "To make nature democratic," as Montesquieu does here with the stroke of a pen, is to give it the limits of ancient democracy as it once existed. The idea of virtue may sum up the viewpoint of Greek philosophy on political and human life in general, on man as man, but Montesquieu's formulation suggests that Greek philosophy is linked to the Greek city as a plant is bound to its ecosystem, an ecosystem that is now extinct. "The political men of Greece who *lived* under popular government" apparently had little desire or capacity to look beyond the walls of their city. Thus, beneath an apparent appeal to convention, Montesquieu shows his less naïve or more attentive reader that Greek political and moral philosophy, guided and so to speak held together by the notion of virtue, has nothing pertinent to say to those who do not *live* under the popular government of a Greek city.

Montesquieu perpetuates as he modifies the thesis of Thomas Hobbes on the virtues of the moral life, just as he also modifies the teaching of Machiavelli. As is well known, Hobbes, in rejecting the old moral philosophers, the writers of moral philosophy, who saw in virtue the *"finis ultimus*, utmost aim" of human life, individual as well as political, makes of the virtues "the means of peaceable, sociable, and comfortable living."[9] There is no doubt that by "politicizing" or "socializing" the virtues, by reducing them to instruments, Hobbes degrades them. From ends desirable in themselves because they perfect the soul and raise it higher on the scale of being, they become mere means for protecting physical life. But Hobbes's thesis, like that of the ancient philosophers he opposes, has a universal import. What he says holds meaning in his view for man as man, for human life as such, independent of its conditions in time and space. He claims to speak the truth about man where the Ancients were in error about man. In his critique of the Ancients Hobbes has already consigned them to a place which they could not have overcome. Here is exactly what he writes:

> In these western parts of the world, we are made to receive our opinions concerning the institution, and rights of commonwealths, from Aristotle, Cicero, and other men, Greeks and Romans, that *living under popular states*, derived those rights, not from *the principles of nature*, but transcribed them into their books, out of the practice of their own commonwealths, which were popular.[10]

One can see from the words I have underlined that in condensing these lines of Hobbes, Montesquieu keeps the imputation of particularism but he suppresses the reference to the "principles of nature," which is obviously the decisive point. He is content to "particularize" virtue by linking it to a particular political regime of which it could be the specific means of preservation, without judging, positively or negatively, the general validity of the Greek perspective. He says much less than Hobbes, but beneath the reserve and modesty of his approach he works a radical transformation of the critical enterprise.

It will be said that particularizing virtue is a two-edged sword. To make the virtue the Greek men of politics speak of the expression of the requirements of Greek democracy is to limit drastically the import of Greek moral and political philosophy. It is not necessarily to attain "virtue" as such. It seems that the more Montesquieu particularizes virtue, the more he particularizes his critique. Moreover, since we are on a path that leads us away from the universal and toward the particular, nothing prevents, it seems, conceiving as many types of virtue as there are particular bodies politic, or at least distinct regimes. What we call the critique of virtue then would be very poorly named, since it would entail merely affirming or recognizing the infinite diversity of the human world in which each regime has its own virtue. Although it would be easy to lose one's way, this is not the avenue Montesquieu opens up here. Instead he ends up in effect suggesting that the fate of all virtues and of the whole of virtue is contained in the fate of Greek virtue, the virtue of Greek democracy extolled by the "political men of Greece." His procedure is first to particularize and democratize the idea of virtue and then to turn this "democratic" virtue into the type of all virtue, political as well as moral or religious. Virtue is at first particularized and then generalized. The relation between particular and general thus presents hitherto unseen characteristics that must be pointed out without delay.

According to the traditional understanding, as one finds it in Aristotle, the particular is in some way a real approximation of the general. It has the advantage over the general of really existing, since only the individual is real and not the species, but it has the disadvantage in being only an approximate or imperfect realization. Except perhaps for very rare individuals, if any exist, who are "par excellence" (as individual) what they are (as species), the particular "is less" and has "less being" or "less essence" than the general. In the approach inaugurated by Montesquieu, the distance between the particular and the general is abolished from the start. The general is linked strictly and inseparably to something particular. Virtue is bound strictly and inseparably to the needs of the specific body politic that was the Greek city, which itself is reduced to one of its particular forms, democracy.

In this kind of violent compression the general idea undergoes fundamental modifications. It is in the first place impossible, precisely, to say if we have before us a general idea or a particular reality, since the particular and the general exchange or mix their attributes: the general exists immediately, is immediately real; the particular is immediately intelligible. Previously, the human world was interpreted according to the immovable distance between the particular whose existence one could measure and the essence whose general character one could contemplate. The human mind had only to conduct itself properly; it has no choice as to its position in the world. Henceforth, the distance is abolished, immobility gives way to mobility, and the new notion, neither general nor particular or sometimes both, circulates freely within the world. Amalgamating and confusing in itself the two poles of the general and the particular, the new notion contains at once the process of becoming real proper to the passage from the general to the particular or concrete, and the process of becoming true proper to the approximation by which the particular tends toward the general or universal. The two poles have become its two "moments" and it has free range in the ancient world. From now on, the new notion, covering the two moments and drawing power from their combined forces, becomes, as it were, a magical instrument. In whatever point the mind applies it, the mind finds itself capable of producing, since this notion mixes them, at once the particular and the general, that is to say the human world in its entirety as it is to be found in this point. The mind finds itself in a position of causal sovereignty. It can explain the world at will. The condition of the human mind was to be caught in the tension between the particular and the general. The new idea allows it to see itself or to consider itself outside and above this tension.

These observations remain of necessity abstract at this stage of our inquiry. A more concrete development will be given at a later point and a first and most fruitful illustration in the following section. It was first important to underline, in formal and so to speak scholarly terms, that we are beginning to explore a passage at the end of which the human mind will discover in a new setting new possibilities of accounting for human things.

VI

Montesquieu has fashioned a fiction. He invents an idea of virtue that encompasses not only ancient political virtue but also the "moral" or "Christian" virtues and, in general, every virtue, whatever it might be. His invention, taken up again as is by Rousseau, will have a considerable historical legacy. The modern understanding, our understanding, of virtue and of moral life is shaped by Montesquieu's critique of the Greek city. The key points and the meaning of this critique must be grasped with great precision if we want to be in a position to grasp fully this fundamental trait of modern moral life. For us, who in this respect are different from the Greeks as well as the Christians, virtue can be admirable but it is never lovable.

In the Author's Foreword, Montesquieu says the following:

> In order to understand the first four books of this work, one must note that what I call virtue in a republic is love of the homeland, that is, love of equality. It is not a moral virtue or a Christian virtue; it is *political* virtue . . .

Montesquieu's commentators have readily confirmed these assertions since they meet with the modern prejudice according to which "values" and "spheres" are "autonomous." They are even at the origin of this prejudice, which prides itself in taking them literally. Now it can be demonstrated that when Montesquieu speaks of virtue he means virtue in general, including even the virtues we call moral or Christian. I would like to point out some of his ironical statements on this score.

Here is what he writes in book 3, chapter 6:

> Thus, in well-regulated monarchies everyone will be almost a good citizen, and one will rarely find someone who is a good man; for, in order to be a good man, one must have the intention of being one and love the state less for oneself than for itself.

To "good man" is added this note: "These words, good man, are to be taken here only in a political sense." Montesquieu is not afraid to take advantage of his reader's docility, for what is "good man" taken "in a political sense" other than "good citizen"? Granted that the good citizen of a republic has a different moral economy than the good citizen of a monarchy; the fact that it defines itself by disinterestedness confirms the extreme proximity of the "political virtue" that Montesquieu speaks of and the "moral virtue" as it is generally understood.

Any doubt on this point will be dispelled if we consider chapter 5 of book 4. After noting that despotism and monarchy were founded on passions, respectively fear and honor, Montesquieu makes the following observation on the virtue proper to republics:

> . . . but political virtue is a renunciation of oneself, which is always a very painful thing.
> One can define this virtue as love of the laws and the homeland. This love, requiring a continuous preference of the public interest over one's own, produces all the individual virtues; they are only that preference.

Now what are these "individual" virtues if not the ones we ordinarily call "moral"? The point is all the more conclusive here in that Montesquieu is careful to associate completely *all* "individual" virtues, that is the moral virtues, to love of country, i.e., to political virtue par excellence.

But how does one obtain this continual preference of the public interest over one's own? Here is Montesquieu's reply:

> Love of the homeland leads to goodness in mores, and goodness in mores leads to love of the homeland. The less we can satisfy our individual passions, the more we give ourselves up to passions for the general order. Why do monks so love their order? Their love comes from the same thing that makes this order intolerable to them. Their rule deprives them of everything upon

which ordinary passions rest; what remains, therefore, is the passion for the very rule that afflicts them.[11]

This marvelous passage cannot fail to astonish the reader who comes upon it for the first time. It seems that all of western psychology, the so-called psychology of suspicion, Nietzsche's and Freud's alike, is contained in this epigram. And with the motive arises the desire to suspect the suspicion. Would it not have appeared, by design and as a doctrine, in a very specific political context and in order to meet a very demanding intellectual need: to think about the Ancient when the New was unfolding as yet unmastered, as liberty? Let us for the moment limit ourselves to articulating the decisive point for a proper understanding of the design of *The Spirit of the Laws*, and so of the moral critique that is inseparable from modern politics.[12] Montesquieu tends to liken the ancient city to a religious order and to identify the political virtue of the citizen with the ascetic virtue of the monk.[13] Thus the two types of virtue, whose conflict had made for the complexity and vitality of the European moral tradition, are melded one into the other.

VII

Our analysis is assuredly fastidious, but the history of moral and political life is marked by the introduction of changes that at first can hardly be perceived and that need to be sought in their first intention and color. To do that it is necessary to pierce through the conventions under which they first masked themselves in order to gain a hearing. At least we have shown that in making virtue the hallmark of ancient democracies and especially Greek democracy, Montesquieu seeks not only to reduce the import of Plato and Aristotle, but in doing so he particularizes and politicizes all virtue and above all Christian virtue. It seems that democratic virtue is the model of all virtue and that Christian virtue is merely the phantom of defunct democracy, enthroned on the tomb of the deceased yet soon to be uncrowned.

This prototype of all virtue consists of nothing other than the preference for the general over the particular. Now, this general virtue not only is the characteristic of a particular regime, but Montesquieu ceaselessly underlines the particularly particular nature, if I may put it that way, the exceptional and nongeneralizable nature of the Greek regime. Greek institutions are referred to as "singular" even in the title of a chapter (5, book 7) as though this were an essential trait, in some way a part of their official designation. Their evocation leaves an impression of an improbable, monstrous venture. Montesquieu shows Lycurgus "running counter to all received usages," " confusing," like the Chinese, "the principles that govern men."[14] He describes the Greek city as "a society of athletes and fighters," as an institution whose "ferocity" was only tempered by music or by "a love that ought to be proscribed by all nations in the world."[15] Montesquieu's entire description is governed by his intention of accentuating the strangeness of the Greek city, of arousing in the mind of the reader a sense of distance and even antipathy.

I would like to note other no less important traits. Montesquieu rigorously separates the idea of virtue from the idea of excellence, which among the Greeks were essentially linked. He makes of virtue a sentiment that not only is within the reach of "the lowest man in the state," but also finds its natural bearers among those whose wits, talents, and fortune are "middling."[16] And, in a deliberately muddled sentence, he turns on its head the Greek identification of virtue with happiness, of virtue with wisdom[17], implying that virtue contributes nothing to either happiness or wisdom. "If a republic whose laws have formed many middling people is composed of sober people, it will be governed soberly; if it is composed of happy people, it will be very happy."[18] Democratic laws, whose support and even lifeblood is virtue, can only produce equality or mediocrity; as for happiness or wisdom, they are prior to laws and virtue, and are thus independent of them.

We are now in a position to summarize Montesquieu's theses on virtue. Virtue is the principle of a regime that is not only particular, but moreover singular. It is not founded on the mastery of the passions by reason, but rather on the absorption of the passionate energy of the passions by and in a unique passion, love of country and of equality. It is thus the love of a rule that oppresses and even "afflicts." It has no connection with the grandeur of the soul, but is on the contrary a sentiment that is accessible and even appropriate to the lowest man in the state. It makes a man neither wise nor happy.

VIII

The virtue Montesquieu speaks of is a truly strange thing that has never yet been met with, in this world or the next. It is an amalgam of ancient political and Christian virtue in which each element loses its specific traits and takes on colors that denature it. Benjamin Constant knew very well how to explicate Montesquieu's thought on this point when he spoke of Sparta as a "monastic barracks."[19] What then is the meaning of this shocking fiction?

European moral life was organized and animated by the dialogue fraught with conflict between Greek and Roman civic morality on the one hand and the Mosaic precepts and evangelical counsels on the other; in short, between magnanimity and humility. The two virtues, or two types of virtue, are antagonistic but also in solidarity. I have already pointed out how two moral traditions that proposed to man that he fulfill his nature by seeking out lofty ends are necessarily neighbors and so to speak accomplices. Each one sees man as an arrow aimed at a target in the sky. But beyond that the two traditions are in confrontation and conflict; I dare say that they animate one another. Magnanimity despises humility and humility humiliates magnanimity, as it did at Canossa, for example. Nature is ever anew a candidate for baptism. The demands of grace again and again arouse the demands observed in the major issues of European history before the transition from the Middle Ages to the Renaissance and from the Renaissance to the Reformation and Counter-Reformation. Thus Dante, angered and magnanimous, protests against the humiliation inflicted on our moral and political nature by the overweening pretensions of the spiritual power. Thus Luther revolts against the transformation of the papacy into a pagan temporal force, of the Word of God into an institution of worldly power.[20] Dante affirms nature while Luther affirms grace. Therein lies the rhythm that for a long time held sway in the West. The seventeenth century brought that to an end. Whether it be called classical or baroque, in any event it made a supreme effort at conciliation. It sought to be at once and very deliberately prideful and Christian. Now the instrument, the capstone of the conciliation, that is, the absolute sovereign, at once Hercules or Apollo and the Most Christian King, instead of reconciling and reuniting in his person the two facets of the old world, only succeeded in definitely jeopardizing the one by the other. The spring had been would up too tight and it snapped abruptly in 1715. But there was no resurgence of either pagan pride and ambition or Christian humility and rigor. Something else appeared, which we are trying to identify in this inquiry, something altogether different from Antiquity and the Renaissance and from Catholic or Protestant Christianity.

Despite its grandeur and beauty, the classical project as it unfolded in France—for nowhere else did this take place—had in it something taut, excessive, artificial, and false. As soon as artifice was abandoned, what it sought to unite was itself abandoned: the two ancient versions of the "good life." But there remained what artifice had produced, or at least protected and encouraged: the nation state, henceforth too broad, too strong, too new, to ever accept to defer to the authority of one or the other Antiquity. And thus, linked to the nation state, this supranational society of English, French, Dutch, and Italians, too much citizens to be truly Christians, too Christian to be truly citizens, who find in property, conversation, and commerce those mediating spiritual entities that speak to their situation.

Nevertheless, however definitive the disappearance of the classical project after the death of the great king may appear to careful observers, many upright minds and noble hearts continued to take their bearings from Antiquity and Christianity. The social and intellectual current that runs through Europe no doubt heralds something altogether new and unheard of, but just what is it? And will it be strong enough to liberate people ever after from the attraction of those dead or dying stars, Athens and Jerusalem?

To prevent any return of or to the Ancient, to secure the authority of the New, the dialectic of nature and grace must be brought to a complete end. To accomplish such a plan, what is more daring yet more unstoppable than to merge them? Montesquieu squarely superimposes city and church, citizen and Christian one atop the other. Their common denominator is obedience to a rule that mortifies the passions. Now bringing to light this common denominator contains in itself the critique of the two traditions, since obedience, which is common to both traditions, is henceforth devoid of motives, of proper ends that justify it in each tradition. It now appears as the simple oppression of nature and no longer as the education of nature for its perfection, as the means to attain higher goods. To love passionately the rule which afflicts, precisely because it afflicts, is admittedly *against* nature, however nature is understood. A virtue understood in this way can be judged, which is to say rejected, without the need to specify the characteristics of an action that would be "in conformity with nature," or without even having to presume anything in general terms regarding human nature. This notion tends to make us think that the ancient city and the Christian church are equally, though in different ways, repressive or "afflicting," and it encourages us to rest content with this thought as purely *polemical.*

IX

The preceding analysis has underlined, I think demonstrated, the deliberate and artificial character of Montesquieu's elaboration, its quality of fiction. But the fictions of a philosopher, especially one so sober as Montesquieu, are never arbitrary. They fix and make explicit and real a possibility already inscribed obscurely in the political and spiritual configuration.

I was speaking earlier of the dialectic of the two traditions, pointing out how magnanimity and humility, nature and grace combat and call forth one another. But, if we take each critique literally and follow it to its logical conclusion, if we consider what nature and the city say or imply about grace and the church, and what the church and grace say or imply about the city and nature, we see that each one tends to strip the adversary of legitimacy and rid it of substance. In the eyes of the citizen, what value is there to the mortification of the Christian, when what matters is not to fall on one's knees but to mount one's horse, and the sins one ought to expiate or rather correct are not the sins one commits against chastity and truth, but military and political errors?[21] In the eyes of the Christian, what value is there to the political and military endeavors of the citizen, when he believes that, victory or defeat, whatever the regime, this world is a vale of tears ravaged by sin and that states are nothing more and better than vast bands of robbers?[22] To each of the two protagonists, the sacrifices the other calls for are vain.

I am not overlooking that in practice cities, kingdoms, and even republics accord some place, at times a great deal of place, to the churches and that churches more often than not recognize the consistency and legitimacy of earthly cities, and that the most authoritative statement regarding the relations between nature and grace holds that grace perfects nature without destroying it.[23] But we are concerned here with the offensive edge of the argument when it is pushed to its logical conclusion and a situation of conflict prevails as often happens in political and religious life. We are concerned all the more in that such a situation produces more effects, more changes, more "history," one might say, than it brings about conciliation or compromise in a fine-tuned harmony. Then no doubt each side views the sacrifices and obedience of the other as vain, such that if we take either argument literally at the same time, man seems fated to a useless obedience, an empty virtue, whether he wears the citizen's toga or the Christian's hairshirt. For centuries the spiritual forces turned on one another like two grindstones. City and church, nature and grace wore each other down as they went from conflicts to conciliations. Each one's efforts to return to its original truth had strangely wrought its own defeat. The Renaissance brought an end to the city's life and the Lutheran Reform disarmed religion in the face of temporal power. What does this erosion leave in its wake if not the reciprocal imputation of useless service and vain obedience? Once nature and grace have spent their force against one another, they leave behind them the confused traces of an almost common law. It is on such a foundation that Montesquieu works out his notion of virtue, his fiction of a prototype combining pagan political virtue and Christian virtue. His artifice is made both possible and fitting thanks to the spiritual situation generated by the reciprocal action of the two traditions and it rests on that situation. The virtue examined in *The Spirit of the Laws* is not chiefly an author's invention, however marvelously ingenious it is. As sketched and depicted by Montesquieu, it is a grand Figure of European History that draws its force and its meaning from the spent force of the two traditions, ancient and Christian, after the last and vain effort of the classical age to affirm the two together.

X

Does what has just been said mean that Montesquieu is equally hostile to
the two great traditions, or to their "repressive" effects? Not at all. When,
instead of developing the fiction of their fusion, he takes as his theme their
conflict, he underlines the advantages of the pagan or civic tradition,
which at least does not divide man. His beautiful passage on Epaminondas witnesses to this preference.[24] Indeed, any exposition of Montesquieu's
thought should give adequate attention to his satire on the division introduced by Christianity.[25] However, what is important for our inquiry is not
how Montesquieu adheres to or continues Machiavelli's critique of modern
religion, but the intensity and radical character of his critique of the ancient city. What matters to Montesquieu is that a third possibility be allowed to appear, a very different and novel authority.

No doubt it will be asked why, if our thesis is correct, Montesquieu has
multiplied the passages, like the one I have just mentioned, that have led
so many good readers to consider him a sincere admirer of classical Christianity.

Montesquieu was most certainly a sincere admirer of what is admirable
in Greek and Roman antiquity. Since he was supremely capable of understanding all things, he admired in it a thousand beauties that will escape
our petty souls. However, in his eyes the ancient way of life was no longer
a real possibility. It belonged irretrievably to the past. Whoever reads
Montesquieu today needs to make an effort to grasp fully the novelty expressed in these statements that seem so modest. This is so because the
contemporary reader always, without any effort or particular scruple,
leaves or sends the past behind because "all is historical" and "history is
irreversible." But until Montesquieu's time, to recognize the authority of
the Ancients meant precisely to admire an always present model because
it was founded on the permanent capacities of an unchanging human nature. Henceforth, to reject the authority of the Ancients meant to reject the
criterion of Nature, which they had discovered and recognized as valid. If
the principle that elicited their highest adherence is rejected, then the
heart of ancient spiritual life is robbed of its truth. Once can no longer
admire them without grave reservations, at least as long as one has any
concern for truth. I cannot fathom just how admiration and reprobation
could each find a place in Montesquieu's spacious mind.

In any event it is certain that Montesquieu deliberately veiled his critique of virtue and that a minimum of attention is needed to become alert
to his irony and perceive the extreme radical character of his attack. There
is in these precautions a lofty political prudence and a moral prudence as
well. In effect, how will the sincere reader, the reader of Plutarch and of

The Imitation of Christ, respond if the two great versions of the "good life" are subjected to a perilously sharp critique that finds both at once lacking? He needs an image of man that can occupy his mind and his heart. That is why Montesquieu, content to have decisively weakened the authority of the two traditions in the eyes of his reader, asserts with a noble boldness that he never intended to speak of Christian virtues and turns with deliberate bombast to the conventional praise of the greatness of ancient lives. The authority that is to replace the authority of virtue brings with it no new idea of man and his nature, possibilities, or vocation. The writer who will defend this authority, if at least he retains any humanity, and Montesquieu was humanity itself, cannot destroy or subvert purely and simply the image of virtue and of the "good life," the noble image of Epaminondas. It must go on living, in a sort of limbo, in order to provide, in spite of everything, the new humanity with a representation of man, a moral foundation devoid of any authority to direct his actions but able at least to occupy his imagination. Montesquieu's boundless art destroys the intellectual and political authority of ancient virtue, but it preserves or rather invents its imaginary, "aesthetic," or "historical" authority that will remain at the roots of the best part of European education up to the 1960s.

The significance of this achievement should not be underestimated. Although it may appear to carry little weight, this consistent and powerful imaginary construct plays a real moral role that Montesquieu views as necessary and wholesome. One has only to think of what will happen in Eastern Europe, when modern man, inebriated and, as it were, possessed by the sole authority of History and the Future, completely wipes out all ancient images from his imagination and undertakes to bring into existence the unknown quantity of a New Man.

But History had a strange irony in store for its ironic champion. The virtue he invented was to haunt European man in an altogether different way than he had foreseen and willed. Before long his invention was made to serve the opposite of what he intended when Jean-Jacques Rousseau turned Montesquieu's fiction inside out like a glove.

XI

We have underlined how in identifying the common denominator in ancient and Christian virtue, Montesquieu makes a radical satire of one and the other by depriving virtue of its specific motive. Virtue is now no more than an unnatural obedience to a repressive rule. He offers in sum a self-criticism of virtue. But at the same time this "democratized" virtue that joins the equality and austerity of Christianity to the austerity and activity of the Greek city opens or appears to open a hitherto unforeseen possibil-

ity. Such a democratic conception that fulfills or appears to fulfill both the
nostalgia for ancient and civic greatness and the Christian taste for equality will be able to evoke a positive attraction once the novel authority of
modern experience is rejected as it was by Rousseau. By a singular reversal, the repressive and unnatural character of virtue that Montesquieu had
delicately suggested in order to steer his readers away from it, was emphatically proclaimed by Rousseau to the great acclaim of his readers. The
fiction that was intended to keep the prestige of the past and the authority
of Antiquity at a distance came to violently challenge the authority of the
modern experience it sought to establish. The interpretive principle that
was meant to close an epoch of history became the active principle capable
of opening another period that was no longer "modern" but "revolutionary." Robespierre will proclaim the reign of virtue that Montesquieu invented and critiqued and that Rousseau confirmed and celebrated.

What is most striking in Rousseau's feat is the ease with which he over-
turns Montesquieu's intention and the thoroughgoing assurance, with an
element of enthusiasm, with which he describes the cruel character of civic
virtue.[26] Will one say that the two philosophers share the same concept of
virtue, but make different and even squarely opposed "value judgments"
about it? If the answer were to be yes, we would have come upon a rare
instance, a problem, a situation where appeal to the notion of "value judgment" is indispensable to understanding the human world.

Montesquieu himself was aware of the other possibility his invention
entailed, the possibility developed by Rousseau. How could the writer who
shows us the monk who ardently loves the order that oppresses him because it oppresses him, not have foreseen the image of the citizen thanking
the gods for the victory that took her five sons? Moreover, he notes explicitly or rather he forges the following maxim: "By the nature of human
understanding we have in religion everything that presumes an effort, just
as on the subject of morality, we love in theory all that has the character
of severity."[27] This is perhaps the most general statement in *The Spirit of
the Laws*. The awareness of this possibility was no doubt another motive,
the inverse of the first, for veiling the critique or self-critique of virtue. The
sincere reader was not to be driven to despair, but he was also not to be
tempted.

But Rousseau himself does not love the virtue he celebrates or he only
loves it without his natural goodness enabling him to practice a virtue that
is contrary to nature. Indeed, he does not love it, since he imputes to it
what in his eyes or rather in his heart is the most unforgivable flaw, its
cruelty.[28]

Both Montesquieu and Rousseau equally perceive the ambivalence of
the law and its cruelty. What makes it odious is also what can make it
lovable or rather the object of a strange intellectual desire. If we truly loved

it, we would practice it and our love would not remain merely "speculative." Each thinker makes use of this ambivalence to lead the reader toward the thoughts and sentiments that seem to him true or desirable. But
perhaps neither Rousseau nor even Montesquieu, who is nonetheless master of himself, determines fully what we must and can think of the law.
The ambivalent sentiments and even the conflicting judgments are the
result of the undetermined character of the essence and understanding of
the law. We must be attentive to the difference between the extended
meaning Montesquieu gives to the law and the one Rousseau gives it.

The fiction about virtue fashioned by Montesquieu encompasses both
the ancient pagan world and the Christian world. What he says about
virtue concerns the human world as it always has been up to the present
appearance of the English regime, the new regime of modern liberty.
Rousseau further extends this extended meaning, if I can put it that way.
This virtue or law is imbedded in man's very humanity. From that point
onward, it is not a matter of passing from the rule of ancient law and
repression to that of the new law, which is merely instrumental, and of
liberty, but of at last establishing the law that is both purely law and pure
law and that blends with moral and political liberty.[29] The disagreement
between the two philosophers is a philosophical disagreement over the
meaning and place of law. Montesquieu seems to envisage a society where
the repressive law that modifies nature would be abolished, while Rousseau believes that man cannot live in society without obeying a law that
deeply mutilates his soul. Rousseau has so little affinity for the cruel law
that he prefers to flee into solitude.

XII

Virtue as construed by Montesquieu and confirmed by Rousseau is pure
repression because it is fashioned or "feigned" as the common element in
Greek and Christian law. It is defined in a purely negative way; it consists
in the negation of the individual's attachments and interests, in the denial
of nature inasmuch as nature is individual. If we follow Montesquieu, such
a sacrifice of the individual's attachments and interests has no other outcome than sacrifice itself and the strange satisfaction the soul finds therein.
It goes without saying, as I have noted, that this virtue has little to do with
the conception of it held by the Greeks and the Christians themselves, each
of whom had a different view of the life of the soul. What could be more
different than nature and grace? Yet, the Christian and Greek ideas of
virtue overlap a good deal. For both the philosophers and the Christians,
virtue is the subjection of the passions to reason, of the soul's lower to its
higher parts, an ordering and an order wrought by the soul.[30] This idea of

virtue can entail a mortification of the attachments and interests akin in breadth and content to the mortification implied in Montesquieu and Rousseau's idea, but it has a very different meaning. For the philosophers and the Christians, asceticism is the necessary means to a higher life, whereas for Montesquieu it is an end in itself. Rousseau keeps something of the traditional idea of order in the soul, but he emphasizes to an even greater extent how virtue and law denature the soul.[31] Without wanting at all cost to condense very complex phenomena in a few short formulations when what matters is to uncover and preserve complexity, it might be useful to suggest the following summary account.

Ancient virtue and law, in both their pagan and Christian versions, have man passing from a certain state of his nature to a more elevated state (even, in Christianity, to a "supernatural state") as he rises in his own being toward greater degrees of Being. His virtues unfold, as do his vices, on a scale of countless steps and nuances that reaches from the abyss of degradation to the height of perfection. The new virtue and new law entail the denial of individual nature, without it being clear whether this negation brings with it any higher or lower state for the man who practices virtue. This incertitude is the decisive element in the new determination. Unable to find or to conceive any place in the degrees of Being, the new virtue and law will forever be eluding the old ontology.

Before venturing any further, we need to ask what it is the Greek and Christian ideas have in common. We have insisted that their common denominator, according to Montesquieu, was obedience as an end in itself. But we have just said that they also had in common something altogether different, the idea of an order in the soul. What then is their true common denominator? The question is not without foundation.

The notion of an order in the soul cannot be extracted as a common denominator, even though it is in fact common to the soul. Since it is necessarily a substantial or "material" notion, it must receive a content that determines it, a content which it evokes and reflects. Whatever order there is must be specified. No order of the soul can be conceived or even less brought into play that would remain unspecified, merely the idea of order. But, it will be said, could there not be some clearly determined aspect of the soul's order common to both traditions? What prevents the philosopher and the theologian from saying the same thing, for instance, about anger or lying? Perhaps nothing prevents it, but whoever perceives and adopts this common element must also situate it within a whole. Then the disparity between nature and grace emerges once again. What one thinks of anger or lying, he thinks as a Christian or a philosopher, and, given that, even if it is the same thing, it is not the same thing. Otherwise, in order to make of this partial agreement something that resembles a unified whole, one must formulate with the greatest care a teaching that can at one and the same time accommodate both the philosophical and religious positions. The Christian centuries saw numerous syntheses of the Greek and Christian notions of order in the soul, the broadest and most coherent of which is no doubt the one worked out by St. Thomas Aquinas. In a synthesis of this kind, however, one of the wholes, if I may put it that way, necessarily embraces and subordinates the other. For Thomas Aquinas, theology makes philosophy its handmaid. In any event, constructing a synthesis is not the same thing as extracting a common denominator. It is even the opposite in that it adjusts and adds disparate objects rather than reduces them to a common element. On the other hand, in the sacrifice of individuality and obedience to law because it is law, there is a perfectly clear common denominator for the very reasons we have given. It can be summarized in one word: law is *formal*.

In dealing with the order of the soul, it is necessary to say precisely what kind of order the human soul knows or ought to know: Stoic, Epicurean, Aristotelian, or Christian? Regarding the common denominator, it is enough to hold that the soul, or individual nature, is negated or must negate itself in its empirical attachments and interests. The eventual specific motives of obedience to law and negation of nature can be left aside. The notion of the soul's order as such is unspecified and cannot become operative for either thought or action unless it is first determined, but virtue conceived as a negation is immediately operative since it is defined by a negative determination. Human thinking is inclined to negative determination instead of indetermination, but its desire for a positive determination remains greater. If then it is impossible to determine even in some small way the content of the soul's order—whether this impossibility be essential or the result, if I may put it that way, of an inherent accident— the tendency of thought is to fashion, simultaneously or successively, the most rigorous negative formulation possible and to seek the positive determination that corresponds or even merges with the negative. Much of modern philosophy has been taken up with this twofold and unified quest.

I spoke in section 9 of the two great traditions, the two great spiritual entities that constitute Europe, and their reciprocal action. This action can move in the two opposing directions we have distinguished. It can give rise to syntheses that add and adjust things, as with St. Thomas Aquinas, although there is something essentially unstable and fragile in a synthesis whose elements are as disparate as philosophy and revelation. It is only held together by its author's architectonic genius, later reinforced by the approval given to it by some institution as, in the case of Thomism, the Catholic Church, the institution par excellence. The other direction of reciprocal action thus is tendentiously and irresistibly the stronger. It extracts the common denominator by carrying ever further and pursuing ever more rigorously the reciprocal critique of the virtues, the self-criticism of virtue. From this permanent critique that nature and grace, the city and the church make of one another there emerges Law, the Form of law, as the consequence and the locus of their discord but also as their common achievement. Unlike the synthesis of St. Thomas Aquinas, it can never be defined in positive terms. More precisely, as a negative determination it is always seeking its positive formulation. In this development and quest, the common achievement, which remains the locus of the discord, does not cease to obey its internal necessity, to fall neither on the side of pagan nature nor of Christian grace. This twofold pressure gave the modern mind the lively impulse, the violent and enduring movement that characterizes it. Hamlet's paralysis is the moving force of modern philosophy and politics.

XIII

These considerations are far from conclusive and remain only an introduction. The most they can claim is to draw attention to certain aspects of the Phenomenon. Yet they nevertheless find a confirmation in the central element of the modern development that are the construction and unfolding of the modern state. The state was unthinkable and could not come about apart from the polemical relation it has simultaneously with the Greek city and civic life on the one hand and the church and Christian religion on the other. We will have to speak at greater length, in sections 7 to 12 of chapter 5, of the artificial elevation of the modern state above and in some way against both natural communities and those nurtured by grace or the idea of grace. It suffices here to note that this polemical relation is explicated and even aggressively proclaimed by the author of the blueprint of the modern state, Thomas Hobbes. Hobbes sees in the writings of the Greek and Roman political men on the one hand, and in the Christian Scriptures on the other, the two great causes of the disorders that affect "Christian commonwealths."[32] How does Hobbes proceed, on what basis does he erect the state that will establish civil peace by taming democratic claims and ecclesiastical pretensions alike? As is well known, his edifice is founded on one and only one element: the human individual's entitlement to rights. The individual finds his fundamental right in the commanding need he has for survival. He experiences the pressure of this necessity with a striking clarity when there is no state or the state lacks force, that is, when the state of nature prevails. The state of nature is an accurate image of the internal contradiction of each tradition: it is the ultimate actualization of the factional disorders of the Greek cities and the wars of religion of Christendom. In the state of nature, where man discovers himself as an individual, he discovers that he is something prior to being a citizen or a Christian, something more fundamental than either. Before his submission to either political or religious law, the individual is a whole, since he has in him the sufficient source of all his actions, *de facto* as well as *de jure*. Every man is a whole sufficient unto himself prior to the existence of the law.

The idea that man is all that he is prior to any law, political or religious, will be a central element of democratic man's self-consciousness. Our concern is with the identity or rather the genesis of this radical man, the individual prior to the citizen and Christian alike. He emerges, as we have just said, as the result of the internal contradiction in each tradition, and even more of their reciprocal critique. With the citizen and against the Christian, he is of this world; but with the Christian and against the citizen, he belongs to no city of this world. Or, to repeat a remark made above, since the city and the church reproach one another with the vanity of their sacrifice, the individual is the man who rejects each form of sacrifice and defines himself by this refusal. He accepts each tradition's critique of the other and concludes that he never has the duty to die or to suffer, or again that the right to live is the foundation and the entirety of his moral being.

This does not mean, of course, that the individual, who by nature is a perfect and solitary whole, can live without law altogether. He needs law, but only to protect his nature as it is prior to the law. The law of the modern state, liberal law, is a simple instrument of nature and does not, in principle, modify or perfect nature. Montesquieu sees this new law, which is purely instrumental, appearing and at work first in Protestant, commercial, and liberal England.

We are now in a position to provide a broad sketch of the human world at the moment Montesquieu formulates and brings to light the self-consciousness of the Enlightenment.

Modern man understands the promise of the New. It is at once the promise of eternal nature, which is at last itself, only itself and entirely itself; and of the new law, nature's efficacious and docile instrument. The promise of the New is the indictment of the Ancient, of ancient nature because it is modified and mutilated, and of ancient law because it is pure denial or repression of nature. Modern man is ever interpreting his past as Montesquieu interpreted the Greek city and Greek virtue. His past never passes away completely since it lives on in the present. The world ought to be—it will be!—a free state of nature; it was and still is a law against nature. The earth does not cease to be the "ascetic planet."[33]

The ancient law and the new law, the one pure repression and the other a mere instrument, are obviously at the opposite poles of human experience, like slavery and freedom. Yet they have in common that they are both strictly external and extraneous to nature, the one as its despot, the other as its servant. In some way they are the same law, since each is a law that has no substantial connection with nature. Law can become nature's mere docile instrument because it was at first its pure negation. If, in the old regime, nature essentially needed law in order to be fully nature, to become what it is, then law could never afterwards sever itself completely from nature to be its instrument and the modern regime of law would be inconceivable and incapable of coming into being. But the law that is pure repression contains the promise of the complete liberation of nature, since nothing essentially connects it with nature except negation, which is the contrary of essence. This complicity between the two opposite poles of the law constitutes the identity and the unity of the human world of the Enlightenment. Law is no longer substantive; it is no longer a means of expressing or fulfilling man's nature or his supernatural vocation. It is the continual oscillation between despotic negation and servile instrumentality; or rather it is the historical movement and dialectical dynamic between these two poles. The one who inhabits this "ascetic planet" is both free and everywhere in chains.

Through their reciprocal critique and turning on one another, city and church, nature and grace, thus foment both pure law and pure nature. The city and the church are two associations, each one inseparably uniting human nature and a specific law. The pressure of the two associations upon one other dissociates nature and law, perhaps in each one but at any rate in the city become state. It separates what is by nature united. The dialectic of city and church produces its broadest and at the same time most intimate effect when in this way it severs once and for all the two halves of the human condition.

But let us return from these depths to the surface of the blue sea crisscrossed by the ships that bear our wealth and our hope! Montesquieu subverts the authority of the ancient city and ancient virtue to make room for and to glorify the modern experience, which in his eyes is epitomized by commerce, to which we turn our attention next.

XIV

The opening chapter of book 20 of *The Spirit of the Laws*, entitled simply "On Commerce," from the beginning takes as its theme the opposition of the Ancient and the New, of virtue or "pure mores" and commerce. There Montesquieu writes:

> Commerce cures destructive prejudices, and it is an almost general rule that everywhere there are gentle mores, there is commerce and that everywhere there is commerce, there are gentle mores. . . .
>
> Commerce has spread knowledge of the mores of all nations everywhere;

they have been compared to each other, and good things have resulted from this.

One can say that the laws of commerce perfect mores for the same reason that these same laws ruin mores. Commerce corrupts pure mores, and this was the subject of Plato's complaints; it polishes and softens barbarous mores, as we see every day.

Montesquieu's prosaic and modest observation that commerce softens mores is the starting point and the focal point of his interpretation of European history. He suggests quite clearly that commerce is basically the only thing that softens mores as a "general rule." This no doubt means that this happy evolution need not be ascribed to Christianity. It also means that we have before us one of the major moving forces, and perhaps the principal one, of historical development and that, more fundamentally, history is moved by such a force.

By putting people in contact with one another and thereby getting them to compare their respective mores, commerce has brought about "good things." Montesquieu leaves it for us to determine what these good things are. We can conjecture that each people has been led to cut itself off in some measure from its particular traditions, or at least to dislike less the ways of life of other people, and so has become less savage. Nevertheless it seems that these "good things" have their counterpoint in the fact that commerce corrupts pure mores. Without explicitly stating it, Montesquieu suggests a correspondence between "pure mores" and "barbarous mores" on the one hand, and "corruption" and "perfection" on the other. Basing himself on the tastes of his readers who, already educated and transformed by centuries of commercial progress, cherish gentleness and perfection, Montesquieu proceeds with virtuosity to substitute new criteria in place of traditional criteria, both pagan and Christian. For the reasons we have discussed in the previous section, replacing a new authority for the ancient one cannot be done by way of demonstration, nor even in a forthright way. Montesquieu must appeal to a kind of clandestine art of persuasion. What is authoritative for us, "Plato's complaints" or what "we see everyday"? There is no doubt about the answer Montesquieu implies and expects. Who will prefer the distant authority of plaintive Plato to the authority bestowed on it by evoking the experience "we" have "every day"? Montesquieu knows well that, whatever we say, we prefer ourselves to Plato and even our judgment to his, and that only a residue of human or religious respect keeps us from acknowledging this preference. He does not hesitate, this man who thinks in the company of Plato, to encourage this preference, to induce everyone to admit it to himself; he seeks everyone's complicity and cooperation in favor of the new and against the old philosophy. Whoever is sensitive to the gentleness of the present, as we all are, has begun to prefer himself to Plato and to cast doubt on Antiquity itself. Montesquieu will persuade him to dare to love what he loves, what the present time, our time, has brought. The gentleness and perfection of mores, not their purity, is the new criterion that must and will hold sway. The effects of commerce must and will be appreciated according to the criteria that commerce itself has introduced.[34]

What more precisely are its effects? Montesquieu writes a little further: "The natural effect of commerce is to lead to peace. Two nations that trade with each other become reciprocally dependent; if one has an interest in buying, the other has an interest in selling, and all unions are founded on natural needs."[35] Thus, if political virtue, the virtue of the ancient cities, is willingly belligerent, commerce is naturally peaceable. The advances of commerce, which we see "every day," promise, better yet they entail, corresponding advances in peace. Ancient virtue's logic of war gives way to the logic of peace of modern commerce. Man thus appears under the two successive guises, which are also exclusive and contradictory, of the warrior and the merchant. Naturally the question arises which is man's true face, or more precisely, which activity, the warrior citizen's or the peaceful merchant's, best permits man to develop his abilities and fulfill his nature? It is important to note that Montesquieu never asks these questions. Does he then suggest an indirect answer? It is true, as we have seen, that he indicates subtly but firmly how ancient virtue is "contrary to nature," but he does not affirm that commerce is "according to nature," even if he gives a favorable account of its "natural effect." Montesquieu's reader acquires a knowledge and dislike of what is "against nature," but not, it seems, any knowledge and taste for what is "according to nature."

In refraining from asserting that commerce is natural to man, Montesquieu differs markedly from his nineteenth-century disciples, who would hold that the passage from war to commerce, which is the law of European history and so in the end of all human history, was rooted in human nature itself. Benjamin Constant writes as follows:

> We have finally reached the age of commerce, an age which must necessarily replace that of war, as the age of war was bound to precede it. War and commerce are only two differrent means to achieve the same end, that of possessing what is desired. Commerce is . . . an attempt to obtain by mutual agreement what one can no longer hope to obtain through violence. . . .
>
> War then comes before commerce. The former is all savage impulse, the latter civilized calculation. It is clear that the more the commercial tendency prevails, the weaker must the tendency to war become.[36]

One can see how for Constant the history of humanity is contained in man's acquisitive nature. War and commerce are two different and successive ways to the same natural end of man, which is to attain what he desires. On the one hand, Constant makes war sound dull and prosaic; he says not a word about honor and glory. On the other, he turns commerce into war. But the acquisitive and commercial viewpoint is already at work in the warrior's activity, although men do not yet know it. Constant commercializes war much more than he renders commerce warlike. Man is accordingly an acquisitive animal who attains self-consciousness by gradually discovering that commerce is the most reasonable means, because it is the most regular and the surest, of obtaining what he naturally desires. Such is the doctrine of modern commercialism, at least to the extent that it is concerned to develop a doctrine.

For his part, Montesquieu never attempts to make a psychological connection between war and commerce, to give them a common natural foundation that could explain "naturally" how history develops going from one to the other. At the very beginning of *The Spirit of the Laws*, in chapter 2 of book 1, he does assert against Hobbes that man is not by nature dominating or warlike; but, unlike Constant and Adam Smith,[37] he does not see man as commercial by nature. He brings out the natural and so to speak necessary effects of commerce and he rejoices that they are so salutary, but he does so without deeming it useful to state precisely what connection there might be between commerce and human nature and to seek in the human soul the positive mainspring of this activity. Nevertheless, in according such importance to the effects of commerce, he cannot remain indifferent to its causes and fail to provide an explicit and rigorous account of its appearance and development. In fact, Montesquieu does offer his interpretation of the movement of history in his explanation of the genesis of commerce, whose advances give European history its dynamism and unity. Chapter 5 of book 20 is an essential text that I must cite in its entirety because its strange character makes it decisive:

> Marseilles, a necessary retreat in the midst of a stormy sea, Marseilles, where all the winds, the shoals, and the coastline order ships to put in, was frequented by sea-faring people. The barrenness of its territory made its citizens decide on economic commerce. They had to be hardworking in order to replace that which nature refused them; just, in order to live among the barbarian nations that were to make their prosperity; moderate, in order for their government always to be tranquil; finally, of frugal mores, in order to live always by a commerce that they would the more surely preserve the less it was advantageous to them.
>
> It has been seen everywhere that violence and harassment have brought forth economic commerce among men who are constrained to hide in the marshes, on islands, on the shoals, and even among dangerous reefs. Thus were Tyre, Venice, and the Dutch towns founded; fugitives found security there. They had to live; they drew their livelihood from the whole universe.

The activity of commercial cities, or economic commerce, does not have its origin in a positive choice made by the individual or group. No one chooses to engage in economic commerce for its own sake, but only in response to the need to survive. It is in fact less an activity than a reaction to the location of hillsides and reefs and to the demands of sterile nature. One does not even choose which virtues one will practice, since zeal, justice, moderation, frugality are all born of the need to survive in hostile circumstances. By means of economic commerce, or commerce simply, virtue becomes the necessary means to a necessary end, a necessary escape.

I referred earlier to Hobbes's critique of traditional moral philosophy and its teleology. For Hobbes the moral virtues are not ends to be sought in themselves, but means to one's self- preservation. The commercial cities Montesquieu describes corroborate Hobbes's theory by concretizing it. As we have seen, Montesquieu also transforms the virtue of the Greek warrior cities from the universal human end it was for the Geek philosophers into the means to preserve a particular political regime, democracy. But if in the warrior cities the preservation of the body politic and the preservation of the individuals who compose it tend to be mutually exclusive, in the commercial cities the birth and maintenance of the body politic are rooted in the individual's desire for self-preservation. Whereas the citizens of warrior cities possess virtues in order to know how to die, those of commercial cities possess them in order to know how to survive. In both instances, however, the virtues and passions are ordered solely in terms of the need for preservation as it affects the individual or the group.

The preservation of the warrior group often entails the sacrifice of the individual. We have seen in our analysis of virtue how a sacrifice such as that of the monk could be the object of a ruling desire or need, in a word of a "passion." In a comparable arrangement Montesquieu sees how the desire proper to warrior cities is rooted in the desire for glory: "For people who have nothing but the necessities, there is left to desire only the glory of the homeland and one's own glory."[38] The glory the warrior citizen seeks in the sacrifice of his nature is the residue of the desire of the human animal when it is left unsatisfied.

Is commercial activity, contrary to the love of glory and obedience to law, the spontaneous or at least rational expression of this desire and hunger? Is it in the end the only truly rational activity of social man? Does Montesquieu agree with as well as foreshadow his admirer Constant? This is not the case at all since all of a sudden we learn that the cause of commerce—what makes it necessary and salutary—does not reside essentially in the natural hunger that seeks to eke out its food from stingy nature, but in "violence and harassment," that is, in certain human actions. It is in order to flee "violence and harassment" that one seeks refuge in Marseilles, as Montesquieu has it, and there starts to engage in commerce.

The founders of commercial cities are outcasts, exiles, and refugees who no longer have any land on which to subsist. But they do not take new territory for themselves; instead, they might even settle on a reef. Commercial activity is remarkable in not having or needing any territory of its own. It transforms the whole world into a land of survivors. Thus commercial cities such as Tyre, Venice, or the Dutch towns are specific and even strange bodies politic, whose operating principle is the inverse of that of other bodies politic.

Political bodies are ordinarily defined by frontier boundaries within which they draw the essentials of their livelihood and, more generally, the goods that make up the common life of people. Self-sufficiency is not only the condition of the city's life; it is also in a well-defined way its very goal.[39] Commercial cities, on the other hand, draw their subsistence from outside; or rather, commercial activity robs the distinction between interior and exterior of its hitherto decisive importance. Montesquieu can thus say with complete accuracy that commercial cities draw their subsistence from "the entire universe." Elsewhere bodies politic are generally founded, consolidated, and reformed to defend their citizens against enemies; in commercial cities, defense is essentially a matter of escaping. The bodies politic founded on economic commerce, such as those described by Montesquieu, are in some way the opposite of those where most men until then had sought their protection. The violence inseparable from traditional political bodies gives rise to new bodies politic. Commercial cities are thus not particular political regimes among other political regimes: they are born and live out of another logic of human action than the one at work in ordinary politics.

Thus we start to see some content to the formal observation we made above in section 4. In making us see that the English regime cannot even be integrated into the radically new classification he has fashioned, Montesquieu places "before our eyes" the fact that the world of politics cannot be adequately or exhaustively covered by any classification of regimes whatever. Classifying regimes presupposes that the problem of political life is essentially the same everywhere and always but that it can take different forms that combine the same elements in different ways according to disparate and often incompatible criteria that are the object of rational debate and evaluation.[40] The analysis Montesquieu offers of commercial cities shows that they function morally, socially, and politically in essentially different ways than do other political bodies that always tend to be warlike. This is not a question of two political regimes, but, one is tempted to say, two regimes of political life.

The new regime of political life, the alternative ordering of human action, could be characterized by saying that good results, even "virtuous cities," are more assuredly attained in politics by fleeing evil than by pursuing good. When men aim directly and naïvely at attaining the good city of virtue by law according to the best regime, they impose on themselves very harsh constraints—they "afflict" their nature—and condemn themselves to a life of war against other men and against their own nature. The greatest good that can befall men is the one they derive from the evil that besets them.

XV

But is the genesis of commercial cities the genesis of commerce itself? After all, the benefits of commerce enjoyed by commercial cities are found only in the breaks in the general violence fanned by traditional warrior politics, politics "as usual," and even seem to depend on this violence. Can the benefits of commerce be universalized or are they rather destined to remain the special preserve of a limited number of cities favored by geography? Montesquieu leaves no doubt that the benefits of commerce can be generalized and, beyond that, that their generalization is the salutary moving force of European history, as he shows in what is perhaps the most important chapter in *The Spirit of the Laws*, chapter 20 of book 21, entitled, "How Commerce in Europe Penetrated Barbarism."

Montesquieu's point of departure is the commonplace topic of moral philosophy and theology: lending at interest, which Aristotle and the Schoolmen condemn. In Montesquieu's eyes this condemnation is absurd and counterproductive, "for, whenever one prohibits a thing that is naturally permitted or necessary, one can only make dishonest the people who do it." He does not specify here whether lending at interest is "necessary" or "naturally permitted," but in the chapter specifically devoted to it, chapter 19 of book 22, Montesquieu states that it is necessary and that if it is not available at a modest price then the rate will be usurious. As he says there, "the business of society must always go forward." Montesquieu does not deny that religion can legitimately render its own, negative judgment on lending at interest, but it must express it only as a counsel of perfection and not as a positive command that can be promulgated as law: "To lend one's silver without interest is a very good act, but one senses that this can be only a religious counsel and not a civil law." Lending at interest in some way supplies the crucial test of Montesquieu's moral philosophy, since its prohibition produces its aggravation, which is usury, about which Montesquieu says that "extreme laws for good give rise to extreme evil."[41]

Because of the disgrace engendered by its prohibition, lending at interest, or usury, became the specialty of Jews who concentrated wealth in their hands. They thereby aroused the envy of princes, who often plundered them and at times subjected them to harsh atrocities. Montesquieu has this to say about the Jews and usury:

> Nevertheless, one saw commerce leave this sect of harassment and despair. The Jews, proscribed by each country in turn, found the means for saving their effects. In that way, they managed to fix their refuges forever; a prince who wanted very much to be rid of them would not, for all that, be in a humor to rid himself of their silver.
>
> They invented letters of exchange, and in this way commerce was able to avoid violence and maintain itself everywhere, for the richest trader had only invisible goods, which could be sent everywhere and leave no trace anywhere.[42]

As we have seen, commercial cities fled violence by establishing themselves "in the marshes, on islands, on the shoals, and even among dangerous reefs." At first they hid, then made themselves useful, and finally indispensable. In the Middle Ages Jews did not have the opportunity to found such a city, even in the most hospitable places, and so they found the way—the letter of exchange—to make their goods altogether invisible.[43] They are, as it were, a commercial city which is or could be present everywhere and whose wealth is nowhere visible. The invention of the letter of exchange frees commerce from the limitations that circumscribed it. It is no longer the activity of certain specialized cities. Every individual who engages in it tends to be as impregnable as Marseilles in its bay or Venice on its islands. Thanks to the revolution produced by the letter of exchange, commerce can be universalized and it does indeed become more and more universal. Over against the ordinary political world with its boundaries, sovereigns, and armies, commerce constitutes "another world" that is invisible, without a head, without territory, or rather whose territory is the universe, with no coercive physical force at its disposal but always imposing in some measure its law on political sovereigns. In its rapport with the world of politics, it behaves like and resembles the world of religion. But if it has the good effects that religion has or should have in softening the mores of subjects and princes, it has none of its bad effects. It does not "divide" human life by establishing a second sovereignty; on the contrary, it does not nurture fanaticism, as we saw at the start of the preceding section. Where religion seeks, commerce finds.

Montesquieu draws the lesson and formulates the irony of European history in the following terms: "Thus, to the speculations of the Schoolmen we owe all the misfortunes that accompanied the destruction of commerce; and to the avarice of princes we owe the establishment of a device that puts it, in a way, out of their power."[44] What matters is to determine just what preserves and saves and it is evident that evil does so more than good does.

Montesquieu's analysis of European history shows us the human world divided between two regimes of action. One regime seeks the good, but once this quest comes up against necessity, it produces evil: "extreme laws for good give rise to extreme evil." The other flees from evil, and thanks to necessity—how could one not flee from another who seeks to kill or rob him?—this flight produces good. Necessity corrupts the good and corrects the evil. Since necessity will always be at work among men, the more judicious and salutary regime of action is the one that, instead of seeking to humiliate necessity by affirming the good or surpassing the best, knows in a humble way how to make of it a permanent ally and to benefit from its boundless energy. Men will always flee suffering and death.

It is true that the wholesome regime of action has its origin in the results of the ruinous regime. The sublime speculations of the Schoolmen that ruined ancient commerce provoked the social dislocation and violence that gave rise to the letter of exchange and to modern commerce.[45] But humanity is not condemned to experience indefinitely the presence or threat of evil in order to find whatever avenues to the good lie within its ability. Once the ingenious method of payment is invented, commerce tends to become in some way invulnerable. A mechanism is unleashed which replaces the indefinite alternation of good and evil with the moving force of progress. Montesquieu's faith in the enduring effects of this mechanism is contagious:

> Since that time princes have had to govern themselves more wisely than they themselves would have thought, for it turned out that great acts of authority were so clumsy that experience itself has made known that only goodness of government brings prosperity.
>
> One has begun to be cured of Machiavellianism, and one will continue to be cured of it. . . .
>
> And, happily, men are in a situation such that, though their passions inspire in them the thought of being wicked, they nevertheless have an interest in not being so.[46]

What most recommends commerce to observers of the mutability of human things is the cumulative character of its effects. As the network of invisible wealth spreads and consolidates, as what Adam Smith will call "the system of natural liberty" develops, the motives princes have for misbehaving lose ground little by little. Once a crime becomes a fault, a lack of tact, an imprudence, it is committed less and less frequently. The collapse of exchange or the retaining of credit effectively excommunicates the criminal prince from reasonable society and he will soon come to repent his ways.

The way things happen according to modern experience, which is to say its "effectual truth," gives princes other counsels than those which they "would have thought of themselves" or that even Machiavelli would have offered them. Machiavelli urged them to take the initiative in "great coups of authority," the "spectacles" that leave citizens or subjects "at once satisfied and stupefied."[47] But modern princes have recourse to these less and less, not because they are more virtuous than their predecessors, but because they have, in fact and "in the event," much greater interest than their predecessors in conducting themselves in a somewhat decent way.

The interest of princes or the demands of necessity thus speak a different language in Montesquieu's time than in Machiavelli's. According to Machiavelli, "it is necessary to a prince, if he wants to maintain himself, to learn to be able not to be good, and to use this and not use it according to necessity."[48] Not only must the prince learn not to be good, he must also "know how to enter into evil, when forced by necessity."[49] When he renounces being good or decides to be evil, the Machiavellian prince always only obeys the necessity of his own preservation. Now if necessity might command at times a prince to oppress or to kill, it always commands his subjects, at least some among them, real or potential victims, to try to escape oppression. The desire to escape death and suffering is in all respects more general, more imperious than the necessity of killing or the need to torment. Commerce is the practice that makes it possible to benefit from this necessary inequality and to institutionalize these benefits by universalizing them.

As I observed in section 14, Montesquieu makes every effort to shed light on the positive effects of commerce, but he is not concerned to indicate the source or root of commerce in the human soul. That observation can now be made more precise. Montesquieu never describes commerce as the expression of a positive natural desire, whether it is the desire to possess that Benjamin Constant will speak of or "the desire of bettering one's condition" that Adam Smith will see as the principle of the moving force of "improvement" that cannot in the end be resisted and that gives European history its meaning.[50] Commerce is not at first desired or willed for its own sake but as the means to escape death or misery. Beyond this initial impetus and so to speak under its protection, the natural desire for the goods of this world, for "enjoyments" as Constant will say readily or for "the commodities of life" Montesquieu already speaks of,[51] will have full sway to develop. But, taking everything into account, it must be maintained that commerce is not the object or the project of a fundamental natural desire of the human soul.

Thus, what gives rise to and directs the development of European history is a process that is not immediately or directly rooted in man's nature. Man is not, according to Montesquieu, a commercial animal, as he was a

political animal for Aristotle. What befalls man in the wholesome development of commerce is only indirectly linked to his nature. This perception
or interpretation qualifies the authority Montesquieu gives to the present
moment, to history.

XVI

We can now take a synthetic view of the two great regimes of politics and
human life between which Montesquieu perceives, or rather introduces,
such a profound difference.

Until the eighteenth century, European men essentially lived under the
regime of virtue and law, either civic or Christian, that enjoined a man to
risk his life or mortify his nature. But more and more they tend to live
under the regime of commerce and liberty that was set into motion and
maintained by the desire and the necessity of avoiding death and misery.
They place themselves more and more under the authority of the modern
experience.

As we have seen, these two regimes can be described, the first as the one
where the wellspring of human action is the quest for the good and hence
of the best, and the second as the one where what matters above all is to
flee from evil. These two possibilities are evidently "inscribed within
human nature." Everyone every day has a hundred occasions to do both,
choose good and flee evil. But precisely if we take our bearings from the
idea of nature, we do not understand how nature can present two so different and almost contrary faces such that these two possibilities that by
definition are permanent really characterize, respectively and disjointedly,
two successive epochs and regimes of human experience. Since these two
equally natural possibilities succeed one another and also exclude one another, they cannot be brought back to the unity of nature, which appears
to be transformed and guided by something stronger than itself. By their
very succession, in the "history" they form, they show the inadequacy of
the concept of Nature as well as of classical philosophy rooted in the idea
of Nature. Consequently, Montesquieu cannot give a rigorous answer to
the question whether the regime of law or the regime of liberty conforms
more to nature. Nor does he have to give an answer because the question
of human order is no longer raised in these terms.

Perhaps it will be said that these theoretical considerations are too scrupulous and that everything really points to a simple answer: the old regime
that oppresses nature is liberated and thus fulfilled in the new. This impression is misleading, however. If Montesquieu in fact grounds his teaching in the well articulated idea of progress we have sought to elucidate in
this chapter, he overlooks any "progressivist" naivete. In particular, he

looks askance at the satisfactions human nature can find in England. The mainspring of the English regime is "impatience" with regard to evil. Consequently, the English, to whom "everything" is "intolerable," are unhappy "while having so many grounds not to be so."[52] Modern liberty is not moved by the attraction of the good or the best, but by a force that comes from behind: the fear of evil, real or imaginary, the "feeling of ills." Montesquieu offers the following sketch of the freest people on earth: "Servitude always begins with drowsiness. But a people who rest in no situation, who constantly pinch themselves to find the painful spots, could scarcely fall asleep." English liberty is the vigilance of a people whose hypersensitivity keeps them from falling asleep. Happiness no doubt would be content with a more "moderate" liberty, but such liberty, which is the hallmark of the French monarchy, is always threatened by despotism, this "insult" to human nature. If one wishes to definitely banish despotism that is the fatal weakness of monarchy, one must accept to be "extremely free." One must thus accept the moral effects of commerce and liberty, which are not all favorable to the greatness or the happiness of man in his nature.[53]

Now that we have dealt with the objection that progressist good sense raises for the strict doctrine of progress, we can go on to formulate the synthesis that is the concern of this section.

If the regime of virtue or law can legitimately be termed "contrary to nature," the regime of liberty cannot be said to be strictly speaking "in conformity with nature." It cannot be the unifying element of the different possibilities of human life. The classification of political regimes according to their greater or lesser conformity to nature gives way to the succession of the two great regimes of law and liberty. To call these two regimes political is anachronistic; it is much more appropriate to call them historical. History, and no longer Nature, is the umbrella under which the two regimes are joined in their succession and their incompatibility. In revealing the new element of History, the modern experience is not only the experience of the effects of commerce and liberty, but also of their incompatibility and thus its own incompatibility with the earlier regime. The modern experience is forever severing itself from the past and dividing the past and future world in terms that reinforce their separation. It discovers that in the knotted tissue of human life with its goods and evils there runs a seam that joins and disjoins two possibilities in life. One of these seeks an uncertain good exposed to corruption and the other, faced with necessity, seeks to escape the evils of which it has first taken careful stock. In opposition to and in the place of the desire to seek the good to attain it and so to perfect oneself arises the urgent need to flee from evil in order to be safe and free.

The evil can be death, pain, or above all simple discomfort, which sums up the effects of all evils from which one needs to be delivered. This involves a moral and spiritual act that has the energy and simplicity of a physical movement and consists in turning away from the law and the good one has been given in order to expose oneself fully to the painful pressure of discomfort, the force that comes up from behind to push us forward into an ever more open space. Intent on methodically taking all the steps that are destined to free him from all discomfort, whether of feeling cold or guilty, modern man is concerned only with the instruments of his emancipation project or with the obstacles to it. Nothing substantial, be it law, good, cause, or purpose, either holds his attention or holds back his advance any longer. He has become a runner and will go on running until the end of the world.

The monk was not aware that his cell was "uncomfortable." He might die of cold without letting that interrupt his prayer. There is no chance this will happen to modern man, whose first *thought* is to light a fire. Such is the modest exchange of priorities and the liberating deed of the modern experience, which, as it becomes widespread and sharper, makes all the elements of traditional life appear all the more subjected to a law contrary to nature. The family and the city appear as closed as a monk's cell. The man who once sought to expiate his fault now wishes to escape from discomfort and guilt. The supreme discomfort is the one that gives rise to law itself, which afflicts and is hostile to nature. For whoever has changed priorities and who therefore no longer loves the law above all else,[54] the law is for him among the dead and sad things that constrain, irritate, and perplex him and from which he now turns away. Fleeing from the law is altogether different from disobeying it. Men have always disobeyed the law, but fleeing the law is proper to modern man and sums up his whole experience.

Because modern man continually experiences within himself the succession and incompatibility of two moral attitudes, two directions of attention and intention, he concludes implicitly but irresistibly that there are two successive and incompatible humanities, the ancient and the modern. Self-consciousness, the consciousness of being modern, is thus the consciousness of this division. Once this consciousness is formulated explicitly and objectively, it comes to see that the two distinct humanities, incompatible and successive, are bound and borne by neither nature nor law, but by the mother and sum of all successions, which is History.

But does not this affirmation of History as the ultimate element and Whole also denature the modern experience? As the experience of division, modern experience holds within itself a double negation whose expression and activity are brutally overshadowed by each and every affirmation of History. With respect to the old law that oppresses nature, the new regime affirms it. However, the old regime presupposes a certain understanding and affirmation of nature that is necessarily mingled with the law, with respect to which the new regime aims at being pure liberty that no natural finality can jeopardize. Modern consciousness negates the ancient regime of life under the law in the name of nature and at the same time it negates nature in the name of liberty. Precisely because it is unaware of it, this equivocation gives common consciousness its singular confidence and its capacity to be diffused. Thanks to the double negation, modern man feels very sincerely and very modestly superior to all things which are either law or nature and above all else to all the humanities that came before him. But does not modern philosophy, which is forever concerned to reveal an ever more radical historicity beneath the progress that excites popular opinion, itself remain deceived by this duplicity that is otherwise very evident?

CHAPTER II

The Sociological Viewpoint

FROM A CERTAIN point in time onward the feeling of "living in history," and no longer in nature or creation or under the law, imposed itself as the determining element in European consciousness before whose brilliance all traditional authorities pale. How could anything possibly resist the "demands of the present time"? Montesquieu established the new authority's credentials with subtlety and rigor as early as the first half of the eighteenth century, but it was only after the revolutionary period and in the following century that it imposed itself in all quarters. One has only to compare Montesquieu's refined play on the words "seek" and "find" in which we have located the first philosophical elaboration of the idea of the authority of history, with Lamartine's proclamation of the emerging new humanity that has all the appearances of a *fait accompli* and the awesome prestige of a revelation:

> C'en est fait; la parole a soufflé sur les mers;
> Le chaos bout, et couve un second univers,
> Et pour le genre humain, que le sceptre abandonne,
> Le salut est dans tous et n'est plus dans personne!
> A l'immense roulis d'un océan nouveau,
> Aux oscillations du ciel et du vaisseau,
> Aux gigantesques flots qui croulent sur nos têtes,
> On sent que l'homme aussi double du cap des Tempêtes,
> Et passe, sous la foudre et dans l'obscurité,
> Le tropique orageux d'une autre humanité.[1]

Between Montesquieu and Lamartine "history" had found its support and vehicle in "everybody" and "society." While Greek man came into contact with and came to know his nature through the political regime of his city, it is by means of society that modern man comes into contact with and comes to know his new element, history. Contemporary society is history that has become the route that is followed, the truth that is accepted, and the life that is shared.

It is true that commerce, in Montesquieu's interpretation, already has most of the traits that will soon be conferred on society.[2] However, its authority still needs to be made manifest and explicated by the philosopher and political men need to know how "to take advantage" of its benefits.[3] It does not have the aura of triumphant irresistibility that will subjugate all parties in the wake of the French revolution. I might say that commerce still retains civil and courteous manners that its two big sisters, History and Society, will never adopt.

Precisely what does it mean to say that society would have access to the heart of modern life? The feeling of living "within society" is the effective expression of the feeling of living "within history," both of which are of central importance for us. The former found itself and its depiction in the novel and gave rise to a new science: sociology. Nothing will be said here of the novel, but an effort will be made to penetrate the meaning of sociology, the approach or perspective that allows and requires one to speak on any subject "from a sociological viewpoint . . ."

II

As is well known, this science was officially established at the start of the nineteenth century with the urgency of putting an end to the revolutionary crisis. Whereas the French Revolution had been the grandest undertaking ever conceived by men to found deliberately a rational political order in which the fundamental liberties to which they have a right would be guaranteed, sociology gave itself the task of extricating law from social necessities. The French Revolution thus becomes a construction site between two periods of political thought that seem to lead in two political directions as squarely opposed to one another as the ideas of the free social contract and social determinism. This contrast originates in part to be sure in a "reaction" to the French Revolution and to the social dissolution induced, it was thought, by the individualism it brought with it. But too much importance must not be given to this reactive, or even at times frankly "reactionary," aspect of the postrevolutionary discovery of society.[4] The grumblers of the Reaction notwithstanding, society and social determinism were discovered with the same enthusiasm that had accompanied the proclamation of human equality and liberty. The blossoming of humanity, which is still the issue at hand, is no longer to be sought in the deliberate construction of a free and rational political order, but in the obedient grasp of the social determinism, or more precisely the salutary development of human society through a succession of necessary stages. On this score Karl Marx and Auguste Comte are in agreement. A fulfilling and just human order is less the work of liberty than the effect of necessity acting in history and society.

In the nineteenth century the partisans of liberty and the contemplators of necessity, the liberals and the sociologists, are less hostile toward one another than it appears. Whereas the liberals struggle with pains and rebuffs to establish and consolidate in France liberal institutions comparable to those of England and the United States, the sociologists tend to see in liberalism a continuation of the revolutionary disorder. Accordingly Comte applauded the coup-d'état of Louis-Napoleon before proposing an alliance with the general of the Jesuits against "the anarchic irruption of Western delirium." As real and substantive as this discord is, it must nevertheless be observed that the liberals admit and even proclaim that the new society born of the revolution is established definitively and only needs to be perfected politically. It is impossible to go back to the Ancien Regime or, more generally, to an inegalitarian society. In the eyes of the liberal there is an irresistible movement, a necessary progress of human societies. Diverse as they are, Constant, Tocqueville, or Chateaubriand are equally convinced that human history is happily ordered by the law of the progressive equalization of conditions. In upholding the idea that an irresistible process is at work in history and society, liberalism and sociology agree on a fundamental point.

As the century advances a third group appears and grows in influence: the socialists. Like the sociologists and the liberals, the socialists maintain that the essential element of the human world is society, as opposed to the state and, more generally, the political order, which some even foresee will wither away. How close socialism and sociology are on this essential point can be seen in the "personal union" that the two doctrines achieve in the person of Émile Durkheim.

After the French Revolution, these three great schools of political thought—the liberals, the sociologues, and the socialists—are joined in the notion of society and the idea that society—again, as opposed to the state and political institutions—is the locus of the irreversible and irresistible movement of history. In this sense, the sociological viewpoint penetrates and dominates all modern political thought.

III

Émile Durkheim laid bare the fundamental presuppositions of this viewpoint in a particularly clear way. I shall here consider his Latin dissertation of 1892,[5] where the master of French sociology presents in a remarkably succinct way what distinguishes the sociological viewpoint from that of classical political philosophy.

> Before social science could begin to exist, it had to be assigned a definite subject matter.

At first sight, this problem presents no difficulty: the subject matter of social science is social "things," that is, laws, customs, religions, etc. However, if we look into history, we find that until quite recent times, no philosopher ever viewed these matters in such a light. They thought that all such phenomena depended upon the human will and hence failed to realize that they are actual things, like all other things in nature, which have their particular characteristics and consequently call forth sciences that can describe and explain them. It seemed to them sufficient to ascertain what the human will should strive for and what it should avoid in constituted societies. Accordingly they sought to know, not the nature and origin of social phenomena, not what they actually are, but what they ought to be; their aim was not to offer us as true an image of nature as possible, but to confront our imagination with the idea of a perfect society, a model to be imitated. Even Aristotle, who devoted far more attention than Plato to experience, aimed at discovering, not the laws of social existence, but the best form of society. He starts by assuming that a society's sole object should be to make its members happy through the practice of virtue, and that virtue lies in contemplation. He does not establish this principle as a law which societies actually observe, but as one which they should act upon in order that human beings may fulfill their specific nature. . . . The political thinkers who came after him followed his example more or less. Whether they completely disregard reality or pay a certain amount of attention to it, they all have a single purpose: to correct or transform it completely, rather than to know it. They take virtually no interest in the past and the present, but look to the future. And a discipline that looks to the future lacks a determinate subject matter and should therefore be called not a science but an art.[6]

The objection which dominates this admirable page is that the viewpoint of classical political philosophy and even of political philosophy in general "up to a very recent time" is an active or practical point of view. This is indeed what Aristotle himself affirms, for example at the beginning of *Nicomachean Ethics*.[7] For social science to be truly scientific, to be a true and pure science, it must, according to Durkheim, be pure theory. The task of sociology is not to depict the desirable political order, or best regime, that Durkheim, in a revealing fashion, calls "the best form of society," but to determine, to define, and to classify the forms or types of society. He cannot deny that Aristotle in great measure has recourse to the most precise and complete classification possible of the different forms of human association. Precisely, as he states a little further on, Aristotle confused the diverse types of society with the different forms of states, and was concerned to classify only the latter, leaving in a confused state whatever pertains to morality, religion, commerce, the family. But these elements have profound connections with the nature of societies; they even constitute the true matter of life and, consequently, of social science.[8]

There is a close connection between the practical viewpoint and the almost exclusive interest in the state as distinct from society. The philosophers were interested above all in the state, or in politics generally speaking, because the political domain seemed to them to be the proper locus of human activity and initiatives.[9] That is a "superstition" which the philosopher, the political man, and the ordinary citizen all hold in common and from which only the sociologist, it seems, is exempt. The superstition gives credence to the causal or causative capacity of human action, man's capacity to bring about something new and unforeseeable. In reality, Durkheim says, social life develops according to rules that are independent of the will of man. If it were otherwise, no science of society would be possible: "The subject matter of science can consist only of things that have a stable nature of their own and are able to resist the human will."[10] Human action is contingent, but necessity is found in the sociologist's knowledge.

As a scholar, the sociologist discovers necessary laws, comparable to those of nature. But laws of what and laws that regulate what? Since the will and action of men are only contingent, these laws can only be those of the nature of man, which is expressed, one can think, in what man wills and does. However, the fact is they belong to another nature, to social nature; they are the laws of society.[11]

Émile Durkheim has brought us to a decisive observation. Sociology is constructed as a science comparable to and parallel with the sciences of nature in taking as its object something other than the nature of man and in deliberately refusing to take man's nature as its object. It seeks to and must abstract from this nature. Sociology as a science, or "science of man" as it will soon be called, exists only by refusing to be a science of the nature of man.

IV

We can summarize what we have learned by saying that classical political philosophy, and perhaps political philosophy as such, takes its bearing from the *viewpoint of the actor*, the citizen or statesman, the practical viewpoint, whereas sociology adopts the viewpoint of the spectator. The *viewpoint of the spectator* is all the more pure and scientific in that it accords no real initiative whatever to the agent or agents, but considers their actions or their works as the necessary effect of necessary causes. Such is the original thrust of sociology, which determines its whole history.

What the individual does produce by his will is in Durkheim's terms "fortuitous," "capricious," or "contingent." Not only is it not truly efficacious, without causative capacity, but it is also deprived of reason and not apt to being fit into a truly intelligible, which is to say scientific, scheme. Reason is entirely concentrated in the gaze of the spectator, in the trained eye of the sociologist, and so is all the efficacy in society as a force essentially distinct from and independent from the real individual actors who make up society. Reason, or science, is in the sociologist; force, or cause, is in society. The sociologist observes society and in him reason is joined to force or cause. Nothing of importance can escape this alliance of reason and cause that uncovers and promulgates the true order beyond the insignificant chaos of individuals animated by capricious human nature.

To be sure, in the confusion wherein we live, the social or moral agent, the citizen, the father, the single person, the merry widow, the master swimmer, the philosopher, the jack of all trades, all do things for certain reasons. Each is a force or cause that acts for certain motives. In each one, whether he be Caesar or my neighbor, cause and reason are present and intermingled. The trained eye of the sociologist disentangles this confusion. The sociologist, or at least the sociological viewpoint, appropriates the whole of reason; force and causality are vested entirely in society. The consequence is that naturally there is little rapport between what the sociologist describes or demonstrates and what real men live out. Whether Caesar or my neighbor, their motives are not to be found in the sociologist's reasons or his causes.

The sociologists were not able to perceive this difficulty, and a considerable part of their discipline is occupied in seeking to resolve it, or at least turn it around. This is the case in particular with that part of the discipline based on "methodological individualism." The most impressive effort in this direction no doubt was accomplished by Max Weber.[12] Weber sought to preserve and even solidify the viewpoint of the scientific observer or spectator who considered only the objective linkage of causes, while giving a rightful place to what the real man lives, thinks, and wills, the individual who chooses among diverse possible actions and produces real effects. Max Weber impressively accorded the real individual his "values."

Before inquiring into the attempts made by sociology to overcome its original handicap, it is appropriate to investigate why its first project straight off throws this science so far from any correlation to reality that it then ardently desires and takes all the pains in the world to regain that connection. The "methodological" intemperance that characterizes it, and that spreads to the other "human sciences," stems first of all from this twofold contradictory movement: a deliberate and forceful distancing from any familiarity with what is real in order to achieve the distance and height of Science, and a no less deliberate and forceful effort to recover that familiarity. Durkheim shows his awareness of this problem when he writes that "either social phenomena are incompatible with science or they are governed by the same laws as the rest of the universe."[13] In fact, whether one conceives of sociological law as identical with or analogous to the laws of nature or as altogether different from them, the sociological viewpoint consists of this distancing in order to draw out the law of causality. The sociologist knows society as a cause by drawing out the laws of social nature. We cannot proceed with our investigation without examining closely the notion of sociological law. On the decisive point, as Durkheim himself tells us, our guide must be Montesquieu, who was the first to place the notion of law at the center of social science.[14]

V

Let us turn anew to Montesquieu, who says the following in the Preface to *The Spirit of the Laws*:

> I began by examining men, and I believed that, amidst the infinite diversity of laws and mores, they were not led by their fancies alone.
>
> I have set down the principles, and I have seen particular cases conform to them as if by themselves, the histories of all nations being but their consequences, and each particular law connecting with another law or dependent on a more general one.

Montesquieu's starting point is the "infinite diversity" of human things, which is also the starting point of sociology and the human sciences generally. Nothing human is alien to them. They do not hesitate to study, for example, "the symbolism of penis sheathes in the Upper Oronoco," or "the feeling for the infinite along the shores of Lake Chad." Durkheim the sociologist reproaches the philosopher Aristotle with speaking of man or of human nature in general, while "completely neglecting the reality" of the infinite diversity of human things. A more refined version of this critique will make of philosophy and its inquiry into the general and universal the expression of a particular society, for example, the "technological West," that is just as particular as the Nambikwara of the Amazon and the Semarang of Java. But what is often overlooked, though it stands out in the Montesquieu passages cited above, is that this diversity is underlined by the sociologist only to be soon erased. At the end of the scientific procedure, the particular facts, as diverse as they appear at first, will be no more than particular cases of general laws. Shall we say that diversity only attracts the sociologist's attention because it is a stumbling block to him? Or that the affirmation of diversity is only a polemical tool in his debate with the philosopher? In any event two stages need to be distinguished in the sociologist's procedure. In the first he brings out and emphasizes human diversity in order to remove any plausibility from the philosopher who claims to be able to draw out the essential traits of human nature or the primordial articulations of the human condition. In the second stage he abolishes this diversity or deprives it of its meaning by drawing out the general laws under which all particular cases fall and which thereby regulate the functioning of human societies.

Passing from philosophy to sociology is not to pass from abstract and monotone generality to concrete and diverse reality. Rather it is going from the universal as the nature, condition, or "existence" of man, to the general as a law under which all particular cases fall. Particular reality is the pivotal point in this passage that rejects the universal and makes the particular case the basis of the general law. It can play this pivotal role only because it has an altogether different relation with the universal as understood by philosophy from the one it has with the general in sociology. Without taking up one of the thorniest questions in ontology, one can make the following observation. According to classical philosophy, for example, the universal that is human nature is present in the human world in each particular individual as well as each particular deed, work, event. It is eminently and supremely present when it has been placed in a condition to act, to produce specific effects of justice and happiness, that is to say when a political regime has been instituted "in conformity with nature." In the technical language of Aristotle, the universal is at once the formal and the final cause of the particular. According to the sociological viewpoint that discloses the general law under which all particular cases fall, the general is the cause of the particular in an altogether different and, it seems, greatly weakened sense. A good example of this is the law that appears fundamental to Durkheim and which, according to him, Montesquieu discovered without being able to formulate it in all its rigor and to draw all its consequences, the law according to which the forms of society—its institutions, mores, and laws—depend on its volume.[15] Let us assume that this law is as verified as Durkheim asserts it to be. It is at the same time clear that the social volume is neither present nor "causing" in each society as is the political nature of man in the Aristotelian city. Durkheim makes it perfectly clear that it is the cause of the *differences* among societies. This means that all things otherwise being equal, the social volume is the principal cause of the differences among societies. But, "all things otherwise being equal" means assuming society and social man, or man being what he is. The elaboration of the general law presupposes a universal which it excludes from consideration. It follows that, in the example before us, the "volume" can be said to be "cause" or "source" only in a restricted sense. As the cause of the difference, it is only a secondary cause that presupposes and is subordinated to the first cause, the humanity of man, the cause of likeness which conditions and holds together all the differences. Should it not be said that secondary causality as illuminated by the sociological law presupposes the primary causality of the human universal that philosophy seeks to investigate?

Perhaps it will be objected that, in every investigation in the human sciences, the humanity of man is obviously presupposed; and that, leaving it to philosophy to rehash sterile tautologies, these sciences, and particularly sociology, press onward to more heady discoveries. Perhaps that is the case. It may also be that this view shows an unjustified disdain for tautology. After all, what is man, taken up with being what he is, with saying what he thinks and understanding what he says, desirous of expressing his being ever more exactly, if not a living and ardent tautology?

What is more, the intellectual quest resembles a human battle in that it is extremely risky to leave behind an essential objective without investigating it. This abstention or postponement will not cease to haunt later investigation as a principle of both energy and uncertainty. Whoever refuses to raise the principal question and yet continues to search, will raise it in spite of himself without recognizing it, with an anxiety and an ineptness whose source he is unaware of. The primary question of the human universal is not absent from sociology. It is hard to recognize yet it is recognizable. It becomes the question of the generality of the law, which nurtures the search for the most general law possible.

Montesquieu and Durkheim are very concerned to subject the diversity of cases to the unity of law, to an ever more unitary and general law. Consequently, both strive to reduce the role of chance to a minimum. On that score, the two sociologists are explicit and even emphatic.[16] The affirmation of sociological causality is one and the same as the denial of chance. It is true that if one refuses to grant an explicative and causal role to the humanity of man, if one scorns the tautologies of human nature, if one then abandons the most capacious generating and integrating principle, the intelligible chain must be tightened all the more. Thus in effect, either the social world is regulated by a strictly necessary causality, or it is pure confusion rebellious against all science. Either the sociologist lays bare a necessary causal link or he has nothing to say, at least nothing properly scientific. On the other hand, whoever grants primary causality to human nature, to man's very humanity, can give chance a large role to play, as all philosophers and historians did until the eighteenth century and as everyone still does today, from the greatest to the least and from the most foolish to the most learned, when no one is looking over his shoulder. Two examples will illustrate the solidarity between the causality of human nature and chance (or the causality of chance) on the one hand, and between the causality of society and strict determinism (or the denial of chance) on the other.

If, for example, one attributes the English resistance of 1940 to the great soul of Churchill, one at the same time attributes it to chance; it was by a great "chance" that a man such as Churchill found himself at that very moment in a situation to take action. In order to understand 1940, one does not need to "search for the cause of Churchill": Churchill himself is the cause. Human nature is here at once the primary cause and the limited or finite cause. Consequently, the effects it produces are at once fully intelligible and altogether unnecessary and, in this sense, altogether fortuitous. Inversely, if, for example, one attributes the defeat of Robespierre on the Ninth Thermidor to the chance rainfall that scattered his partisans, in doing so one puts human nature in the position of a collateral cause that is very low on the scale. Even though they are patriots and virtuous men, people detest staying in the rain. The causality of chance does not act without the input of the causality of our human nature. Thus, since the highest human causality is ever fortuitous itself, the most trivial chance summons human nature.

If now we seek to give a "sociological explanation" of England's behavior in 1940 (this time leaving aside the sans-culottes, who have received more sociological attention than any social group, past, present, or to come), we shall invoke for example the "pigeon-hole social structure" of that country that is particularly apt to preserve those virtues which "anomie" had eroded in France. But the link between social structure and political and military behavior must then be strictly necessary. If the first does not necessarily entail the second, there is no sociological explanation at all. One is dealing merely with more or less judicious considerations, which can be called "sociological" if one holds to it, but which hold meaning or validity only in the framework of another type; they do not constitute an explanation of scientific sociology. If the causal link is verified, the sociologist will conclude that, given their social structure, the English could not do otherwise than refuse to submit to Hitler's aggression as well as to his attempt at seducing them.

This is not the place to decide between one and the other explanation. Our subject is not the Battle of England. But one sees just how the sociological explanation does not hold up on its own the way the explanation by human nature does. The "pigeon-hole social structure" of England in 1940 cannot be the primary cause that was Churchill's noble nature. It, too, in turn has its cause, for example, the social volume of King George III, or of the Saxon heptarchy, which, in turn, has its cause. . . It is doubtless necessary to come to an end at some point, as Aristotle observed in another context, but why stop at this cause rather than another? Is it even possible to stop, once the human world is only comprehensible as a causal chain without a first cause? Or shall we elaborate the system of Society, the General Theory that exhaustively deploys the network of effects and causes and explains all that has to be explained in the social world? At this point nothing stops the volubility of the human mind.

It will be said that I am exaggerating the necessity of necessity in sociological argumentation, and that, whereas I cite Durkheim's clearest passages, the discipline has distanced itself a good deal from the rigor of its earliest assertions. It is true that in practice what so-called "sociological" scholarship most often offers are causes that are not truly causes, at any rate not by themselves but only when considerably reinforced by conditions, that is, supplementary and complementary causes. Yet it is not clear how sociology could depart from Durkheim's rigor and still retain its scientific ambition. Let us read the master once more:

> In consequence of the society's particular situation, communal life must necessarily assume a certain definite form. This form is expressed by the laws, which thus result with the same inevitability from the efficient causes. To deny this is to assume that most social phenomena, particularly the most important, have no cause whatsoever.[17]

One can sense anxiety in these last words, where the validity and very possibility of the sociological viewpoint are at stake. Aristotle's error, as we saw above, his "superstition," is to make any science of man impossible. It is also the error of the statesman and the ordinary citizen alike, and that of everyone with the exception of, precisely, the sociologist. But why? Doesn't the principle of causality hold in both senses and can't science move just as well from cause to effect as from effect to cause? Such is not the case, as sociology has understood very well. If man is posited as a cause, he will be the cause of a multitude of possible effects. He will be an undetermined cause. This indetermination, which drives Durkheim mad, will only be removed, and human causality only become operative, through the mediation of human intelligence and liberty. As soon as the humanity of man is posited as a cause, another viewpoint than the causal viewpoint is taken on the human world, one which sees man as an agent confronting the uncertainty of the future. Such an agent is by nature the addressee of a "practical science" or an "art";[18] he cannot be the object of a causal science or pure theory. To a man who is to act or to one who, considered as a cause, is essentially a man who can act, one would in truth only have "advice" to give, more or less well informed, judicious and pressing, but one would be at a loss to place him in a necessary causal chain. On the other hand, if one considers man as an effect, everything is different. There is no longer any real uncertainty, only a scientific difficulty. It is up to the observer, the spectator, the researcher to designate clearly the cause. He is free to make the cause as clear and even clearer than the effect; in fact, he is free to designate whatever he wants as cause, provided only that the subject of his research displays the causal necessity, which is to say that it gives the appearances thereof. Such is the reversal accomplished by the sociological viewpoint. So that the human phenomenon can be the object of science, all that is needed is that sociological laws be general and necessary. The necessary and sufficient cause of such laws is that man, instead of being the naturally free source of his deeds and works, be rigorously necessitated to do what he does, the way he does it. For the sociological spectator, man appears no longer as cause, but as effect, no longer as causing but as caused.

VI

Man appears in this light for the first time in *The Spirit of the Laws*. Here is how Montesquieu expresses himself:

> Many things govern men: climate, religion, laws, the maxims of the government, examples of past things, mores, and manners; a general spirit is formed as a result.
>
> To the extent that, in each nation, one of these causes acts more forcefully, the others yield to it. Nature and climate almost alone dominate savages; manners govern the Chinese; laws tyrannize Japan; in former times mores set the tone in Lacedaemonia; in Rome it was set by the maxims of government and the ancient mores.

These remarkable, even extraordinary lines by themselves constitute a whole chapter of *The Spirit of the Laws*, chapter 4 of book 19, entitled "What the General Spirit Is." Let us consider the first words, which seem so innocuous, almost expletive: "Many things govern men." Men are presented straight off as being passive rather active, subjected rather than free in their conduct. This formulation, so deliberately and strictly neutral, suggests the equal dignity or lack of dignity of each of the things that govern men.[19] In the subsequent enumeration, all things are placed on the same level, climate along with the maxims of government. One and the other govern men. Accordingly, if I live in a very cold climate, I must work hard to survive: I am "governed" by the climate. But if, on some sunny island, the government orders me to go take part in harvesting sugar cane even though I am a violin maker, then I am "governed" by the "maxims of government." The perspective thus formulated for the first time by Montesquieu tends to erase the specific and eminent role of the political order such as the Ancients conceived of it, the role of "laws" and "maxims of the government," since these are only two among numerous instances that "govern men." Here is manifest in striking and even provocative fashion the essential trait of the sociological viewpoint that, in discussing Durkheim, we underlined in section III of this chapter. The real human agent is deliberately ignored. In Montesquieu's inaugural formulation, the trait is pushed as far as the bizarre, so much is it evident that for a real human agent, a living man, it is in no way the same "thing" to receive an "order" from the climate, which, moreover, he in no way perceives as an order, and to receive an order from the government or, more generally,

from a man or group of men. Accordingly Montesquieu's first act is to
erase the distinction that matters most to men, the one they recognize or
establish, between those beings endowed with intelligence and will and
those deprived of them.

The various "things" that "govern men," or as we would say today,
more abstractly, the various "social parameters," are thus placed on the
same plane. Their combined effects, the result of combining their influences, characterize each body politic in forming what Montesquieu calls its
"general spirit." Since there is apparently no discernible natural hierarchy
among the different "things," one is tempted to say the "general spirit" is
determined, as with a sum of forces or a chemical compound, by the relative weight or proportion that prevails among the diverse ingredients. This
proportion is established at the conclusion of a sociological analysis, once
the sociologist is in a position to conclude, for example, that such and such
a society is governed by religion, and another by its ancestral mores.

Such an analysis, precisely because it is sociological and not philosophical, scientific and not metaphysical or dogmatic, does not presuppose any
judgment concerning the place, for example, of religion in human existence in general, and even less, if that is possible, concerning its truth or
the truth of any particular religion. It even excludes such a judgment in
principle. The requirement of scientific neutrality raises a difficulty for the
researcher which it is important to assess precisely. The sociologist, who
chooses to be and believes himself incapable of saying anything about the
truth, for example, of Christianity or Islam under any of their forms or in
general about the place of religion in human life, on the other hand wants
to and believes himself able to arrive at scientific, that is, rigorously demonstrated conclusions on the role, for example, of Calvinism in Western
economic development[20] or of Shiite Islam in the social and political development of Iran. Not wanting to say anything about the universal or the
general, he wants to and thinks he can be demonstrative about the particular. It seems that whoever cannot attain the least can achieve the most. Or
must one think that the particular is susceptible of being known without
any prior or at least concomitant knowledge of the universal and the general? The sociologist, it will be said, far from stopping at the particular,
also aspires to a general knowledge, but of a new kind of generality that
expresses itself, as we noted in section V, not by the general law under
which the particular cases are made to fall. But how does one proceed to
elaborate such a general law in order to arrive at this new generality? The
birth of the new understanding could, I believe, be sketched in a very
schematic way in the following terms.

In a given society or body politic we observe the active presence of a
religion, Islam for example, of a family organization, polygamy for example, of a type of political power, despotism for example. In another society,

we observe the active presence of another religion, such as Christianity, of some other family organization, for example monogamy, of some other type of political power, a moderate monarchy. This set of observations naturally gives rise to a series of questions. "Naturally," which is to say that our mind, which, as Aristotle says in the opening sentence of the *Metaphysics*, by nature desires to know, asks these questions spontaneously and irresistibly. These questions that press upon us are the very ones formulated by classical philosophy, or, if one wishes, scientific thinking, which is more aware of their complexity. For example: which is the true religion, Islam or Christianity? or another religion? or none whatever? Which family organization, polygamy or monogamy, or which political ordering, despotism or moderate monarchy, is more in conformity with nature or the vocation or right of man? Or is a third form more so? The sociologist does not raise questions of this sort. He asks an entirely different question, whether Islam, polygamy, and political despotism properly go together according to a law of reciprocal causality in the same way that Christianity, monogamy, and moderate monarchy necessarily go together, and the same among religion R3, family structure F3, and political type P3, and so on indefinitely. If such relations or laws are effectively measurable, one would be in a position to arrange the diversity of the human world by determining the "types" of society thanks to these relations and laws. This is how Montesquieu proceeds in *The Spirit of the Laws*. As the first philosopher to adopt this approach, he is also the first sociologist.

Now in focusing all of one's scientific attention, that is, all one's legitimate attention, on the relation proper to a type of society one observes among Islam, polygamy, and despotism, among Christianity, monogamy, moderate monarchy, among such and such a religion, family structure, political form, one leaves in the shadows or rather necessarily obscures, by excluding it from legitimate scientific inquiry, the most natural if I may say so, and most essential rapport that prevails between Islam and Christianity as two religions, that is, as two forms of life and thought that both equally claim to give access to the true God; between polygamy and monogamy as two family organizations that seek each one equally to fill the need for the perpetuation of the species as well as the desire of each sex for happiness; between despotism and moderate monarchy as two political forms whose comparison requires us to raise the question of the just political order. Once the mind's attention is focused on relations, the mind loses even the memory of the most essential question bearing on the human meaning of each of the elements it is supposed to connect. And within a given type, the sum of the different parameters appears as a system, to such an extent that each type ends up resembling an animal species, distinct from other species and without any true communication with them.[21] The necessary tendency of sociology and anthropology, as of the human sciences in general, is to consider that "societies" or "cultures" or "civilizations" are closed and essentially incomparable wholes.

This observation confirms and even makes worse the trait we brought out in section 5 when commenting on the role Durkheim assigns to social volume: sociological science is science about what is different inasmuch as it is different. Therefore the way it goes about its work is the opposite of philosophy, which is knowledge of what is universal inasmuch as it is universal. It is contrary to the very definition of science as such. The example we have just studied even incites us to ask whether the conservative proposition we then formulated, that sociology presupposes the humanity of man without further inquiry into what constitutes his humanity, is not too timid or complacent. In reality, this discipline is so taken up with classifying social types and for that reason in doing an inventory of the indefinite range of their differences, that one can and must ask if it is still legitimate for it to speak of "social man," if the societies it studies still have it in common that they are human. It would undoubtedly be more rigorous, and only rigorous, to say Persian man, Western man, primitive man, specialized worker, member of the lower upper middle class, scientific researcher, asylum inmate, and so forth indefinitely, always designating the object under study by its difference. How then can the sociologist speak of his discipline with a calm conscience as a science *of man*?

VII

Perhaps it will be said that we are dramatizing the difficulty, that the conceptual tools of sociology have as their goal precisely to master this diversity and to prevent it from becoming truly indefinite. Is that not precisely what the general law achieves? If the sociologist confronted pure diversity without any "general" means at his disposal, he would be reduced to having nothing to say or write. We can all testify that such is not the case, however. He knows how to make use of all-encompassing parameters, of gathering multitudes of facts under the heading, for example, of the influence of demographics on the economy or politics, of religion on demographics or the economy, of the economy on demographics or politics or religion. What else does the philosopher and sociologist Montesquieu do in *The Spirit of the Laws*? One sees therein nothing that is unacceptable or simply disturbing to reason. And must one really suggest that industrious and conscientious sociologists pose a threat to the unity of the human species? I will not here take up again the distinction I noted between the philosopher's universal and the sociologist's general. I recall only that the latter is characterized by a weak causal power and thus by a weak capacity to integrate human experience. We shall attempt to grasp more closely the difficulty of sociological work.

Let us suppose we have observed in a given society reciprocal causal relations among several sociological parameters, for example an influence of demographics on religion and of religion on demographics, or of political institutions on trade or of trade on political institutions. Of all these relations, these influences, these causalities, which is or which are the most important, the most decisive, the most general? The natural movement of sociological investigation, as indicated in the passages from Durkheim and Montesquieu which I have cited, is to seek the most general laws and the social causes that cause the most, if I can put it that way. The natural tendency of sociology thus will be to posit a sociological determinant "in the final analysis." This is eminently the case of Marxism which, as is known, makes of "productive forces" and "relations of production" the determinant in the final analysis of the structure and life of every society. Many are the sociologists who rebuked Marx for thus exceeding the epistemological limits of social science and of substituting for the latter, which knows and can know only of reciprocal influences and causalities without thorough analysis, a "dogmatic philosophy" or "social metaphysics" that claims to hold the secret of human life and history. The objection is sympathetic and seems to tow the mark of rigor, but it comes up against the fact that in proceeding and concluding in this fashion, Marx is only bringing to its logical conclusion not only the natural movement of the human mind, which, as Aristotle states in the *Metaphysics*, is to seek the "highest" and "deepest" causes, but also, as we have just now recalled, the very movement itself of sociology, which is to seek the most general laws of social phenomena. Modern philosophy has taught us to distrust this "natural movement" of the human mind that draws it beyond the "limits of reason," in ways that are perhaps innocent but also ruinous for science. And one generally does not omit in this context to recall how Kant has definitively put us on our guard against any "transcendental usage" of the concepts of understanding.[22] It is not certain that the Kantian critique can be applied to the present difficulty. The problem of social causality in the final analysis is bound up with the question of the relative weight of the various sociological parameters. To this question, which has nothing transcendental about it, something of an answer must be given if there is to be a social science.

Whatever the case, the most respectable sociologists of the methodological rigor speak willingly of the "influence" of religion on the economy or of the economy on religion, for example. Without asking here how one could give an exact definition of this influence—this intermediary between the relation and the cause on an ever-growing ontological scale—we will note that before evaluating the influence of one sociological parameter on another, they first must be rigorously distinguished. This means that one can avoid asking the Socratic question about the nature of religion or of economy. If one refused to meet this requirement or neglected this precaution in doing case studies, one would run a great risk of confusing what belongs to religion or economy with, for example, what belongs to politics. One might even risk, despite their apparent distance, confusing religion and economy under one or another of their aspects. After that, all the methodological rigor in the world would be like all the instruments and skill of a surgeon operating in the dark. The sociologist's work of distinguishing and defining seems to be the same as the philosopher's, but it is in fact much more difficult. The Socratic philosopher sought out and marked out the articulations of our experience, and distinguished the different goods that man naturally desires. But these different aspects of one's self-understanding, these different objects of human desire, coexist and even belong to one another in unity because they all point to the same ordered and hierarchical nature and above all to the nature or soul of man. Nature, like the soul, is the goal of thought because it sets forth how man and the world are bound together; it brings to life Parmenides' equation of thought and being[23] and assures the unity of the human world. One could say, by stating more precisely the tautology we spoke of earlier, that for the Ancients, for classical philosophy, man, as nature and as soul, is the cause of the human phenomenon. But as soon as this ordering and integrating principle is abandoned, the human phenomenon becomes plural; it becomes pure plurality; it becomes social phenomena; and each one of these appears as the result—a plurality of the second power—of the encounter of several social causes. How can one evaluate the relative force of each of these causes that are so diverse and disparate that nothing seems to hold them together? According to what criterion can one arrange them in a meaningful constellation and attribute a particular importance to one rather than another? In their diversity without principle, sociological parameters are necessarily equivalent to one another, or they are worth only as much as the ingenuity of the sociologist who makes use of them is worth. This indetermination is not only causal uncertainty; it affects the contents, the very definition of each parameter. Without a principle of order that can unite the different elements of the human world, each one undetermines itself. In the face of this, how can one tell if the phenomenon at hand is economic, political, or religious? But the sociologist overlooks these questions; he ceaselessly keeps the mill of sociological causes, laws, or influences turning, without concerning himself to define precisely in what politics, economics, or religion consists, or even suspecting he ought to be concerned with doing so. Often, of course, he begins by proposing a nominal "definition," a "criterion" for locating the aspects related to the parameter under consideration; but this definition or criterion is explicitly deprived of any substantial or real import. It is only a "conceptual tool" that allows for the classification of phenomena. Should it be said that the sociologist's very life consists in not raising "the question he should naturally raise"? He nonetheless cannot remain in complete indetermination. He is obliged to have recourse to a principle of the unity of human experience or at least to something resembling that. He will have to do what he forbids himself doing and speak as a philosopher, or at least in the manner of a philosopher, of social conditioning, social stratification, social reproduction, and above all of society. The uncertainty that weighs on the definition of each instance is easy to bear once the instance is an element of society. Why bother to distinguish precisely, for example, between politics and religion when both only have significance as two aspects or components of society? While rejecting Marx's precise dogmatism that posits the forces and relations of production as the sociological determinant in the final analysis, the sociologist is forever falling prey to a vague but more misleading dogmatism that consists in positing *society* itself in the final analysis.

Sociologists who know their craft and the risks it runs put us on the alert when they say that to speak of "society" is a dangerous commodity or perhaps a dangerous necessity and that above all the concept of society ought not to be "reified." In fact, for the rigorous sociologist, "society" is only the sum of its internal differences, with no common substance.

Yet, sociology retains its plausibility only thanks to this tendency of our intellectual nature against which it does not cease to put us on our guard. It is indeed a good thing for it that the human mind irresistibly "reifies" its concepts. If "society" did not of necessity take a little, or much, of the causal density proper to a "substance" or "nature," if the modern sociologist's society did not in that way resemble the classical philosopher's nature, the sociologist would have before his eyes only the indefinite and indeterminate sum of the differences, a sum or a series obviously recalcitrant to any scientific consideration. In truth, the sociologist himself cannot be confident in his science. He cannot believe himself saved inasmuch as he maintains an implicit and obscure faith in the social nature of man, in the old Nature. He believes he knows what he is doing because he does not know what he believes. The scholar's refinements hang on the faith of the coal miner.

VIII

It is now time to study the difficulties of sociological demonstration with the help of an example. Following what Charles Péguy called "the method of pre-eminent cases," we shall consider the most famous text of sociology, *The Protestant Ethic and the Spirit of Capitalism*, published in two parts in 1904 and 1905.

Max Weber, as is well known, frames the hypothesis that there is a spiritual affinity between a certain Protestantism and a certain type of economic activity. The "Calvinist" experiences anxiety over his salvation all the more keenly in that he can place no confidence at all in his "works." This can make his interior life intolerable. Following a train of thought that is psychological rather than theological, he will look for signs of his election in "the world." This is how, Weber asserts, "Calvinists" ended up finding proof of God's choice in temporal, particularly economic success.[24] By his own admission, the "Calvinism" or the "Puritanism" Weber speaks of is no longer the authentic religion of Calvin.[25] As R. H. Tawney will observe, it is rather a "Calvinism" that would have horrified the reformer and his earliest disciples, a "Calvinism" that had already made its peace with "the world."[26] What Weber describes, following a very suggestive mental and affective logic, as the transformation of a religious belief and energy into a type of economic behavior—a transformation exemplifying the influence of religion on economy—can also be analyzed in an inverse sense as the result of the pressure of "worldly" attitudes on an already emasculated religion. The intelligible or "meaningful" relation between religious attitude and economic behavior, assuming Weber has described it correctly, is susceptible of two "sociological," "scientific," and "causal" readings that are incompatible and even rigorously opposed. Weber asserted that his thesis in no way claimed to establish the character of causality in the final analysis of religion for the explanation of social and economic phenomena, in this case of the development of capitalism. That would have been to fall into the same metaphysical dogmatism and one-sidedness he objected to in Marx.[27] In fact, far from Weber refuting Marx here, it would be enough to change very little in the scientific grounds in order to make of his work a one-sided Marxist thesis on the determination of a later Calvinist ethic by the spirit of capitalistic acquisitiveness. Its title would be simply, "The Spirit of Capitalism and the Protestant Ethic." Weber's scientific protestations do not make his argumentation more rigorous, only more uncertain, and even altogether uncertain. Whoever takes literally the methodological reservations at the end of his essay can only draw the conclusion that *The Protestant Ethic and the Spirit of Capitalism* does not, properly speaking, contain any thesis, scientific or otherwise. If it did, one would have to formulate the thesis as follows: it is possible that there is some relation between the Protestant ethic and the spirit of capitalism or between the spirit of capitalism and the Protestant ethic.

It is repulsive to draw such a meager and fleeting teaching from such an impressive intellectual undertaking that seems to kindle like a bush of flashing flares when we abandon ourselves to its enticing charm. But Weber's methodological exorcisms, vehement as they are, are not to be taken seriously because they are not serious. They are undoubtedly sincere, and Weber himself was a "serious man" if there ever was one. That they are not serious means that what Weber presents as scientific precautions rendered provisionally necessary by the incomplete state of research is in fact an intrinsic weakness of the sociological approach as such. Unwilling and incapable of drawing even the most approximate sketch of the respective place the various parameters occupy in the human order, in this case religion and the economy, how would he ever arrive at a rigorous demonstration, one bearing moreover on a particular case?[28]

Let us set aside the scientific apparatus and ask a simple and naive question. We do not wish to know what the sociologist Weber demonstrates rigorously or under what conditions a sociological argument is conclusive, but simply what makes *The Protestant Ethic and the Spirit of Capitalism* such a fascinating work. The answer, I believe, is contained in one of its last sentences: "The modern man is in general, even with the best will, unable to give religious ideas a significance for culture and national character which they deserve."[29] A few pages earlier, under the relative discretion of a note, Weber had advanced this trenchant and almost aggressive proposition: "religious ideas themselves simply cannot be deduced from economic circumstances. They are in themselves, that is beyond doubt, the most powerful plastic elements of national character, and contain a law of development and a compelling force entirely their own."[30] One cannot imagine any more "general," "metaphysical," "one-sided" propositions; deprived of the barest beginning of proof, they are for the taking or leaving. If Max Weber's historical description is forever giving the impression that he places the religious parameter in the position of cause and the economic parameter in the position of effect, that is because he judges religion to be more interesting and more basic for man than economics. But Weber cannot state bluntly that this judgment, which bears on the human order as such, is the primary inspiration of the entire investigation; even in the statements we have just cited, Weber formulates it in historical and sociological terms. Religion is important and perhaps decisive, not in and for itself, not for man as man, but for "culture and national character" or the "national mentality." Scientific honor is saved as Weber shifts this conviction that he has no right to form, this thought he has no right to think, to a scientific or causal plane that gives the impression of proof or of what can be proven, but that on the contrary forbids it, since the conclusion is referred back to the indefinite conclusion of indefinite investigations. In order to be able to speak of what passionately interests him, Weber is forced to make believe he is practicing a scientific discipline and to believe this fiction. Throughout his inquiry, he must silence what constitutes its motive and source. All the erudition in the world will never rectify, complete, or verify such a committed approach. Max Weber claims to impose upon himself a neutrality that is the contrary of true science, since it fetters the mind's movement toward its object. Is it at all surprising that the object finds itself burdened with the subject's involuntary avowals? In few works of thought is personal confession so involuntary and irrepressible as in Weber's.

In reading *The Protestant Ethic and the Spirit of Capitalism* we rediscover, through Weber's vibrant soul, the man or one of the men we were, the Puritan for whom the concern for external goods was but "a light cloak, which can be thrown aside at any moment," and who appears wondrously free and human to us for whom this light cloak has been transformed into an "iron cage."[31] In an extraordinarily vivid way Max Weber sets before us a part of our religious and moral history. It is just to recognize our indebtedness to him; but it is also possible to overlook what he tells us about science and about his theory, in general and in this particular case.

IX

An objection arises at this point. The most we have just established, it will be said, is not that Max Weber was not a scholar, but that the social science he developed and put into practice implemented is of a different type than Durkheim's "causal" or "objective" science. Weber recognizes the "subjective" side to human experience and thus his science is more human, but it is not less scientific. It is true that Weber was the great promoter of the notion of value which is today at the center of sociology and the human sciences, where one might suggest it has replaced the notion of law as the organizing concept. However, "Weberian" sociology, centered on the notion of value, is not that different from "Durkheimian" sociology, centered on the notions of social object or sociological law. The subjectivity of values and the objectivity of laws are opposed only in appearance. In fact, the same thinking is at work in both, as I would like to show.

In every society, as one can readily see, a certain hierarchy of activities is established; as we like to say, some are more "valued" than others. In one society, for example, commerce is highly prized as a useful and meritorious activity, while in another it is despised and virtually proscribed, subsisting only as in the clandestine fashion of illicit activities. The only thing that the sociologist can say, as a scholar, about the hierarchy of values is that one finds it one way in one society and a different way in another society. In his eyes, it is sheer "metaphysical" arbitrariness to affirm that a society, at least a society capable of functioning in a lasting way,[32] is inferior or superior to another equally capable of enduring. The values that respectively inspire them cannot be compared, since they hold nothing in common by which to measure them. The sociologist who observes diverse societies cannot, as a scholar, attribute any value to values. He thus cannot rank societies in any hierarchy, even if he needs to know how to observe and describe in what manner each one of them distributes its own values and relates to them. He must "understand" the values of the society he studies and at the same time scrupulously abstain from the least "value judgment." Such is, summarized in simple terms, Weber's conception, which is today largely dominant in the social and human sciences.

Indeed, there is a considerable and even stark difference between the sociological parameters or "things" Montesquieu and Durkheim speak of and the values Weber speaks of. The first underline the passivity of men in their subjection to sociological parameters, to the "things" that "govern" them, whereas the sociology of values insists on the active and even creative role of men. A value is what is valorized by a society. Thus it is the product of a valorization or the activity itself of valorizing, precisely because it does not exist by nature outside of the human act of valorization. A value has no "natural" value. Consequently, there is no greater contradiction than to view man as subject to sociological causes and laws and as a "creator of values." By what right does one affirm, as I just did, that these two propositions come down to the same thing, that they are two expressions of the same basic position?

Let us begin with the critical observation that the two propositions share the same enemy. They both reject the classical idea of an objective hierarchy of ends and human goods inscribed in human nature, even in the very order of the world. Montesquieu places sociological parameters, the "things" that "govern" men, on the same plane, whereas the sociology of values maintains that all values carry value objectively. A value becomes a value, and thus has value only in a subjective way, from the viewpoint of the will of the one who posits and affirms it, from the viewpoint and by the will of the one who values. The two propositions judge things in the same neutral and egalitarian way and that is how one can pass from one to the other, from the objective sociology of Montesquieu or Durkheim to the subjective sociology of Weber.

As I noted in section 6, Montesquieu and Durkheim, or sociology *tout court* in its original impulse, adopts the viewpoint of the spectator. Only from the spectator's viewpoint is it possible to say with a minimum of plausibility that climate "governs" men as do also in their own way the "maxims of government." It should be emphasized that from the viewpoint of the actor, the man of flesh and blood, these "governments" are so different that it is absurd or nearly so to employ the same word. Montesquieu deliberately proposed such a confusion because it was indispen-

sable in constituting the sociological viewpoint. Once it is set up, the sociologist will be able to contemplate the difficulties of the situation in which
he has placed himself. He will strive to take into account that the sociological parameters do not actively intervene in the human world unless they
are first reflected in the consciousness of the actors. They cannot be causes
unless they first are motives. But it is not so easy to recapture common
experience, as "methodological individualism" in particular seeks to do.
The sociologist cannot simply make sociological parameters the motives of
human action, rejecting as "perverse effects" what does not correspond to
any motive or is the contrary of motives. More generally, the coherent
analysis of the social world in terms of motives is not allowed him. At this
point we come to the reason why the sociological grasp of the social world
is necessarily mutilated and confused.

   To describe and interpret human behavior in terms of motives is to
conceive of it as the result of deliberation, at least implicitly. The motivated action that is the result of this deliberation is in its turn the natural
motive of another deliberation that inquires into the validity—the perti-
nence, honesty, justice, nobility—of the first. The reason that discerns and
weighs motives is the general means of one and the other deliberation. As
it goes about its work of evaluation, reason must have recourse to one or
some universal criteria that define what is honest, just, noble, in conformity with the natural hierarchy of human ends or with the moral law
proper to man. One can see such an undertaking at work especially in the
great works of moral philosophy, however diverse and contradictory they
might otherwise be, for example, Aristotle's *Nicomachean Ethics* and
Kant's *Foundations of the Metaphysics of Morals*. But it is already vaguely
present in all the circumstances of ordinary life where we are concerned
with human actions, ours and those of others.

   This approach, common in some way to both the philosopher and the
ordinary man, is forbidden to the sociologist. More precisely, he himself
has forbidden it to himself. The sociologist who has grasped the motive of
a behavior must, as a sociologist, refuse to take the natural step that would
bring him to inquire into the validity, nobility, or justice of that motive.
Whatever acuteness and force of mind he has mustered to discern it and
then describe it, he must cut short and rip the motive from its natural
element that is the whole or totality of the motives that can feed human
deliberation. He must refer it exclusively to the actor who bases his conduct on it as the value which he as the actor valorizes. The motive's reference point is no longer the constellation of human possibilities but the
actor's solitary choice. This choice is solitary even if it is taken as a fact for
a society of countless men, for it does not refer to the implicit universality
of human deliberation. From this viewpoint, the choice of values of a bil-
lion Chinese has no greater importance than my cousin's idiosyncrasy.

The sociologist who wants to rediscover the actor's viewpoint can transform the sociological parameter or cause into a motive only by transforming the motive into a value.

To measure the distance that separates the sociological viewpoint from the philosophical approach as well as from the ordinary man's spontaneous attitude, it is good to note that the position of the objective spectator championed by the sociologist, whether in describing "reference to values" or establishing "laws," is foreign to the ordinary man and clearly rejected by the philosopher as contrary to the fundamental human situation. It is not so much that the spectator can never be perfectly "pure" or "objective"—sociologists willingly agree on that—but more radically that man cannot be the spectator of man.

As I indicated above, every observation of human behavior necessarily brings us to consider the deliberation at the origin of this behavior, however cursory this deliberation may be, even if it consisted only in yielding to passion. Since it is the deliberation of one man, the other man who is the observer considers it spontaneously and naturally as human deliberation, that is to say, of the kind he could have engaged in himself. The observer spontaneously and naturally asks himself if he would have done well to engage in it and come to such a conclusion. He thus asks himself if he could have justified it before another man, hypothetically before a wise and just man capable of judging human actions. Thus, either as an ordinary man he defers to the authority of the one he takes to be wise and just—depending on the situation and the times, to the pastor, the teacher, the representative, the television reporter; or he strives to become wise, that is to say to judge of human actions and to act himself in conformity with a universal norm inscribed in nature or promulgated by reason. The sociologist takes neither of these routes. He neither defers to any established authority nor seeks to rise above all authorities to arrive at a perspective over human things that is accurate because it is universal. The sociologist does not follow the natural movement of human inquiry, but rather breaks with it abruptly and arbitrarily. In refusing to judge, he "abstains from all value judgments" and thereby confuses the borrowed and unexamined judgment of the ordinary man and the well-founded judgment of the philosopher.

The sociologist reckons he is giving sufficient due to the viewpoint of the actor he is observing in assessing and affirming that what moves him is a certain "value" that this man has chosen or posited and even created. In fact, the sociologist has some reason here to be satisfied with himself. It seems there could be no greater generosity than this almost divine, or perhaps even more than divine, liberality that grants man the right and the capacity to "create his values." But the reverse side and the condition of this extreme generosity is that the sociologist makes of the actor and the value he chooses, posits, or creates, a Whole, a self-sufficing Whole that no longer has reference to a greater Whole in which the observer would also have his place. The Whole made up of the actor and the value he posits or creates has no reference to the great Whole of the universal human. It is pure particularity, one particularity among an indefinite number of particularities, the other actors who create other values. In practice, it is important to note, this particularity is the "subject of investigation" of the sociologist, among the indefinite number of "subjects of investigation" of other sociologists. Once the question of the universal is taken out of consideration, the particular Whole can in effect constitute an object that is completely outside the spectator and on which he can fix his trained eye.

The sociologist who interprets human behavior in terms of values does so exclusively within the spectator's viewpoint. Only within the narrow limits authorized by this viewpoint does he give any rightful place to the actor's viewpoint. More exactly, it is to preserve its sovereignty that the spectator's viewpoint arbitrarily accentuates the arbitrary character of the choice or "creation" of values by the actor. If what the actor says or does were recognized as the possible object of a rational debate, that is to say with reference to a motive in the ordered constellation of motives and not to a value in a nebulous indefinite realm of values, the sociologist would have to abandon his position of spectator and abdicate his sovereignty. The sociologist of values in the end follows the rules of the sociological method without seriously transgressing Durkheim's prohibitions. Human reason remains concentrated in the science of the sociologist who has nothing in common with the values of men and certainly not with reason. One could even maintain that the sociology of values represents an extension to new territories of the rules of the sociological method. Many aspects of society that did not lend themselves to explanation in terms of laws can be understood, at least with some plausibility, in terms of values. But it is the same science that is at work and it is only the accent or style that has changed in Durkheim's stark and forceful prose.

Weberian man, who chooses in full liberty and sovereignty the values to which he wills to devote his life, is the double of Durkheimian man, who is subject to the necessity of sociological causes and laws over which his liberty has no control. These are the two opposed yet overlapping figures of the man deprived of reason by the sociological perspective. In order for social science or the human sciences to be possible, reason must be eliminated from real human actions and concentrated in the scrutinizing gaze of the scholarly spectator. Thus the tissue of implicit common deliberation connecting every man to the men he seeks to understand has been torn.

No effort of methodological refinement will succeed in opening the eyes of an intellectual discipline that seeks to interpret the human world by indifferently bringing into play one *or* the other or one *and* the other of two definitions of man: he is a cause like an object or he is a creator like a god—a god who could be nothing but will, and devoid of intellect.

X

Thus, the sociology of values, which claims to give the actor's viewpoint its due, leaves intact the sovereignty of the spectator's viewpoint. We shall now examine more closely this sovereignty, which is constitutive of social science. Again this time, Montesquieu, the modern philosopher most capable of losing us as well as saving us, will be our guide.

Those who know nothing else of *The Spirit of the Laws* know that it deals with climate and that the author makes a great deal of it. Public opinion in this matter is an indicator to be followed. Montesquieu's theory about climate in effect does give us a particularly direct access to the sociological viewpoint. One would willingly say that it is its most naive expression if science could ever be naive. As we have already noted, Montesquieu ranks climate among the "things" that "govern" men. What is more, by listing it first he places it in the forefront, a position he confirms elsewhere: "The empire of climate is the first of all empires."[33] In the series of sociological parameters, climate is the only one that is not human. What significance is there to the exorbitant role attributed to climate?

If we set aside a possible and frequent misunderstanding, we will be in a position to understand the significance of this "empire." The power of climate in no way eliminates human liberty; on the contrary, one of the traits of the good legislator is that he knows how to combat the bad effects of climate.[34] The proclamation of this empire signals that man's nature, but not his liberty, has just suffered a definite deathblow.

If a factor so completely nonhuman as climate exercises such a power on man, it is because the nature of man, or one might say the humanity of man, does not suffice to determine or cause his actions. The acting man is not only the nature or the humanity of the acting man, but the acting man *plus* the causality of climate. Human nature itself remains undetermined or under-determined. With its vicissitudes climate supplies the determination that is lacking in the humanity of man and that allows the social and human world to be what it is. In understanding and making known how humanity is determined by climate, the scholarly spectator displays and achieves his superiority over the acting man.

Thus the sociologist's rapport with human nature differs greatly from the philosopher's. One might say of the philosopher that he discovers the lofty power of human nature. His very superiority over other men, a genu-

ine superiority that makes him a proud man, consists in that he alone
understands the superiority of nature over the conventions that men confuse with it, the superiority of the highest Good over the subordinate goods
beyond which other men do not reach. True, his thinking does not always
follow the paths of Nature. He can hold that whoever thinks of man in
terms of nature, even a rational or otherwise "superior" nature, blinds
himself to what properly constitutes the humanity of man. It matters little
in our present context. The difference between the philosopher and the
sociologist remains the same. The philosopher strives to discover what is
proper to the being of man, beyond the confusion, the bondage, the alien-
ation and oblivion that mar him and make him a stranger to himself—
what is proper to man, or, not to leave aside any philosophical approach
or thought, what is proper to the one whose most usual name is "man."
The sociologist, on the other hand, does not inquire into what is proper to
man and is in no way concerned with it. Such a difference is at first hard
to understand. How can there be a "science of man" that excludes from
consideration the question about what is proper to man? The sociologist
proposes various reasons in answer to this question. For one, in the name
of rigorous science he rejects such a question as "metaphysical," a question that "does not come up," nothing more than the deplorable and
slightly ridiculous remains of a happily surpassed stage of the human
mind. Then again, in less trenchant terms but always rooted in the requi-
sites of science, he admits, as though regretting it, that the sciences of man
are still too little developed for it to be reasonable to countenance answering such a question at the present time. Much interdisciplinary work, en-
listing teams of investigators in the different human sciences and employ-
ing all the current means of compiling and handling information, is the
indispensable prerequisite to dealing with the question. These reasons and
others alleged by the sociologist are not convincing. Since nothing can be
said about man or men that is not the beginning of an answer to this
question, we have here only pretexts that are as vain as they are varied.
The truth is that the sociologist has already answered the question in his
heart. Whether he is arrogant or modest, whether he judges that the question is not to be raised, or no longer, or not yet, he has already answered
it. More precisely, he has put himself in a certain position with regard to
it, a position of essential superiority whose device Montesquieu's theory of
climate has shown us. What the sociologist knows with certainty as a
scholarly spectator is the determinability or causality of our nature. He
knows, and his task is to know, the determinants of this undetermined or
underdetermined reality that is the nature of man, of the humanity of
man. He very willingly accepts to overlook what it "is"—and thereby he
establishes his scientific credentials and his innocence of every "dogmatism" or "metaphysics"—for he knows something better yet. He knows

what is stronger than man's nature, what determines it, and thus he knows more than if he knew man himself. Besides, man is nothing more than the sum of the determinations which only the trained eye of the sociologist is capable of unraveling. Thus the sociologist, who sees, for example, how man is "governed" by this nonhuman "thing" which is climate or by this human "thing" that is religion, rises above all things human! Would one not say that his mind, taking inventory of and adding up the sociological parameters of the determinants of man's humanity, forms and fashions it, creates it so to speak? The arrogant philosopher is superior to other men, but the modest sociologist is superior to the very humanity of man.

If man's humanity is then an unknown "X" subject to be determined by an indefinite number of sociological determinants, the sociologist is sovereignly free to choose the point from which he will "observe" this determination of the unknown by the sociological determinant. Any aspect of nature, human or nonhuman, referred to in current research or in history, can become the sociological determinant that the sociologist observes acting upon other aspects of human nature, which immediately face into indetermination and become this unknown "X" that needs to be determined. But every aspect of the human condition—nonhuman nature is out of the picture—can be this unknown "X" to be determined, for the determination of which all the other determinants can be employed, though only some among them are actually used each time. One can thus do sociology of the family, for example, in two ways: either by taking the family as a social cause that determines religion, economy, or politics; or by taking it as a social effect, determined by religion, economy, or politics. The two directions of the approach are equally scientific, since in both cases the sociologist brings to light a sequence of determinant-determined. A mixture of the two approaches would come to the same thing, under the aegis of "reciprocal" causality or influence. The one necessary element is that at each point man appears as caused, as we saw in section 5. All combinations are possible, the only rule of the combination being that it is never allowed to come to a stop. To stop and assert that social man is determined by *this* social cause is to claim to determine definitively and exhaustively the undetermined "X." Man indeed remains "caused," but a recognized and stable cause begins to look like a nature. Without answering the Question, the sociologist comes close to the philosopher. Then he has learned not to succumb to the temptation that was so pressing in the beginnings of the discipline, as we saw in section 7. Research that has now gone on for several generations has given sociology the resources to put forth a combination that is beyond suspicion. The innumerable aspects of the human phenomenon come to light and then pale in the roles of determinant and then determined as the kaleidoscope of social science goes on turning.[35]

The refusal to say anything or know anything about man as such, except where and when he is the effect of a social cause, ought to have discredited, it seems, the science of man that imposes on itself this refusal as a matter of conscience. But as we know well this is not what happened. Its prestige has only grown with its works, to such a point that sociological language has become in some way the official vernacular of modern democracy. This is so because social science plays a decisive role in the deathblow to nature that characterizes our regime. It is supremely revealing that, among the things that govern men, Montesquieu does not mention, not even as one cause among others, their nature. Sociology was born at the same time as the conviction that the true nature of man is to be free. The claim to be unable to say anything of "man" is intimately linked to the will to define man as liberty. More precisely, for these terms are too vague, the sociological viewpoint is constituted the moment the notion of liberty becomes the cornerstone of the human world and the decisive theoretical expression of this transformation.

It would be misleading to focus attention on the all too obvious contradiction between the ideas of human liberty and sociological determinism. It makes perfectly good sense to ask what point there is to exalting human liberty, to seeing in liberty what is proper to man as we have done for the past two hundred years, if the central science of the human world presupposes and claims to prove that human behavior is regulated by necessary laws, or at least cannot be understood except as the effect of social causes.

Let us first make the simple observation that if the will to liberty and the sociological viewpoint indeed coexist and even overlap for modern man, the two would not be simply or solely contradictory. Without assuming that society is a coherent system, but simply because man is a thinking being, it is probable that the spirit of a society, the spirit of its laws—to be bold enough to use these fine and grand sociological expressions—would not direct its attention and its intention in two patently contradictory directions for very long. As we have just recalled, the sociological viewpoint and the modern will to liberty both presupposed the lowering of nature, but to say that is nothing more than mere tinkering and even if this observation is on the mark, it does not do justice to the situation since it is a question of explaining the fundamental movement of the human mind. It is as though modern man all of a sudden got it in his head to resolve this problem of human geometry: given freedom, society, and nature, under what conditions would one find that at the same time liberty would be pure and complete, society would be ordered by necessary laws, and human nature would be subject to being determined but not capable of determining?

We have already gone over the explanation again and again when we read and reread what the master of the labyrinth says: "Many things govern men. . . ." To maintain that man is determined is at the same time to assert very forcefully that he is determined in many ways, each of which is distinct from the others and is not to be confused with them. It seems that respecting each one of the many things that affect human life is the very program of modern liberty. At least it is Montesquieu's program.

Let us consider for example chapter 16 of book 19, entitled "How Some Legislators Have Confused the Principles that Govern Men." Here Montesquieu is concerned particularly with the Greek legislators such as Lycurgus, who confused "laws, mores, and manners." As Montesquieu states more precisely a few chapters later, these things are "naturally separate," although "they are still closely related."[36] The authority of nature, let us note in passing, no longer enters into play except to separate human things, never to unite them. The most important difference is the one that exists and must be allowed to exist between laws and mores: "The difference between laws and mores is that, while laws regulate the actions of the citizen, mores regulate the actions of the man." This sentence draws our attention only because Montesquieu's manner of speaking is more than usually calm and simple, yet its air of majesty and silence strikes us. It is only the world turning on its hinges.

Among the separations that foment and feed the sociological viewpoint, the one between man and citizen is decisive. It brings with it and establishes the rupture of the human world, the division of the One. Classical philosophy, of course, made a clear distinction between man and citizen. It was even particularly attentive to the tension that emerges between the "good citizen" and the "good man," between the man whose "goodness" is relative to the regime and the one who is good absolutely. The two come together only in the best regime, which is the same as saying that in most cases they remain distinct. But then, in defining man as a political animal, classical philosophy saw the city as a Whole where man finds all the goods proper to his humanity. A man is truly a man only inasmuch as he is a citizen. As a citizen, he is distinct from those who are not his fellow citizens only by his allegiance to the law of the city. Whether the law is made by one man, by a few, by many, or by all, it sums up, as it were, the active truth of the city, and for that matter of what it means to be human. By placing political law on a par with the many other things that govern man and thereby eliminating the unifying and integrating role of law and also of the city, sociology situates itself in a dismembered human world or rather dismembers it in order to find its place in its own good time and fashion.

In separating the "government" of mores from the "government" of laws, Montesquieu emancipates mores. In fact, one can "do sociology" only about mores that are "free." Were they not free, they would be only a part, however specific one would like, of the body politic's law. But one cannot "do sociology" about political law in the strong and full sense, the original sense of the term, since law is the ruling element in a body politic.

What is true about law is true of the political arena as such. The political actor is the cause of his actions. This causality is at times as opaque and complex as the causality of the most intricate social dynamic, but our perplexity surrounds the uncertainty of motives and human ends. In all instances, an actor is a cause and in no way caused. Caesar crossing the Rubicon is supremely a cause and for that reason supremely devoid of interest for social science. But the senator Caius Placidus, who was the first to make his submission, is just as much a cause and just as devoid of interest for social science. The world ordered by political law knows only the action of men upon one another. All men are causes, the one who obeys as well as the one who rules, even if their powers are unequal. All depends on the human will, as Durkheim explained in an enlightening way in the text that gave the impetus to this chapter's discussion.

It will be said that the contrast as I have formulated it is arbitrary and harsh since there is in fact a "political sociology" and that moreover Montesquieu devotes a good deal of attention to political law as such and numbers it among the things that govern men. As one social cause among other social causes, why would it not be a concern of sociology? These observations are reasonable, but they lack any solid foundation until once the human world is dismembered or political law is debased, that is, once society has been separated or is in the process of being separated from the state.

The world turns on its hinges when political law ceases to rule over an essential part of the world. But far from finding itself lost in the darkness of chaos, the world turns to another law, of a different sort, the sociological law. Once the hold of political law is decisively loosened, one part after another of the human world will leave the clear light of the spoken word that rules for the obscure government of social causes. Because this government holds sway outside the natural political light, it can be seen and its workings understood only through the lens of a particular viewpoint, the sociological viewpoint. The critical moment comes when religion severs itself from political law or is sundered from it.

XII

Montesquieu sees the relation of religion and law in the following terms:

> Human laws made to speak to the spirit should give precepts and no counsels at all; religion, made to speak to the heart, should give many counsels and few precepts.
>
> When for example, it gives rules, not for the good but for the better, not for what is good but for what is perfect, it is suitable for these to be counsels and

not laws, for perfection does not concern men or things universally. Moreover, if these are laws, there will have to be an infinity of others so that the first ones will be observed. Celibacy was a counsel of Christianity; when it was made into a law for a certain order of people, new laws had to be made every day in order to bring men to observe the first one. The legislator tired himself, he tired the society, making men execute by precept what those who love perfection would have executed by counsel.[37]

This text takes up the traditional Catholic distinction between precepts and counsels and draws its political consequences in terms that appear both reasonable and orthodox. Simply stated, since counsels cannot be made obligatory, they are not the object of political legislation. At the same time, however, Montesquieu lets the accents fall in such a way as to lead us to think in ways that are hardly traditional. If the counsels of perfection, or more broadly the concern for the higher life that is proper to religion, must be left to the free pursuit of those who love perfection, then not only must the church be separated from the state but also the power of the church's hierarchy over the members of its clergy, in particular the power to mandate celibacy, must be abolished.

The statement's formal orthodoxy is subtly but profoundly challenged by its tone. Choosing or rejecting the path of perfection seems to be no more than a matter of personal taste, like choosing to go to the sea or the mountains, a choice made with a sort of amiable spontaneity, with no great concern or seriousness. In any event, the pursuit of perfection cannot be a burden to those who love it. By affirming it, by maliciously exaggerating its ease and spontaneous character, Montesquieu separates those who love perfection from all others who, presumably, do not love it. He therefore separates the counsel from the precept, while remaining silent about, or rather annulling by his silence, the intimate bond between precept and counsel. Obedience to the precept is a preparation for perfection and even a part of it; it has no religious meaning save from the vantage point of perfection. The Christian religion gives itself or understands itself to have as it mission to lead men, all men, to perfection.[38] But what regular and permanent means does the church have to convince men of the urgency of this mission, that is, to fulfill it, if its teaching is completely separated from the majesty of the law? It will be said that the only legitimate and effective persuasion is the one effected by the words and above all the deeds of the saints. But will those who have not encountered saints along their path or who have turned their backs on them be deprived altogether of the presence of the Word? In any case the church has never had the confidence in the spontaneous love of certain men for perfection that Montesquieu seems to manifest in this passage. It believes that all men are called. For that reason, while scrupulously preserving the distinction between precept and

counsel, the church ceased to claim the right to command in certain particularly grave matters in order to affirm the need for religious law to a be
a part, at least in part, of the political law.

The separation Montesquieu posits here is fraught with consequences.
For both Christian theology and Greek philosophy, the perfection of being
is the raison d'etre of every human being, even if he is still or will always
be far from attaining it. One and the other affirm a continuity between
ordinary, even decadent, nature and its sublime end. A blind slave could
become a brilliant philosopher or a flawless saint. Montesquieu's separation ruptures this continuity. Who would have said that modern liberty
would browbeat such delicate points of Being that even despotism respected?

XIII

Thus the sociologist's analytic scrutiny separates the state from society
and from the church. The body politic that the ancient law held together
is dismembered into three great parts, each one subject in turn to further
subdivisions. The state is divided according to the "separation of powers";
the church is divided into sects; and society is divided into an indefinite
number of "groups." From now on life will be lived in the "age of separations."[39]

But where did the sociologist find the boldness it took to separate in this
way the political law from other "governments," of reducing the Whole to
but one part among other parts? It is tempting to say that he simply took
stock of the European political development and was merely reflecting it.
However that may be, Montesquieu, who established and formulated the
authority of the contemporary historical moment, constructed the sociological viewpoint on an interpretation of the present moment and the history that led up to it.

According to Montesquieu's diagnosis, the monarchies of continental
Europe are marching irresistibly toward despotism.[40] But one needs to
understand just what that means. It means that as the power of the king
becomes a specifically political power, it emancipates itself more and more
from mores and from religion. Until that time, the peoples of Europe were
governed by mores, as they still are at the time Montesquieu is writing.
The analytic core of his diagnosis is that the king separates the law from
mores and religion.

The peoples of Europe recognized a certain distinction between law and
mores, but traditionally political law properly speaking did not weigh
upon them at all. This is not to say that it was secondary or subordinated,
but only that a small portion of the commands the Europeans obeyed

stemmed from it specifically or exclusively. The rest, the essential ones, were mixed in together with their mores. As despotism progresses, however, the Europeans are more and more governed by royal power but less and less by mores and religion. The peoples of Europe thus find themselves in an absolutely unprecedented situation which can be understood by comparing it with what Montesquieu writes about despotism properly speaking, or oriental despotism. In such a regime, religion and mores, or customs, have immense force.[41] But whereas oriental despotism is the friend of custom, Western monarchies tending toward despotism are its enemy. The Europeans are the first members of the human race to experience simultaneously the growth of political power tending to despotism and the decline of the power of mores and religion.

Thus on the one hand Montesquieu asks that the "counsels" of religion be very neatly distinguished and even separated from law; on the other had, he regrets the weakening of the political power of religion which, as bad as it might be in itself, is a barrier against despotism when there is no other. This apparent contradiction means only that there is no solution to the formidable problem raised by the growth of royal despotism, which is to say of specifically political despotism, in the religious and customary framework of continental monarchy. Now, in the chapter to which we have just referred, Montesquieu makes this remark: "In order to favor liberty, the English have removed all the intermediate powers that formed their monarchy. They are quite right to preserve that liberty; if they were to lose it, they would be one of the most enslaved peoples on earth."[42] This last phrase gives the impression of hostility or low esteem for the English, but it means on the contrary that the English have successfully broken out of the stereotype of European monarchy. It is true that they pushed to its end, further and in a more coherent way than the French, the logic of a monarchical despotism, which is to say despotism of a specifically political stamp, since they suppressed intermediary powers such as feudal justices and religious and customary powers, but they did so on such political grounds—the separation and distribution of powers—that instead of the anticipated slavery arising, the sure result was the greatest liberty men have ever known.

This is not the place the examine how Montesquieu understands and describes the English regime.[43] What interests us is to grasp the historic dynamism underlying his considerations. European monarchical despotism is much less inhuman than despotism properly speaking, oriental despotism, but it is incomparably more powerful. It either destroys or inexorably erodes what the first spares or even lovingly preserves. The history of oriental despotism is the monotonous chronicle of human nature mistreated, whereas the history of European monarchy is a regular process, the uninterrupted and growing transformation of the condition of the Eu-

ropeans which now places them before the alternative of a servitude and
a liberty that are equally unprecedented and equally extreme.

Other mores and other religions, of course, have lost strength or even
disappeared, but it was because either the body politic lost its ground and
they disappeared along with it, or they gave way to another religion that
was now perceived as the true religion and in its turn governed a people's
mores. In Europe, for the first time a religion loses strength over a long
period of time at the same time that the body politic grows strong, without
any new religion appearing to replace the first.

In Montesquieu's eyes, the English experience an extreme political liberty, whereas the Europeans and notably the French, although still enjoy-
ing a moderate liberty filled with amenities, are threatened with extreme
servitude. In both regimes religion is subordinated, however unequally
and in different ways. Whatever constraining power religion retains, it
borrows in both cases from the sovereign or arbitrary power of the state.
Henceforth, it is less a principal part of the law than the occasional tool of
the state that has elevated itself decisively above religion. Religion persists,
to be sure, as Catholicism, Anglicanism, or some form of Protestantism,
but it no longer rules in any proper sense. It is only a great thing or even
simply a thing that directs the actions of men or at least a large number of
them.

The Europeans witness something unheard of in the chronicle of humanity. An essential part of their life is in the process of breaking away
from law because, in becoming purely political, the law raises itself irresistibly above the contents of life.

One may ask how it happens that this elevation of political law is reflected in or absorbed into the sociological consciousness (or the self-consciousness that is sociology) by reducing the importance of politics to a
mere parameter among others. This is because the new regime requires
that all other regimes be considered in another perspective. Politics is so
elevated, so separated, and thus so intellectually distinct that all the other
regimes appear confused. From such a lofty vantage point, Sparta and
China look alike.[44] Each of the other regimes seems to be governed by that
with which the political law finds itself "confused," Sparta by mores and
manners, China by manners and mores. Politics is so "distinct" in France
and England, the two countries in the forefront of European development,
that it is no longer to be seen in the "confused" state it takes on elsewhere,
and thus the other regimes appear governed by something other than political law. This effect of perspective is inseparable from the sociological
viewpoint and merges with it. Political law is but one of the things that
govern men. The historical moment of which we speak is marked by the
fact that the real elevation of politics entails its theoretical lowering. An

elevation that was pursued over centuries has brought political law to this point of humiliation.

It makes little sense to reproach Montesquieu with equivocating on the notion of law. If at times he gives the impression of oscillating between two incompatible meanings of the word, as pure political command and law as pure sociological constant or necessity, he is only describing and confirming what is in the process of happening to the law.

Traditional law, both Christian and Greek, expressed certain contents of life in the form of commands. It was the "imperative" reflection of the ends of human nature according to a certain interpretation of human nature and it produced a modification in the soul. According to Montesquieu's description of what the law undergoes and the consequences he draws from this, the law extricates itself from this confusion with nature by dividing itself into two halves. One part separates itself, emancipates itself from nature, raises itself above all the constituents of nature, becomes properly and absolutely sovereign, in such a way that it can, according to the situation, either govern it despotically or threaten to do so as in France, or allow it be extremely free as in England. The other part reabsorbs itself into the human matter which, once it is abandoned by the political command, becomes the dense and opaque chain of social causes accessible only to the sociological viewpoint that holds back and fetters individual liberty, the trials and bondage of which the modern novelist depicts for us. Each of the two poles between which ancient law divided itself can be apprehended in terms of the other. One can say, in the language of command, that different sociological parameters govern men. One can also say, in the terms of matter subjected to necessity, that the political law is one social "thing" among others. Many things govern men.

The Economic System

I

LIKE MONTESQUIEU before him, Adam Smith had a vivid sense of the significance for the future of what was taking shape in England. But whereas Montesquieu cautiously established the English experience as a new authority, Adam Smith complacently accepted it as an established authority.[1] Whether he is speaking of propriety or liberty, Smith always assumes what he calls "the present sense of the word."[2] In place of the complex dialectic Montesquieu uses to describe and explain the good effects of commerce, Smith asserts a linear progress that can be summed up in the one word that serves as the leitmotif of his great work: *improvement*.

For Smith, the economic growth taking place in England and Scotland, especially since the Restoration, is of the greatest importance. In explaining this kind of improvement, which in one sense differs from Montesquieu's notion but also anticipates Benjamin Constant, Smith appeals to a universal psychological factor that lies at the heart of human nature, "the desire to better one's condition." Man's desire to better his condition is always at work, in whatever historical circumstances or political or economic institutions. The "extravagance of government" and the "greatest errors of administration" cannot stop the "natural progress of things, even if they can slow it down."[3] Improvement constitutes a general law of history, at least of English history.[4] Smith, who is ordinarily so scrupulous and careful in documenting his economic assertions, has such confidence in the irresitibility of improvement that he sees it at work in periods that are hardly accessible to research, asserting that England "certainly" was more developed in the time of the Saxon heptarchy than in the era of Julius Caesar.[5]

Smith admits nonetheless that political institutions can place limits on improvement, although only in a purely negative way.[6] The best they can do is not to hold back the action of this universal wellspring by encumbering the free use of property or compromising its security. Thus, Smith does not concern himself with the bothersome fact, so well noted and commented upon by Hume and Montesquieu, that the security of property is about as great in France as in England while economic development is stronger in England.[7] Thus, progress for Smith is as easy to grasp as an addition: it is the increasing sum of the identical effects of a similar cause. There could be no simpler account of the New.

II

The desire to better one's condition, the efficient cause of economic progress, constitutes the central wellspring of human nature in which, so to speak, nature and history are joined. Smith believes in the possibility, which Montesquieu did not consider, of a dialectical linear deduction of "history" starting from "nature," or an analytic inclusion of "history" in "nature." In going beyond Montesquieu, Smith the moral philosopher concurs with Hobbes the moralist in bringing to light a fundamental desire that both defines and resolves the human problem. The language Smith uses to characterize the desire to improve one's condition seems to echo the language Hobbes used to depict the desire for power. Smith speaks of the first as "a desire which, though generally calm and dispassionate, comes with us from the womb, and never leaves us till we go to the grave," adding that "[I]n the whole interval which separates those two moments, there is scarce perhaps a single instant in which any man is so perfectly and completely satisfied with his situation, as to be without any wish of alteration or improvement of any kind."[8] In shorter compass, Hobbes affirmed of the second moment: "in the first place, I put for a general inclination of all mankind, a perpetual and restless desire of power after power, that ceaseth only in death."[9] One is tempted to say that the desire to better one's condition is the "dispassionate" desire for power. In fact, Hobbes had placed a stumbling block for Smith's modification when he wrote that "the passions that incline men to peace, are fear of death; desire of such things as are necessary to commodious living; and a hope by their industry to obtain them."[10] Smith himself refers to Hobbes in this context:

> Wealth, as Mr. Hobbes says, is power. But the person who either acquires, or succeeds to a great fortune, does not necessarily acquire or succeed to any political power, either civil or military. His fortune may, perhaps, afford him the means of acquiring both, but the mere possession of that fortune does not necessarily convey to him either. The power which that possession immediately and directly conveys to him, is the power of purchasing; a certain command over all the labour, or over all the produce which is then in the market.[11]

From Hobbes to Smith, the desire for power has become the desire for purchasing-power, whether to purchase the products of labor or labor itself. Although appearing to correct Hobbes's thesis, Smith actually develops it by simplifying Hobbes's simplification. The wellspring of human nature and the process of history are condensed in a desire that can be named without fear. Once the fundamental human desire has become the desire to better one's condition and then the desire to increase one's purchasing-power, nature and history come together in what was beginning to be called the economy.

Consequently, Smith does not believe that economic calculation yields the secret of the human world. In spite of the fact that he simplifies things greatly, as I have just emphasized, he finds the central human desire to be very complex. It behooves us to explore this complexity carefully, since in analyzing the desire to better one's condition we are brought to the edge of the abyss that conceals the thinnest of all beings, *homo oeconomicus*.

III

The desire to better one's condition is presented in very different terms in Adam Smith's two great works, *The Theory of Moral Sentiments* of 1759 and *An Inquiry into the Nature and Causes of the Wealth of Nations*, published in 1776.

Let us consider first this crucial passage in *Theory*:

> What are the advantages which we propose by that great purpose of human life which we call bettering our condition? To be observed, to be attended to, to be taken notice of with sympathy, complacency, and approbation, are all the advantages which we can propose to derive from it. It is the vanity, no the ease, or the pleasure, which interests us.[12]

Now let us read the corresponding passages in *The Wealth of Nations*. These are found significantly in chapter 3 of book 2, entitled "Of the Accumulation of Capital, or of Productive and Unproductive Labor." The chapter is organized around the distinction and contrast between prodigality and frugality. The first of these employs capital in frivolous expenses, thereby turning it from its proper use as capital, whereas the second, by saving and accumulating capital, uses it in a productive way or allows for such a use. The reasonable, that is to say productive use of savings, and thus the disposition to be frugal, to make annual savings, arises from "a very powerful principle, the plain and evident interest of every individual."[13] The expenditures of the prodigal man, who is moved by vanity, are then denounced in accents of holy indignation:

> By not confining his expense within his income, [the prodigal] encroaches his capital. Like him who perverts the revenues of some pious foundation to

profane purposes, he pays the wages of idleness with those funds which the
frugality of his forefathers had, as it were, consecrated to the maintenance of
industry.[14]

But such a disgrace is rather rare. The great majority of men economize
because that is the "most vulgar and the most obvious" means of aug-
menting their fortune.[15] This calculation of interest, arising from dissatisfaction, can have only a distant connection to vanity, since capital was
accumulated "silently" and "gradually," and accordingly is little susceptible of attracting the attention of the world.

Vanity which incites prodigality is bad and, so to speak, impious. The
pursuit of interest, which leads to economy and accumulation, is reasonable and good. What assures the economic progress of humanity, what
guarantees the continual improvement of public prosperity is the fact that
vain men, or the behavior vanity gives rise to, are much more rare than
frugal men, or the conduct inspired by a frugality intent on personal
gain.[16]

The Theory of Moral Sentiments and *The Wealth of Nations* both evince
the same conviction that the great business of men is the bettering of their
condition. However, this human desire is interpreted in a very different
way from one book to the other. In *Theory*, it is essentially vanity; in
Wealth, it is dissatisfaction and interest without these being explicitly or
implicitly linked to vanity. This change is considerable. Vanity encompasses a relation to other people; the whole of vanity is nothing but such
a link. The dissatisfaction that gives rise to saving and to rational economic behavior neither contains nor implies, of itself, any definite relation
with others. The first version of the desire to better one's condition is social
and moral from the start; it asserts that men see eye to eye in fundamental
matters. The second version leaves in the dark the nature of the satisfaction sought and obtained by rational parsimony; it does not determine the
social and moral context of this desire which it continues to make the
wellspring of human nature and history. Does economic man desire to
become wealthy in order to be admired or to become ever more comfortable? In Rousseau's terms, is he "reflexive" man or "sensual" man? It seems
that, far from providing an answer, Smith's great book—the first monu-
ment of political economy—does not even raise these questions and thus
leaves the nature and character of the social bond completely undetermined.

It will be said that men are linked by trade in its different forms. However, the notion of trade does not contain within itself any idea of its motive. As to why men engage in trade, Smith answers only that they do so
because they have a natural inclination to trade.[17] That is founding the
new science, or the science of the new society, on the narcotic force of

opium! It is hardly likely that political economy rests on such a fragile basis. We must take a broader view of Adam Smith's line of reasoning.

The desire to better one's condition presupposes that a person has a certain image of the better condition he desires and seeks to bring about. To attribute a central role to this desire necessarily implies, it seems, that decisive importance be given to the imagination, which is just what Smith does in putting it at the heart of *The Theory of Moral Sentiments*. One has only to ponder the following lines:

> Our imagination . . . expands itself to every thing around us. We are then charmed with the beauty of that accommodation which reigns in the palaces and economy of the great; and admire how every thing is adapted to promote their ease, to prevent their wants, to gratify their wishes, and to amuse and entertain their most frivolous desires. If we consider the real satisfaction which all these things are capable of affording, by itself and separated from the beauty of that arrangement which is fitted to promote it, it will always appear in the highest degree contemptible and trifling. But we rarely view it in this abstract and philosophical light. We naturally confound it in our imagination with the order, the regular and harmonious movement of the system, the machine or economy by means of which it is produced. The pleasures of wealth and greatness, when considered in this complex view, strike the imagination as something grand, and beautiful, and noble, of which the attainment is well worth all the toil and anxiety which we are so apt to bestow upon it.
>
> And it is well that nature imposes upon us in this manner. It is this deception which arouses and keeps in continual motion the industry of mankind. It is this which first prompted them to cultivate the ground, to build houses, to found cities and commonwealths, and to invent and improve all the sciences and arts, which ennoble and embellish human life. . . .[18]

Thus, our interest in money and power, no less than for the arts and sciences, is aroused by a beautiful image, a disinterested representation at that. The moral philosopher Adam Smith finds that when we are pursuing utility, we are actually seeking vanity, and that when we give in to vanity, it is in effect beauty that attracts us.

But the imagination holds yet other powers. It renders possible a social arrangement that, if it is not founded on justice, produces at least certain of its effects. It is in the framework of his analysis of the powers of the imagination that Smith introduces, as early as *The Theory of Moral Sentiments*, the theme of the invisible hand that will be so decisive for the development of political economy:

> It is to no purpose that the proud and unfeeling landlord views his extensive fields, and without a thought for the wants of his brethren, in imagination consumes himself the whole harvest that grows upon them. . . . The capacity

of his stomach bears no proportion to the immensity of his desires, and will receive no more than that of the meanest peasant. The rest he is obliged to distribute among those who prepare, in the nicest manner, the little which he himself makes use of, among those who fit up the palace in which this little is to be consumed, among those who provide and keep in order all the different baubles and trinkets which are employed in the economy of greatness; all of whom thus derive from his luxury and caprice that share of the necessaries of life which they would in vain have expected from his humanity or his justice. . . . They [the rich] are led by an invisible hand to make nearly the same distribution of the necessaries of life which would have been made had the earth been divided into equal portions among all its inhabitants; and thus, without intending it, without knowing it, advance the interest of the society, and afford means to the multiplication of the species.[19]

Without further comment let us compare this account of the "invisible hand" with the one that Smith proposed in *The Wealth of Nations* seventeen years later:

Every individual necessarily labours to render the annual revenue of the society as great as he can. He generally, indeed, neither intends to promote the public interest, nor knows how much he is promoting it . . .; by directing that industry in such a manner as its produce may be of the greatest value, he intends only his own gain, and he is in this, as in many other cases, led by an invisible hand to promote an end which was no part of his intention.[20]

From one account to the other, the definition of the invisible hand remains basically the same. It has to do with the process by which the selfish passions and actions of individuals produce happy results for the public good of society that have little to do with what each person actually intends. Yet the content of the two accounts differs greatly. In *Theory*, human beings are ruled by their imagination and vanity; in *Wealth*, the imagination and vanity have disappeared and human behavior is motivated only by gain and interest. In *Theory*, the workings of the invisible hand are based on the divisons within society, wherein the imagination and vanity of the great or the wealthy set in motion the economic process and keep it going; whereas according to *Wealth*, the invisible hand functions through the behavior of all participants in the economic process, without any distincion. From one work to the other, we pass from an invisible hand rooted in the prestige of the imagination within a society of unequal people to an invisble hand founded on the prosaic and rational pursuit of gain in an egalitarian society.

Under the same expression, we discover two social processes, two very different moral landscapes. Either the invisible hand makes for unity in the diversity of the human world, or rather, from one account to the other, it becomes so different that it only serves to mask Smith's inability to think of the Ancient and the New together, the hitherto inegalitarian society and the new egalitarian society. Does the invisible hand hold the secret of the modern difference, or on the contrary does it betray it by erasing it? Would it not be the forerunner and type of those fine-sounding formulas that modern thought uses to affirm and deny the new in one and the same breath?

Smith himself may shed light on this matter in a famous chapter of *The Wealth of Nations*, chapter 4 of book 3, "How the Commerce of the Towns Contributed to the Improvement of the Country." There Smith describes the historical process by which inegalitarian feudal society gave way to the egalitarian character of *commercial society*.

IV

Smith's famous account is part of the infused knowledge, or, perhaps one should say, the golden legend of liberal societies. It can be summarized in the following terms. The feudal lord is a great landowner, but he himself can consume only a tiny portion of the surplus produced by those who cultivate his lands. The remainder, the greater part, he can only give away, practicing hospitality on a grand scale and in this way constituting for himself a multitude of retainers and dependents, who owe him obedience in return for supporting them. This organization of the feudal world seems perfectly stable in itself, but it will begin to change thanks to "the silent and insensible operations of foreign commerce and manufactures," whose products will make it possible for the great proprietors to consume on their own the surplus that up until then they had to share with their tenants and retainers. Smith comments:

> For a pair of diamond buckles perhaps, or for something as frivolous and useless, they exchanged the maintenance, or what is the same thing, they gradually bartered their whole power and authority.[21]

In this immense book, this masterpiece of breadth and serenity, the explanation of the passage from feudalism to commercial society and so of the very birth of modern society, rests on an epigram.[22] Is this not a fragile base on which to make history turn?

V

Smith strives to make his interpretation plausible by marshalling the theme of the invisible hand in the following passage, though he does not repeat the expression as such:

A revolution of the greatest importance to the public happiness was in this manner brought about by two different orders of people, who had not the least intention to serve the public. To gratify the most childish vanity was the sole motive of the great proprietors. The merchants and artificers, much less ridiculous, acted merely from a view to their own interest, and in pursuit of their own pedlar principle of turning a penny wherever a penny was to be got. Neither of them has either knowledge or foresight of that great revolution which the folly of the one, and the industry of the other, was gradually bringing about.[23]

Thus, it was the interaction of two very different kinds of human concerns and behavior that at length produced the decisive revolution in the life of Western humanity: on the one hand, vanity, childish vanity, in the great proprietor, and on the other, interest and gain in the merchant and the artisan. If the latter is indeed the logic that is presupposed and affirmed in *The Wealth of Nations*, it would seem that the former is the logic described in *The Theory of Moral Sentiments*.

The psychology of *The Theory of Moral Sentiments*, rooted in the imagination and vanity, cannot, however, explain how the feudal lords would abandon the grandeur of their position to satisfy a childish vanity. It would rather seem to explain how they would defend it fiercely, since the imagination and vanity are so tied to the desire for lofty social position. In this book the philosopher indeed reproves the pleasures of vanity, but he also takes stock that vanity and the imagination with which it is inseparably connected are the source of all that makes up the value of human life, that if they can effectively amuse men and make them be content with baubles and trinkets, they also inspire the most serious and noble of human acitivities,[24] and that, at bottom, what the desire for power and wealth, what vanity and ambition seek, is an idea, "the idea of a certain artificial and elegant repose" that is particularly desirable because it seems to characterize "the life of some superior rank of beings."[25]

Now, if this is how the human imagination turns, how would the feudal lord prefer a handful of diamonds to the power he holds over vast territories and numbers of men, given the prestige that is necessarily attached to it? Would he do so because the diamonds can belong to him exclusively and be altogether his, while the surplus of the produce of his lands must necessarily be distributed to others? But that is supposing that vanity here becomes its own enemy and absorbs or annuls the imagination almost completely. The landlord's imagination no longer embraces large masses of men or fawns with fervor on the idea of a life so radically different from that of common mortals, but shrinks and focuses exclusively on his own person, which it seeks to dress in the costliest fashion possible.

In truth, the psychology of the feudal lord that is set before us is hardly plausible, or rather perfectly inconsistent. When Smith yields to epithets

of increasing indignation in characterizing it, he is only trying to mesmer-
ize his own uncertainty and our vigilance. Forgetting all that he knew
about the powers of the imagination, and that he had so magnificently set
down in *Theory*, he leaves in the dark what goes on in the soul of the great
proprietor prior to its fall into "childish vanity." As he describes it, everything takes place as though the landlords were unaware of their eminent
position, their "feudal" power, and had never given any thought to it.
They have no place in their proud souls for their many dependents, but
surely have them on their hands and bring them together only to sponge
on a surplus they have no idea what to do with.

If we use the abstract language familiar to us, we will say that in this
account the economic surplus by which dependents are supported is not
the indispensable means or the inevitable result of the political institution
of "feudal power"; it is rather the case that the political institution is the
only possible use of the surplus under the circumstances. The proof of this
is that the moment a more pleasant, which is to say a more selfish, use of
the surplus presents itself, the landlords prefer it without the least hesita-
tion. Smith's desire to deduce the political institution from economic conditions is so pressing that it leads him to assert that the proprietor rules
over his clients because he feeds them. Yet the same reasoning would lead
one to conclude that he obeys his peasants because he feeds them.

It will be said that the question whether the political institution is the
instrument of the economic, or vice-versa, is subject to dispute, and that
apparently one is as plausible as the other; that the two theses are not even
exclusive, since there can be "reciprocal causality." The problem that we
are seeking to resolve here induces us to confirm what the preceding chapter suggested, the extent to which this language is shallow and vain! We
are not here dealing with two theses that are equally respectable because
they are equally scientific, one of which would have to be "falsified" and
the other "verified." The thesis that the economic insitution is primary is
not true; but neither is it false; it is simply not thinkable. No effort of the
imagination will allow us to conceive what takes place in the soul of the
great proprietor so that he would burden himself in this way with thou-
sands of dependents he has no idea what to think of or do with. Why in
God's name would he want to feed all these people? And then why would
he want to have this surplus of sheep and fleece? Among the absurd ideas
that would ever occupy any man in his right mind, that of the feudal lord
according to Smith surely ranks among the most absurd.

What gives a certain plausibility to the inconceivable is Smith's speaking as though the feudal lord supported his regiment until such time as he
would be able to use the surplus to acquire what his petty soul truly desires. This is, of course, nothing more than a retrospective illusion. The
rich man does not know that "the progress of commerce and manufac-

tures" sooner or later will offer him goods as desirable as diamond buckles or silk breeches. An interpretation of "feudalism" is tenable, if not true, only if it renders the appropriation of surplus and the support of dependents intelligible in and by themselves, that is, if the lord it describes actually harbors thoughts and sentiments that are inseparable from such a role.

VI

Adam Smith is a profound and subtle psychologist, but the proper relation between his psychological analyses and his political and economic theses remains to be determined. It is possible to make the two come together to such an extent that, as we have just seen, in order to explain, in *Wealth of Nations*, the major event of European history that is the passage from feudal to commercial society, Smith must renounce the doctrine of the imagination and vanity which he had magnificently exposed in *Theory of Moral Sentiments* and that would go a long way in making the intimate life of the feudal order intelligible. He tells a story, the story of improvement, of the advances and victory of commercial society, without at the same time being up to telling the corresponding story of the human passions and ideas. Thus the history of progress is no longer a truly human history. Adam Smith does indeed sketch the human motor of this history, which is the desire to better one's condition. Does the human condition inevitably improve because men have the irresistible desire to better their condition? That presupposes that men know what they want, that they are capable of attaining it, and that they do in fact attain it. Why then speak of an "invisible hand"?

Adam Smith recognizes and celebrates the new society, the modern regime where the watchword by which everything is measured is improvement, the "effectual truth" before which all other considerations pale. This progress, then, and the modern regime as well, must originate in an irresistible desire that is in man's very nature. At the same time, Smith perceives that this smooth quantitative progress conceals qualitative changes and that there is discontinuity between the new society and those that preceded it, enough to make one shudder at the prospect that something has happened or is in process of happening to human nature. But how can one maintain that there is a "contradiction" of this sort?

Montesquieu had resolved the difficulty, or rather he eluded it, by refraining from identifying a fundamental passion in human nature responsible for leading humanity from Spartan virtue to English liberty. As we have seen, instead of giving an account of human nature as the integrating principle of the human phenomenon, Montesquieu distinguished a num-

ber of sociological parameters that came together only in the viewpoint of
the sociologist. He also set up a contrast between two regimes of human
action, of which one, based on the need to flee evil, is the motor of commerce. Despite his admiration for Montesquieu, Smith made no use at all
of his wonderful inventions. This is no doubt because, as I have already
suggested, writing later in the century and with a weaker soul than Montesquieu, the spirit of commerce so ruled Smith that it could not but incite
him to equate it with human nature. It is also the case, consequently, that
the notion of "interest," already present in the French philosophers, at this
point begins to provide such forceful accounts of human behavior that,
beneath the uniform gray of this abstract notion, the qualitative differences start to lose their contours and color.

In fact, if the psychology of the landlord in his feudal role remains to be
determined, or is simply nonexistent, the notion of interest also remains
undetermined despite the many purposes it serves and the frequent use
made of it. What motivates the artisan and the merchant to supply so
simply and reasonably the landlord's luxuries in exchange for good
money? For the sake of gain, because it is their "interest"? If so, do they
want to earn money to live a comfortable life, or to spend with vanity in
their turn, or else to invest money in order to earn yet more? Smith has
nothing to say on this score. In the history of our nature or soul that Smith
is obliged at least to sketch, the only moment where psychology becomes
truly precise, where human bahavior is neatly drawn, is the moment
where the landlord yields to a childish vanity and prefers luxury to this
power for which we were not told he even had any liking.

In the history Smith unravels in *The Wealth of Nations*, the human soul
appears only when the feudal world is passing away, to destroy that world,
not to sustain it and not at all to replace it. Smith's account of its interven-
tion at this point in history is nothing if it is not ironic or epigrammatic.
The landlord, together with his nature and his passions, appears on the
scene only to disappear. The feudal lord, who until that time was the passive tool of his surplus, without passion or ambition, only appears, with
his human traits and childish vanity, at the moment when he disappears
as feudal lord. Only at this instant is there mention of the "power" and
"authority" that he "barters" for a pair of diamond buckles.

Furthermore, it is hard to understand why Smith is so sarcastic. He
himself tells us that at the end of the process the landlord resembles a
wealthy bourgeois or merchant who has "bartered" the embarrassing ab-
surdity of his feudal seignory for a social position in which he will at last
be able to behave like a reasonable man. The landlord's behavior conforms with his own as well as the general interest. Instead of bantering,
Smith ought to seriously celebrate this happy moment that transformed
the landlord from a proprietor of men to a proprietor of costly baubles and
trinkets.

In spite of his official teaching about what is reasonable and fitting, Smith despises the landlord who renounces his seignory. Consequently, he admits that the feudal lord was greater than the richer bourgeois he will become and who is, he says, "insignificant." But he cannot bring himself to penetrate his soul because he would find it too different from the soul of the merchant, that is, of the reasonable and fitting man. Thus he is willing to show us this landlord only once he conducts himself like an ordinary merchant, or rather like an abject milliner.

A serious look at the landlord's soul would make it clear that he has "bartered" power and prestige for carbuncles and pumps only when compelled to do so by the centralized royal power of the sovereign. He was tamed by one stronger and perhaps more intelligent than he! His so-called "childish" vanity only increases as his power decreases. Far from reducing him to impotence, the landlord's vanity is itself the product of his impotence. The landlord is viewed from the narrowest psychological angle, the most reductive and "ridiculous" perspective, because he is not looked at from a political perspective.

VII

But why, in thinking about the Old and the New together, does Adam Smith not have recourse to his conception of the imagination that seems so appropriate to this task? The imagination, as he explains it in *Theory*, can rightly be said to be "creative" or "instaurative." One wonders why Smith does not link the sequence of economic phases to the history of the dispositions of the soul. Why doesn't he give an account of economic history as specifically human by characterizing each phase as ruled by the imagination? Why not see the difference between regimes as produced by the imagination, as is often done today? The constitution of the imagination needs to be examined more closely by taking up again the remarks made above.

What strikes Smith is the disproportion between the real usefulness of the objects and amenities that constitute luxury and the ardor with which they are coveted. He explains this bizarre circumstance by observing that what attracts us in luxury is not its actual usefulness, but the idea of its utility, or more precisely "the order, the regular and harmonious movement of the system, the machine or economy" by means of which luxury is produced.[26] Our desire is moved by an aesthetic consideration which Smith senses he is the first to define exactly:

> But that this fitness, this happy contrivance of any production of art, should often be more valued than the very end for which it was intended; and that the exact adjustment of the means for attaining any conveniency or pleasure

should frequently be more regarded than that very conveniency or pleasure,
in the attainment of which their whole merit would seem to consist, has not,
so far as I know, been yet taken notice of by any body.[27]

Why, for example, does a man seek to acquire the most precise timepieces
possible, when extreme precision in keeping time is perfectly useless?
Smith replies that "[w]hat interests him is not so much the attainment of
this piece of knowledge, as the perfection of the machine which serves to
attain it."[28]

We are now in a position to grasp the radical character of Smith's conception of the imagination.

The imagination that makes us desire wealth and power and aspire to
a life beyond that of common mortals is fundamentally the same as the
imagination that makes us covet high-precision watches and those "trinkets and baubles" that in Smith's time are exactly what today we call
"gadgets." The desires men have for power, wealth, and the products of
technical ingenuity are all rooted in an aesthetic idea that integrates the
diverse human activities in a common ground where they all can find a
place in the same social and moral life. One can champion utility all one
wants, but it is the imagination that gives things their value, makes them
more or less desirable, and associates them with human desire.

Thus the desire for power—the specifically political desire, the greatest
desire—and the taste for gadgets are two expressions of the same aesthetic
matrix, the same faculty of the imagination. The greatest desire is necessarily subordinated to this matrix since it is intrinsically weaker than what
engenders it. And if both the greatest and lowest desires spring from the
same source, if one desires both glory and a watch with the same desire,
then the social world will necessarily end up corresponding to the imagination according to its bent and truth. Since the imagination, which is
basically an aesthetic faculty, is most content in contemplating more and
more ingeniously contrived objects and services, man will find his satisfaction in a society where the ambition for power and glory will have given
way to the desire to acquire more and more products that are more and
more developed. The desire for gadgets can promote the industry of mankind as much as or rather much more and much more rationally than the
brute coveting of power or wealth, a desire that entails little technical so-
phistication.

In *Theory*, Smith describes the human scene as dominated and instituted by the imagination, which can direct human desire, it seems indifferently, toward objects of lofty ambition as well as toward vulgar but developed objects for which a commercial society has a liking. But the imagination is not really that indifferent. The formal idea of utility that fits means
to ends sums up the contagious nucleus of what is desirable. And thus, if
the desires which a society wishes to satisfy most of all depend on what its

imagination turns to, its natural bent is to exercise itself and satisfy itself
in the commercial society where the "aesthetic" motive that moves men is
reduced to its purest and at the same time most recognizable form and is
fully embodied and thus fully available in the developed artifacts themselves.

The imagination is both indifferent to its object, as long as it is formally
harmonious, and fatally led to conform to its own proper form, the idea of
utility that fits means to ends. As plastic or plasmatic as it may be, the
imagination does have a nature. It liberates man from the constraints of
his nature to subject him to those of its own nature. It leads him by the
hand from glory to gadget. But the more it becomes true and pure, con-
formed to its form and essence, the more it becomes poor and petty and
contradicts its own nature. It is purer in the watchmaker's timepiece than
in the soul of Alexander! The imagination which gives things their value
necessarily is unaware of its own value and thus its qualitative difference
from one regime to another.

The imagination conceives so many diverse things and tirelessly popu-
lates Olympus and Tenarus, but it does not permit one to reflect on the
difference among human epochs.

VIII

The imagination of a society devoted to commerce is actively present in the
things that are produced and exchanged, and so also in the medium of this
exchange, which is money. Thus embodied or entombed in artifacts and
money, the imagination disappears as a glorious faculty. It is ever at work,
but it becomes so to speak invisible. Human nature has lost nothing of its
passion for desiring, but what it desires by preference is what is manifestly
desirable, those things that display unequivocally and transparently the
emblem of their desirability, the "useful" things which embody and display the *idea* of utility that fits means to ends.

In the measure that it exercises and satisfies the imagination, the idea of
utility rules over *homo oeconomicus* and also over the one who observes
him. The invisible role of the imagination tended to disappear into the
artifacts that were produced, desired, and exchanged; but it reappears as
no less sharp and even more vigorous in the mind of the spectator who
observes commercial society from without, from which vantage point he
will see it as a grand machine in which the means are perfectly adapted to
the end, a grand system moving itself in spontaneous harmony: the marketplace. The economist's desire and delight extend and fulfill the desire
and delight of *homo oeconomicus*. At least this is how Smith describes his
own situation and sentiments:

The perfection of police, the extension of trade and manufactures, are noble and magnificent objects. The contemplation of them pleases us, and we are interested in whatever can tend to advance them. They make part of the great system of government, and the wheels of the political machine seem to move with more harmony and ease by means of them. We take pleasure in beholding the perfection of so beautiful and so grand a system, and we are uneasy till we remove any obstruction that can in the least disturb or encumber the regularity of its motions.[29]

The same bent of the imagination, the same aesthetic idea incites on the one hand the citizen of the new society to acquire the watch with the most delicate and adjusted movements, and on the other Adam Smith to recommend the removal of "any obstruction that can in the least disturb or encumber the regularity of its motions."

IX

The coarse imagination of the landlord embraced immense fields in a confused fashion. He needed a great many people to fill the gap between his wide-ranging desires and the narrow limits of his stomach. That gap is the wellspring of the invisible hand that opens the hand of the rich. In the new society, the imagination becomes more refined, or rather formalized and individualized. Each man feels keenly the admirable and desirable character of the objects and services that clearly fit the purpose they are intended to serve. Once the imagination has become individualized, every member of society is left alone with the idea of fitness and its indefinite applications. Once every man is moved by this idea, and thus by the tranquil desire to acquire the objects that display it, there is no reason whatever for relations among individuals not to be peaceful and harmonious, unless motives foreign to fitness should intervene, unless the government, temporal or spiritual, should meddle.

As I have noted already, considered in itself, the acquisition of a high precision watch is no more useful nor does it spring from any more reasonable or "philosophical" behavior than the purchase of a diamond clasp. But the watch, even if it is not useful, at least embodies the idea of utility, the idea of fitness, and thus it embodies the specific motive of the imagination proper to commercial society. The vanity of its acquisition is balanced or even reabsorbed by the rationality of the imagination that it embodies. The landlord's purchase of costly jewels provokes excessive moral censure precisely because it expresses an elementary human passion that is not transformed or specified by the abstract idea of fitness. In an inverse sense, Smith's uncertain or ambiguous moral judgment of the behavior proper to modern society—"rational" but "vulgar" like those of a "salesman"—

reflects the abstract character of this behavior. The abstract idea of utility at work in the quest for "gain" modifies vanity or sensuality to such an extent that one wonders whether or not traditional moral censure can still be directed against "flaws" of this kind. But the idea that these selfish behaviors lead to the public good makes the uncertainty perfectly palpable. What the observer contemplates are not individuals acting in a certain way for certain motives liable to moral judgment, but rather a tendentially harmonious system where the natural motives of individuals are no more visible than the grease and teeth of the wheelworks on the face of a watch.

This system constitutes and produces a host of useful effects that correspond to the idea of utility. Whether social or individual, the imagination tends to see an effect or a fact only where means clearly fit the ends they are intended to serve. Whatever each man may want specifically cannot be had as such in the life of society, since the individual is limited to actually obtaining only useful things.[30]

X

The imagination gives things their value, makes them desirable, and since the new imagination is ruled by the idea of utility or fitness, it seems that this idea will provide the criterion or measure of the relative value of things. But what proportion can the imagination discover or establish between the fitness of a precision watch and that of a patrician residence, all of whose elements conspire to nourish the idea of "a certain artificial and elegant repose"? How can one compare innumerable and infinitely diverse objects and services among themselves and arrive at a proper estimate of the rapport between the means and the ends they serve? The commercial imagination reduces all things to useful things in the measure that they embody the idea of fitness, but it does not seem to be able to establish their relative value.

We note, however, that an object is desirable thanks to the fitness it embodies because it has been produced with the idea of fitness in mind. What is pleasing in the watch is the guiding principle of its making. The more delicately fashioned the watch is, the more perfectly it will serve its purpose and be more greatly desired and desirable. We know that a gain of precision in timekeeping does not necessarily add to the watch's real usefulness in practical life, but because the exact measure of time is the raison d'etre of a watch, this gain of precision increases its usefulness in the sense of its fitness, and consequently its value increases. In order to increase precision, greater care must be taken, more labor most be added; and thereby value is added. In general terms, the value of a thing corresponds to the amount of labor it embodies.[31]

The imagination that desires and the labor that produces are alike specified and directed by the same idea of fitness or utility. But the imagination tends to blend with this idea in each object, whereas labor distinguishes itself visibly and objectively in the person and activity of the laborer, even if he is moved by the imagination. Consequently, the laborer can in principle measure what the imagination conceives, which the imagination itself cannot measure. The imagination cannot appear as a measure of value in the commercial society except as labor or under something similar to it.

The commercial imagination puts labor to work and makes it appear as labor—as producing something useful, that is, objects and services displaying the idea of utility. The "theory of value-labor" is no doubt "analytically" false, or at any rate irrelevant,[32] yet it formulates in a very suggestive way a fundamental aspect of the new society, its tendency to value only what is produced by labor, by ever more developed labor. Consequently, because it alone produces value, labor tends to have greater and greater value,[33] it is more and more "beyond price." In the end, a prodigiously well paid handful of Workers will produce what is Useful for all of humanity, the rest of whom will be idle or unemployed.

Once labor appears as the measure or cause of value, the imagination as a universal human faculty capable of reaching beyond the merely useful and embracing the Whole of the world departs from the scene, leaving behind it the insubstantial aura that goes with the products of the Useful and that advertising seizes upon with marvellous ease. Then the "economic viewpoint" confidently settles in, which is in no way a "conception of the world"—with its advent the imagination renounces the "world"—but rather the vital principle and untiring motor of the commercial society.

In the new society, the objects of the imagination and the objects of labor blend together in such a way that the two overlap in an ever more exact manner. The one great object the imagination retains is precisely the harmonious system of production and consumption, the system of commercial liberty governed by the invisible hand of the marketplace. Man as economist is the pure spectator of man become *homo oeconomicus*.

XI

The society we are examining—our own—appears as Economy writ large because it acts as a system of utility, labor, and value. In such a necessarily homogeneous system, where only equal values can be exchanged, there is no place for the power that necessarily introduces difference and inequality, first of all among the haves and have nots. Commercial society nurtures and contains the immanent utopia of a powerless society, a depoliticized city. Yet as we saw in section 2, the economic system allows a particular form of power to subsist: the power of purchasing and in particular the power of purchasing labor. A division runs within the system of labor and labor itself. Labor produces value, and itself has value. It is not only embodied in traded objects; it is also purchased or "ordered" from men who sell it. To begin with, orders have to be placed for the labor that is embodied in the commercial society.

The notion of purchased labor allows for an understanding of how the economic process, that is, the process of labor's embodiment in objects and services, can be maintained and renewed, how human initiative continually animates the system instead of the system, homogeneous and closed, wearing away more or less rapidly and coming to a standstill in things. Purchased labor is at the beginning of the process; it is there for the taking and is the active pivot of exchange. In order for it to play this role, it must produce more value than it consumes. In other words, it must draw a profit.

Just as the notion of power reemerges, in a hardly recognizable way, in the notions of power and purchased labor, so also the imagination reemerges in profit, only this time it is easy to miss it. Here is what Smith has to say about profit:

> The profits of stock, it may perhaps be thought, are only a different name for the wages of a particular sort of labour, the labour of inspection and direction. They are, however, altogether different, are regulated by quite different principles, and bear no proportion to the quantity, the hardship, or the ingenuity of this supposed labour of inspection and direction. They are regulated altogether by the value of all the stock employed, and are greater or smaller in proportion to the extext of this stock.[34]

Thus, the profit is not proportionate to the amount of labor that the capitalist eventually furnishes, but rather proportionate to the stock, that is, the capital he has invested. What accounts for this anomaly in the system of labor and value?

Let us return to our landlord whom we have already belabored a good deal and, just as pitilessly as Smith, let us consider him in his fit of childish vanity when he gets it into his head to acquire a pair of diamond buckles. To make this purchase he will use a part of his surplus, which is in some way the surplus of his surplus, that is, that part of his surplus that he does not need himself, or that at the time no longer serves to maintain or entertain his dependents. This surplus is of an unprecedented kind. It is not allocated, or at least it is not tied up, since the landlord suspends the traditional allocation he makes in keeping with established political order and custom. He will allot it as his fantasy, according to the circumstances his vulgar and childish vanity will suggest to him. He thus conceives that so many head of sheep, or so many bushels of fleece—the freed-up surplus or its value in money—have the same value as a pair of diamond buckles. As

Smith deplores, it is in this "unnatural" way, through the commerce of luxury, that improvement began in Europe, and not by the progress of agriculture that would have been "natural."[35] Everything began with a unallotted, or freed up surplus, an undetermined equivalence that can only be determined by the imagination after custom and nature as well have been suspended or dismissed.

It seems to me that this gives us a direct and simple access to the nature of profit in a developed society. Unallotted surplus makes possible the purchase of any kind of labor like the purchase of any kind of product. Since this surplus can be allocated to any kind of investment as well as to any kind of consumption, it allows for the general equivalence of "utilities," or "works," or "values," that is the precondition for the functioning of the commercial system.

One is strongly tempted to concede that Marx is correct. The profit obtained by an exchange of equal values on the capitalist market is essentially comparable to the surplus extorted in precapitalist societies that was responsible for the inequality in their political and social institutions.[36] But what does that mean?

In a society where all men are by right equal, the differences in the value attributed to or recognized in things, in men, and in the professions are not inscribed in a fixed, binding, "authoritarian" fashion in institutions. They do not translate into differences of "rank"; they are evaluated and measured, for the essentials, by market prices. The value of things, men, professions changes and even change quickly, since they are not officially, that is to say politically, fixed. At all times, the legitimacy of a given relation between social values—of a relative price recognized by society—hinges on the possibility of modifying this rapport at the next instant, if the suggestion of a new equivalence among values receives the endorsement of the social body, if an "offer" counters a "demand." For such a change to be publicly acknowledged and accepted, and so for it to have taken place, the network of equivalencies and proportions must be supple and mobile. If the activities taken together did not produce a surplus, that is to say if certain activities did not produce more than their cost, the network of which I speak would become petrified. No initiative could be given its value on the market. In fact, there would be no market. In order for there to be a market, for money, the universal equivalent of all goods and services, to measure the value of the labors already performed or in progress, it must be possible to measure those works that will sooner or later be undertaken, those which are in a word possible. Thus at every instant a certain amount of money must not be tied up. It must literally be free. For the moment, it remunerates nothing and does not correspond to any labor, although it has the potential to remunerate any labor possible. This free money is profit. If it is proportionate to the invested capital, it is because the imagination first conceives this proportion naturally. In the play of equivalencies, proportions and correspondences it establishes it is simply unimaginable that, all things being equal otherwise, the owner of a big company should register the same profit as the owner of a small company. Although it is true the labor furnished by the first may not be necessarily greater than that of the second. It is a question here neither of justice nor even of economic rationality strictly speaking, but first of all of this evaluating and comparative network without which a society cannot conceive of itself as what it is: a unity constituted by a plurality of diverse elements. Not being able to perceive itself, it could not exist, unless it were held together by brute force alone if that is, in fact, possible.

In precapitalist societies based on the inequality of ranks, there was no profit, or it played only a subordinate role in what Marx called the mercantile "intervals" or "pores," to which surplus was immediately and directly tied. The production of surplus was specified by its use. It would have made no sense to say that labor produced more than it cost, and thus drew profit, since surplus, under the form of revenues or forced labor, was immediately and directly tied to groups and offices whose "value" was considered superior, in fact incomparably superior, to the "value" of labor. What labor "produced," that is, the maintenance of the noble life of the nobility and the pious life of the clergy, was not of its own kind since it was not a product that embodied it.

But in capitalist society, for whom or for what does the proletarian work, or rather overwork? To maintain the capitalist the way John Doe maintained his lord and pastor? This is not at all the case. Rather he works to make capital bear fruit, that is to say to draw a profit. If he did not attain this goal, there would soon be only dead or dying labor, since without profits the Economy is but a valley of industrial dry bones. Only profits, profits proportionate to capital, can give breath and life to the Economy. The imagination conceives this proportion and arouses the desire for it. The capitalist's poetic imagination turns the old words into a new phrase and the elements of the old labor into a new labor that will be truly alive since it will produce more value than it will absorb. The fact is that Marx is mistaken. Profit, not religion, is the spirit of this spiritless world where one must overwork in order to live: the commercial society.

XII

The proposition that surplus is not institutionalized in capitalist society, as it is in earlier societies, gives rise to an objection. Surplus, like profit, is appropriated in private property, which is an institution and even the institution par excellence. This point deserves further consideration.

Those who appropriate to themselves profit can put it to two uses. They can either consume it for themselves by purchasing diamond buckles or necklaces, or they can invest it. In a society based on the idea of equality, consumption tends to be purely private. However vain, pretentious, and ostentatious it may be, it is always only the particular pleasure of one citizen who is no different than all the other citizens, over whom the rich man and his diamonds, furs, and Ferrari have no power at all. Public expenditure in the form of public works or patronage tends to disappear, precisely because it shows a difference in conditions even while seeking to make the difference excusable. Investment no doubt has necessarily good public effects, since it is allocated freely and in any event destined to produce profit whose future use still remains uncertain, but what one can see of it forever points to its invisible essence. The noninstitutionalized, undetermined, floating character of surplus is most clearly revealed in the choice left to the capitalist to use it for his own consumption or for investment. The capitalist is defined by his freedom from having to choose between these two radically different uses of profit. Henceforth, surplus appropriated by the capitalist, either as consumption or even as investment since it is essentially neutral between the two uses, is not visible in the social landscape the way revenue was in festivals and castles. Capital appears as an immense black hole where, it seems, the result of social activity comes to lose itself.

For society to regain mastery over itself, and first of all a thorough perception of itself, is it not enough to abolish the exorbitant liberty of the owner of capital by eliminating the private appropriation of profit? Consumption and investment are two uses so unlike profit that joining them in one and the same person seems a violent blow to the nature of things. Thus the generating of profit for investment will be made a form of labor like all others, remunerated, to use Adam Smith's terms, by reason of the "quantity, difficulty, or quality of the . . . labour of inspection and direction"—a form of labor henceforth separated from all property. The free allocation of surplus by the private owner will give way to its imperative allocation to investment by the collective "proprietor."

This is not a return to the set up of precapitalist societies. Authoritarian investment is not connected to the authoritarian collection of revenue or taxes. The ultimate purpose or use of surplus is not to be found in investment, but in drawing new surplus in order to reinvest it in an authoritarian way, and so on indefinitely, each investment being a part of an indefinite and unlimited investment.

But how is profit to be valued now that the capitalist has appeared? The nature of profit revealed itself in the discretionary choice it offered between consumption and investment. It seems, however, that the abolition of the possibility of choice leaves intact the possibility and reality of profit and that to affirm the contrary would be to attribute magical powers to the capitalist. The capitalist is no magician, but rather, as I have noted, a poet, who speaks in the language of numbers. He can do this thanks to his imagination and his money, his own money, which is the lens through which he sees the world. The imagination weaves correspondences and equivalences and money is the universal correspondent and equivalent, the inexhaustible metaphor. In mocking the merchant who gets stung in the Indies and screams in Paris, Rousseau could see the bottom line: the imagination and money make things felt the world over. Only the owner of capital can conceive endlessly the new correspondences which constitute the life of the Economy, whereas authoritarian or planned investment petrifies the network of social valences and paralyzes the movement of the imagination.

XIII

These few remarks on the structure of modern society suffice for my purpose, which was not, as it ought to be clear, to make a contribution to the science of economics that has advanced a good deal since the time of Adam Smith. Rather I sought only to sketch the plan of the arrangement by which the modern regime took form as the Economy or as an economic System. This development is often characterized as the "emancipation of the economy." The expression is inappropriate, however, inasmuch as the laws and customs that at one time regulated and constrained labor and exchange were abolished, either progressively or brutally, leaving the way free for the extraordinary improvement we have witnessed. But it should also be remarked that what was in this way "emancipated" did not even exist before it was free. The freeing and the founding of the economy took place at one and the same time. From that time it cannot be properly said that the economy is distinct from society; society or the body politic itself becomes the economic system. That presupposes that the social space to begin with takes a certain turn. The imagination turns its sights on labor, which becomes exposed to the imagination.

The imagination, under the form of capital, puts labor to work or rules over it. Labor, or the perspective or irresistible attraction of labor, constrains the imagination to give birth only to useful ideas, at least to ideas that display the idea of usefulness, that are liable to encourage labor. The imagination exercises mastery over labor and labor is master of the imagination. Let us enter a moment into this circle, which is our own.

In earlier societies, labor had two possible purposes. Either one worked "to live," to assure the subsistence of the family or group; or one worked to make possible the noble life of the nobles who did not work. In commercial society, one works neither to live—that is a happy result, but a secondary matter—nor to permit others to live, since the class assigned to showcase the good life has been abolished. One now works only to work, that is, to carry out the ever new useful ideas the imagination conceives and thereby to incite it to conceive yet other ever new useful ideas. Labor never rests.

The imagination, for its part, no longer seeks to embrace as in the past the Being which is "greater than which nothing can be conceived," nor even the lesser divinites who preside over Love and War. It has ceased to build temples or erect statues of a beauty worthy of their greatness. It conceives the new ideas that, once made real by the labor that animates them, will allow the human condition to become better and especially to bring the system of labor to fulfillment. It is still the same imagination. Olympian images still abound in advertising, the images of women and men as beautiful as gods ever young, whose flawlessly quick movements never betray the slighest trace of anything earthly or earthy. But, with its skill and measured steps, bent on our sphere, it no longer knows the disproportionate desire that once led it to make itself equal to the world. The imagination has lost all sense of glory.

PART TWO

The Self-Affirmation
of Modern Man

CHAPTER IV

The Hidden Man

I

THE PRECEDING CHAPTERS have provided summary accounts of the genesis of three major spheres in modern man's self-consciousness: History, Society, Economy. Each of these has two facets: it is a homogeneous set of historical, social, or economic facts; and it is the science that concerns itself with these facts—history, sociology, economics. Each science selects the facts that interest it by focusing its "viewpoint" on the indefinite totality of facts. Whether this viewpoint be historical, sociological or economic, it can be applied in principle to any subset whatever of the whole set of facts. The sociologist has his "viewpoint" on the historian's or the economist's domain and each of these three specialists has his "viewpoint" on the domains of the other two, and on other domains as well. There are, for example, historical, sociological, economic viewpoints on painting, medicine, sexuality, and madness. What is more, these viewpoints can crisscross in a rather dizzying fashion, and only a first-rate methodologist would be in a position to pinpoint what distinguishes a sociological viewpoint on economic facts from an economic viewpoint on social facts. Whatever the subject, just as I have underlined more particularly with regard to sociology, the kaleidoscopic combinations are unlimited. One needs only a very modest amount of imagination to discover or invent endlessly new "fields of research" and to initiate original "scientific projects." Under the constraints of scientific activity, which are more formal than real, the freedom of the scholar in framing his hypotheses and working out his conclusions is so to speak unlimited. He is the absolute sovereign over his province of "facts," which he is methodologically exempt from connecting to other facts, which is to say from the whole of the human phenomenon. He is in fact more than exempt—he is formally forbidden even to sketch such a connection, which would constitute an offense against scientific rigor and a lapse into "literature" or "ideology" or even "philosophy." How fortunate these scholars are to be spared the sole true difficulty of knowledge!

The awareness of this difficulty sometimes surfaces in the abrupt adoption of a position regarding the place of a particular science and the sum of its facts within the Whole of man. Thus, for example, one posits that man is a "historical being," one denies that society determines human behaviors or that *homo oeconomicus* is the truly human man. But the human sciences cannot transform their good, or bad, conscience into knowledge, since they refuse on principle to attempt to take into account the whole of the human phenomenon, to understand the multiplicity and diversity of its aspects in the unity of Nature, or the World or Being, or Man himself. They often evoke the need for interdisciplinary work, as if the sum of the biases they profess could ever yield the unity of an impartial examination. Moreover, in practice, this need is generally only the license given to each discipline to violate its own rules on condition and with the intent that the others do the same. The result is that too often "interdisciplinary research" is to scientific rigor what routing is to military discipline or a stampede to horsemanship.

It will be said that if this science of the Whole were really possible, if only the original claim of philosophy were still plausible, the human sciences would not have emancipated themselves in this way. Must it not be admitted that the idea of a "human nature" has long ago revealed itself incapable of unifying the human phenomenon in an intelligible way? Moreover, have we not seen how the need to give an account of the New led Montesquieu to develop several of the "viewpoints" we are concerned with here? These views, which despair of philosophy, are today shared by almost everyone. Whoever suggests that the case is not closed, and that valid arguments can be advanced in favor of the One, gives the impression of backing up against the wall into a position "objectively surpassed" by the progress of reason and thus "untenable." Isn't this the case?

I have already pointed out in section 5 of chapter 2 that sociology's insistence on the diversity of human things, directed polemically against the idea of a nature identical to itself, was only one moment in an undertaking whose aim was not to save the diversity but to produce uniformity by defining the homogeneous totality of "social facts" regulated by "laws." There is nothing in this, at least, that requires one to despair of the cause of unity, especially, it is important to note, since it is from within philosophy itself—and before the novel English experience would lead Montesquieu to link the fate of knowledge to the authority of commerce and liberty—that there arose a radical challenge to the unity of the human phenomenon, or at least of its unifying comprehension under the compass of nature. Why would philosophy not be capable of redoing what it has deliberately undone? I need to retrace briefly the history of this deliberate dismemberment.

What is commonly called modern philosophy takes shape in the seventeenth century in an attack on the philosophy of Aristotle and, more precisely, his doctrine of "substance" concerning nature in general or human nature in particular. Whether a substance, "substantial form," placed in a hierarchy of substances or forms; or a nature, at once animal and rational, within a hierarchy of natures; or the human soul as the "form" of the human body, it is the teaching of Aristotle, which was essentially adopted by Catholic doctrine, that Descartes, Hobbes, Spinoza, and Locke will implacably destroy. That man is a *substance* and *one* substance, that is the *Carthago delenda* of the new philosophy.

This destruction can be studied in the work of Descartes and the great Cartesians, Spinoza and Malebranche, and also in the English line that goes from Hobbes to Locke and Locke to Hume. This latter route is the more appropriate for us, since it is in England that the destruction of substance is linked most clearly and most closely to the construction of the new body politic, the new world of human liberty. In this context, Locke's work is central in every sense of the word. But it is not possible to take it up without first saying a few words about Hobbes's work.

Hobbes's critique of the notion of substantial form and more generally of Aristotle's metaphysics and politics was direct, trenchant, and even sarcastic,[1] but it did pave the way for a positive redefinition of the human problem. This redefinition no doubt appears as a simplification, analogous to the simplification to be found at the same moment in an author very different from Hobbes, in Pascal, who writes that, "Without examining every particular pursuit, it is enough to comprehend them under diversion."[2] Hobbes, of course, reduces the human complexity, not to *divertissement*, but to the desire for power:

> The passions that most of all cause the difference of wit, are principally, the more or less desire of power, of riches, of knowledge, and of honour. All which may be reduced to the first, that is, desire of power. For riches, knowledge, and honour, are but several sorts of power.[3]

We note that human nature here plays a more direct and, if I may say it, a more concentrated role than in Aristotle himself. In Aristotle nature provides the moving force, the impulse, and the ordering of a human world that is nonetheless described in all its complexity, thanks to a dialectical analysis of opinions and to a phenomenology of the passions. Nowhere in Aristotle does one find a naturalist compression comparable to what we have just found in Hobbes. This compression, moreover, has two aspects.

On the one hand, human diversity and complexity are reduced to the unity and simplicity of a fundamental passion, the desire for power; and on the other, the political order is entirely deduced from this almost unique passion. I will briefly make the second point more explicit.

What sums up both the nature of man and the terms of the political problem is thus the desire for power which manifests itself as vanity or desire for eminence, the desire to be first on the one hand; and on the other hand as desire to possess the things that are necessary to living. Before the birth of the political order, in the state of nature, the two forms of this desire lead with equal necessity to the war of every man against every man. Now, for man to desire to have ever more power presupposes that he is conscious of having power, that is, of being the cause of possible effects. According to Hobbes, men are naturally distinguishable from beasts only by the faculty of science, which is knowledge of the possible consequences or effects.[4] Since together with desire men have the idea of power, and since their desires for power in some way neutralize and nullify one another in the war of every man against every man, men will erect over themselves the greatest power they can conceive of, the sovereign power—the one that characterizes the modern state. In this way, each man will be held back by the fear of this power that is incomparably superior to his power; and henceforth each man will only use his desire for power, which cannot be uprooted, in the industrious search for the goods required for the most comfortable life possible, or in displays of an inoffensive vanity. Once each man's desire for power is held in check by the fear of the sovereign power, the exercise of this desire is nothing more than the exercise of what will soon be celebrated as liberty, as we shall see in section 10 of chapter 5.

There is a wonderful coherence between the analysis of human nature on the one hand and the way the political problem is formulated and resolved on the other. Hobbes is "truly a powerful and systematic political thinker."[5] This is where the commentator, without being aware of it, runs a great risk of missing the critical point that the manifest and almost aggressive role of human nature is here in reality paving the way to its disappearance, or at least its lowering. In fact, the homogenization of the diverse human faculties and passions, transformed into as many different versions of the same desire for power, presupposes a prior work of abstraction and, just as much, of denaturation. The observer or the philosopher speaks of "power," while the real living man with natural spontaneity speaks of wealth, science, honor, or glory. In speaking of it in terms of quantity and desire for power, Hobbes seems to affirm human nature with an altogether distinctive intensity. The later story of the notion of power confirms that his affirmation contains more stridency than power.

Hobbes's bold simplification definitely releases a dense and complex kernel at the heart of our nature in the form of an imperious desire and its obscure and necessary object. However one may reduce it, our nature conserves breadth and gravity. But the wages of abstraction must soon be paid since it destroys what it affirms. Too general, too abstract, too neutral, too little human, power will sever itself from human desire and human nature. What for Hobbes was the center and proper attribute of the human world will dissolve itself into the nonhuman or not specifically human homogeneity of power. John Locke is the witness to or rather the author of this transformation.

III

In its French translation Locke's *Essay Concerning Human Understanding* became the philosophic education of the European Enlightenment. The chapter entitled "Of Power" is the longest in this long essay and the notion of power is at the center of the work.[6] The other main notions are developed by recourse to it. At the same time, as I shall shortly indicate, it is absent from Locke's analysis of human nature, at least of the human passions. Power is expelled from the place where in Hobbes it played the most striking role—the human soul as seat of the passions and desires— but it invades all the other domains. Let us take the time to document these affirmations, even if only in summary fashion:

- the "secondary qualities"—color, odor, etc.—are only the *power* of the primary qualities, or of the invisible particles, to produce these sensations or these effects which we call secondary qualities;
- what we call "substance" is only the *power* to produce a certain number of effects that we perceive empirically, without knowing in the least the nature of this "substance";
- the will is the *power* to prefer one action over another;
- liberty is the *power* to act upon this preference; it has nothing to do with the will for it would then be the power of a power, which is absurd;
- the understanding is a *power*.[7]

Is it possible for such disparate things to be defined as *power*? In any event, one sees that this notion, by the ubiquity of its usage in the domain of matter as in that of man's mental functioning in general strips away the very narrow bond that linked it in Hobbes to the notion of domination or superiority. Its properly moral and human meaning is in some way neutralized. As is clearly indicated in what Locke writes of the connections between understanding and will,[8] it tends to approximate the notion of relation. Power is in sum an intermediary stage—a halfway house—on the road that leads from the world of substance to that of relation.

One of the principal intentions of Locke's *Essay* is to discredit the notion of substance, to put it out of commission, if I may put it that way. As soon as power provides the universal idiom capable of giving an account of what previously had been interpreted by recourse to the idea of substance, the question of human substance or essence, of what is proper to man, can be left aside or at least loses something of its urgency and necessity. We can know nothing but *powers*, that refer in a certain sense to a *je ne sais quoi* as their support, in the case of man to an "agent," to a "substance" if one wishes, but this substance is inaccessible and unknowable. It makes no sense to inquire into it.[9]

It is true that Hobbes had already rejected as completely as Locke the traditional notions of substance and essence, of genre and species.[10] But Hobbes kept the tradition's insistent concern for what is proper to man, even if he interpreted it in an altogether different way than the Aristotelian and Thomist ontology. Locke completely detaches man's aptitude to produce from the effects of the human desire of power, whereas for Hobbes the two are inseparable. Man is no longer the being whose sole concern is with excellence; he is only the being who produces a certain number of effects and knows that he produces them. It seems that this is the same as recognizing and affirming something proper to man, but we need to consider seriously the true import of this definition, if that is what it is.

It will not do to restrict its import to the traditional and very plausible understanding of man as capable of bringing into being, of producing things that were not given in or by nature; in a word, of man as an "artist." Not only has this human property been recognized for a long time, but its manifestation is very closely linked to the very origin of philosophy. Philosophy is born and becomes aware of itself by drawing out the notion of "nature," and distinguishing it on the one hand from law as "convention," and on the other from art as "technique." The arts and the laws are effects of the power of human nature, not of the goodwill of the gods. Philosophy itself, in this sense, arises out of art.[11] Locke's concern, however, does not lie in developing these venerable discoveries. For him, the capacity to produce effects, far from revealing the powers of human nature, on the contrary testifies to its impotence and poverty. What is this mystery?

Let us start with what we know. We know only that man can produce effects. If that is what is proper to man and if we do not engage in adventitious hypotheses, we have no right to assume any other human faculty, any other property of human nature than that one. Let us then attempt to specify the figure of man.

The decisive point is that man's "artistic" character devours his "natural" character. What was considered as the human "given," as that particular man, now appears as an effect produced by man. Or, more precisely, that particular man understands himself only as a product resulting from the transformation of a prehuman matter by . . . by what? By whom? Shall we say yet again by man, when "man" is the result of this production process or perhaps rather merges with the process itself? Man's power and desire for power have given way to an altogether different domination, a "dominion" that is no longer the power of one man over another, but the power to produce man in man. His only activity is his "dominion" over the external world, over brute nature. In both cases, man "compounds and divides the materials."[12] Thus man is labor. Not only does he transform external nature through his labor, but also what is human in him is the result of labor (can we speak of it as the labor of man?) on himself as prehuman matter. At this point, we do not yet know what we may or can say, what it means that what is human in man is the result of labor. But the old man's new name—he is now called labor—starts us thinking unusual thoughts.

IV

The first is that the goodness of nature that was such a great theme of both the philosophical and theological traditions, as Locke likes to recall with malice, comes down in effect to giving man materials that are in themselves "almost worthless."[13] Just as his labor furnishes ninety-nine percent of the value of the things he can own or trade,[14] his labor, although of a different sort, also transforms the "simple ideas" he receives from his senses,[15] the only true ideas that conform to nature, into complex ideas, mixed modes, in particular into moral notions thanks to which he will establish and organize civil society, the human world. Consequently, moral ideas do not correspond to anything in nature; they are the product of the work of man, the "archetypes" created by him.[16]

We would be closing ourselves off to all access to Locke's thought and to any grasp of what is truly at stake in the *Essay*, if we gave a "civil" interpretation to these propositions and held that Locke is concerned here with developing and refining moral notions, a task that is one of the chief wellsprings and greatest benefits of social life. But we simply cannot allow ourselves to interpret Locke in this way when Locke asserts with a poker face that the idea of murder is an "arbitrary" idea.[17] If wonder gives birth to philosophy, then surely Locke rouses us to philosophize!

Locke first posits that men were able to forge the idea of murder before any murder had yet taken place. We do not quite understand what that means or where Locke derives such a certainty. In any case, this singular proposition aims at distancing the idea from the reality which it is supposed to signify and even eliminating any relation between them. One has the feeling that the world of ideas is unraveling, that ideas are being trivialized. Locke specifies that the idea of killing has no more natural rapport with the idea of man than with the idea of a sheep,[18] and that there is no natural rapport between the idea of pulling the trigger and other ideas that make up the idea of murder.[19] He concludes that the idea of murder is artificial and arbitrary because, after dissecting it into its diverse elements, he ascertains that the ideas of these elements have no natural and necessary connection among them.

The proposition itself cannot be challenged, but it is nonetheless hard to accept and makes us suspicious. We have the feeling, as it were, of a moral violence at work in this intellectual decomposition of a notion. Our alarmed conscience asks itself what force or even validity there can be to the law that forbids murder, if the idea of murder is so little consistent and is no more than a patchwork of disparate elements. A moment's reflection reassures us. The sage and virtuous Locke could not cast doubt on the validity of this prohibition. But how must we understand his line of reasoning? Where does his analytical extremism lead?

The argument that the idea of killing has no more rapport with the idea of man than with the idea of sheep is formally unimpeachable, but it is also substantially untenable. In effect, contrary to the sheep, man has an idea of death and a word by which to name it: is that not a very clear natural connection? Even more, death is a primordial concern of man, one so natural that the Greeks called men "mortals." A man knows he is killing a man who knows he is being killed; that is something different from cutting a cabbage or even choking a sheep, whether the choker be a man or a wolf. Locke manipulates ideas like tokens, which differ in shape and color but are of the same kind and weight, as though they are interchangeable. He seems not to see that man has by nature a different rapport with different ideas and that consequently if at least the idea of man preserves some connection with his reality, the diverse ideas have a different rapport with the idea of man than they do with the idea of another living being. It is untenable to posit, as he does, that the idea of pulling or setting the trigger has no natural rapport with the other ideas that make up the idea of murder. The exact contrary is true since this rapport is provided precisely by the idea of murder. The idea of pulling the trigger and actually pulling it exist only in relation to the idea of killing. It can be viewed as a piece of metal with no natural rapport with this idea only at the price of a violent abstraction.

The idiom of ideas, which Locke's *Essay* contributes in a decisive way to develop and accredit in European philosophy, never fails to give a serious and plausible air to whatever thesis one may put forth. The epitome of knowledge fashioned in this way always conveys a plausible image of the world, since for each thing one deduces the idea that one then disposes of at will. This artifice in reality tears apart the human world. The idea of murder, like that of the law that forbids it, is a "whole" that cannot be decomposed and that in effect contains man's rapport to his humanity, as the possibility of murder reveals but also conceals. In any case, in decomposing the wholes that cannot be decomposed and that give meaning to the human experience, Locke would make of it a diversity without any unity, a dusting of disparate ideas, if he did not presuppose a unifying principle somewhere. This principle does not reside within or beyond the world, but in some fashion beneath it, in the source of ideas, in the human understanding.[20]

We do not understand the ultimate meaning of Locke's enterprise, but its hidden violence makes us attentive to its political and polemical import. To say that moral notions are human creations or constructs without model or support in nature is to make it known that since they are defined and promulgated by the political or religious legislator, his commands are without foundation in man's nature. It should be noted in this context that Locke gives the example of sacrilege along with that of murder. We ask ourselves what he meant to say when he affirmed that men were able to forge the idea of murder before any murder had taken place. That also means in any case that men were able to forge the idea of sacrilege before any sacrilege had taken place and even without ever taking place. The idea of sacrilege is an arbitrary creation of the legislator.

V

Thus Locke brings Hobbes's line of reasoning to its logical conclusion. According to Hobbes, political and moral laws are binding only by virtue of the order of the sovereign, the only legitimate legislator. What makes the law is not the truth of its foundations but the authority of the one who promulgates it. Locke turns this proposition, whose tenor and import were chiefly political, into the general philosophical proposition that man as man is the arbitrary creator of his laws and moral notions. For Locke, the Sovereign is not this particular man but man himself, and he is not the sovereign of this particular country but of the human world as such. The political and polemical intention remains present in Locke, as we have just noted; and Hobbes had already very clearly articulated the arbitrary character of moral notions in general, the condition for the possibility and legitimacy of his political project.[21] But for Hobbes the definition of man as artificer, as maker, remains subordinated to his definition as an individual who desires power. Since the human world finds its center of gravity in the brute fact of the desire for power, it is not to be interpreted or constructed as a design of arbitrary ideas.

Hobbes's doctrine contained nonetheless an underlying tension, an implicit imbalance. If what is engaging and efficacious in man's humanity is contained in the desire for power, in which his nature is in some way concentrated, then his moral "ideas," or "thoughts" as Hobbes calls them, can surely be said to be artificial or conventional and to have no other validity than that conferred on them by the legislator. They have so little intrinsic weight that their flimsiness becomes worrisome. If they have no roots in nature and need the external support of the legislator to have value and thus to be, then just what are they and whence do they come? With no support in being, they could only have their origin in that man whose whole nature is to be found elsewhere, in the desire for power. Hobbesian man is on the brink of discovering in himself, but in some fashion outside his nature, a capacity, a power, a dominion, of which he was unaware. Once it is discovered, it will alter the moral landscape and overshadow the natural power coveted by natural man, the pagan power, so to speak, of man over man. The idiom of ideas will progressively ruin the idiom of power and replace it, to the point where Montesquieu declares: "Hobbes gives men first the desire to subjugate one another, but this is not reasonable. The idea of empire and domination is so complex and depends on so many other ideas, that it would not be the one they would first have."[22] Where Hobbes saw the massive natural fact of the desire for power that is not subject to analysis, Montesquieu, and after him Rousseau,[23] uncover the effect and artifice of a "composite idea."

Hobbes's emphatic concentration of man's nature in the desire for power liberated the world of ideas from every natural attachment and ontological bond. Neither nature nor Being will ever take hold of them again, or, if I dare say, recapture them, since the ideas will no longer be attached to the order of the world or to man himself, but from now on to Vulcan's modern workshop, the "human understanding," which nature charges with fabricating what is not natural, with turning simple ideas into complex ideas, into moral notions. Locke's *Essay* explains how the human understanding works.

Since the world of moral ideas is relatively stable and even in some of its parts unknowable, its fundamentally arbitrary character bears no likeness to the disorder of an unforeseeable scattering. The human understanding's elaboration of moral notions obeys rules whose principle needs to be discerned. Thus to the questions why, for example, men call killing a man murder but not killing a sheep, or why men have a specific word for the act of sleeping with one's mother, sister, etc., Locke has a simple and direct answer. What regulates the establishment and credibility of these notions and the words that designate them is their convenience for social communication.[24] Moral convenience is indeed very vague, if not to say very convenient. At one time Locke suggests that men invent special names for what they have frequent occasion to name; at other times he indicates that if men have a specific name, for example, for incest, it is because they judge this act to be particularly shameful. One is tempted to say that we have here two vicious circles for one explanation. The first jumps out before our eyes and the second isn't any less striking.

Let us take the example of incest. Locke reasons in the following way. Is incest, which men condemn so forcefully, shameful or criminal by nature? No, since, like all moral notions, it is an arbitrary creation of men. It cannot be said to be contrary to nature since the notion of incest has no connection whatever with nature. Why then did men create this notion? Because they had an imperious motive to do so? What motive? They judge incest to be shameful and they condemn it forcefully.

The circular development of Locke's argument completely separates the content of the moral notion, which is arbitrary like the content of all "mixed modes," from the moral accent which is ordinarily attached to it. Our mind, or our soul, is left with only two chilling propositions: the ingenuity of the human understanding, whether exercised well or badly, elaborates moral notions without support in the nature of things or of man; men ascribe a positive or negative value to these notions. Locke suggests that the instrument of this valuation can be a sentiment, here the sentiment of shame. Is this sentiment natural or is it as arbitrary and constructed as its object? Locke does not inquire into the human faculty that gives moral notions their positive or negative value. That would be to reintroduce nature and substance. He lets the full burden of the explanation rest on the formal notion of convenience.

Thus Locke's description of the moral world entails three elements. The first and most important is the arbitrary creation of notions. Then, although this second point is left hanging, comes the ascribing of a value to the notions. Finally, these two elements are linked together by "conveniency," which is inseparably the motive for creating the notion and for attributing value. Thus, as the arbitrary construction of ideas regulated by convenience, the human world in its entirety can be analyzed as an artifact. It is not underestimating Locke's philosophical discovery, but on the contrary underlining its extraordinary boldness and significance, to summarize it by asserting that the rules for constituting the human world are fully analogous to the rules for fabricating a table or a chair.

However, a table or chair must be made in accord with more or less reasonably evident natural traits and the needs of its user, that is, man. A table can easily be made which is three times the average human height, but even the most snobbish user will deem it inconvenient. Conveniency and artifice are not indeed completely determined in this instance, but they are at least governed strictly enough by the nature of man in general and, following upon that, by the specifics of the user, with allowance made for the candid imagination's choice of material and form. In the case of the moral notions, where what is fabricated is the constitution itself of the human world, the conveniency of human nature cannot determine things in the same way. That would be to restore human nature to the sovereign position, in the role of substance that it had to abdicate. Consequently, it would be to reduce the arbitrary character of moral notions that has been so greatly emphasized and that was discovered only recently to nothing or very little. What sort of conveniency are we concerned with here?

We can be certain of one thing only, which plays an indispensable and central role in the artificialist scheme conceived by Locke. The construction must be done according to certain rules and the one thing we can be certain of is the rule of construction. Since this rule can no longer be provided by human nature and the contents of life as the Ancients wanted, nor by the law of God as the Christians believed it to be, it must reside in a certain form that compresses the very idea of a rule: not a given substantial motive to motivate the construction, but the idea, the very form of the motive. Man elaborates his world for a motive, and this motive has no other meaning than to be his motive, to be appropriate and adapted to him. The notion of conveniency designates the circle that goes from man to man, from self to self. It will soon be called utility, a notion that is also formal and opens the way to a discreet but fatal return to human nature and its needs and desires, no longer the desire for power but, as we have studied it in the preceding chapter, the desire to better one's condition. Locke is on his guard against such a relapse, and he rigorously preserves the formalism of "conveniency" without substance.

The greatest advantage conveniency has may have to do with the equivocation that it maintains between the universal and the particular. As conveniency *tout court*, its import is universal and it seems capable of ruling over everything. At the same time, it is a rule without foundation or reference point, and thus it must vary indefinitely according to human diversity. It seems, moreover, that the natural movement of the notion leads to setting this second interpretation into motion, the only one that can work in a sense since only the particular circumstances can give a concrete content to conveniency. Thus the way a particular human world is constructed will be analyzed by drawing out how the diverse parameters fit one another, for example, such and such a religion or political organization, according to the social scientific approach that we discussed in chapter 2. Locke does not give in to this natural tendency. Abandoning substance in no way means abandoning the universal for Locke.

VI

It seems that Locke's analysis of the constitution of the human world makes it impossible to establish a political and moral doctrine with universal validity, in short, a political philosophy. If moral notions are arbitrary constructs arising out of and regulated by conveniency, it seems that there will be as many political regimes as the labor of the human mind is capable of inventing, the only constraint being that it must comply with the requirements of conveniency, in whatever way it is understood. It seems also that all these regimes will be equally good and legitimate since there is no natural order by which to judge them and rank them in a hierarchy. According to Locke, however, such is not the case and the very opposite is true.

Since the human mind constructs its moral ideas from the simple ideas provided to it by the external senses and the internal sense—by sensation and reflection—and since these simple ideas are necessarily the same for all men, without which they would not have enough in common to be able to use the term "men," it is possible to elaborate a universally valid political teaching, provided only that the complex ideas be well constructed, that is, that they encompass simple ideas that are compatible with one another and that the complex ideas also be compatible among themselves. Once these conditions are met, moral and political theory can be just as rigorous and demonstrable as mathematics, as Locke insistently emphasizes.[25] It is precisely because the moral and political order does not have its archetype in nature that moral and political theory can be rigorously demonstrative and truly universal. Let us examine how this is so.

It is true that we know nothing of substances, and thus, in a certain sense, we know nothing of man. But if man is unknown as a substance, he is known to us by his powers and his relations. Locke remarks, for example, that the idea of father or brother, the idea of relation, is clearer to us than the idea of man, the idea of substance.[26] Thus when we elaborate moral and political discourse, we have only to combine ideas of relations, or of powers, and to see if they are compatible among themselves. The moral and political problem becomes a problem of logic, of the compatibility of logical notes. According to a suggestion already made by Hobbes, the notion of the "unjust," for example, will come down to the notion of the "absurd," that is to say, of the logically contradictory. Thus for Locke, the maxim "where there is no property, there is no injustice," is not a problematic proposition nor is it the conclusion of a debate on the definition of justice and the place of property in the human order; it is quite comparable to elementary mathematical theorems and the evidence for which is readily perceived by a simple analysis of terms: property is a right to . . ., injustice is the violation of a right, thus . . .[27] The logical analysis Locke provides here may not be irresistibly convincing, but the first condition of his line of reasoning is clear: in developing political philosophy, the nature of the substance, the nature of man, is *presupposed* and is not the subject of investigation.

Despite the sharp and even solemn tone of his declaration, in the *Essay*

Concerning Human Understanding Locke does not move beyond his very general proposition affirming the possibility of constructing a demonstrative moral doctrine to a developed presentation of such a doctrine. He limits himself to a few meager suggestions, the chief among which I have just recalled. Nowhere else in his writings is such a demonstration to be found, unless one thinks that his political *Treatises* contain this doctrine under a simply more "civil" form. The answer matters a great deal to us, since it matters much to know if it is possible to construct a rigorous moral and political doctrine without inquiring into the nature, essence, or substance of man, and even by rejecting any affirmation regarding human essence as presumptuous or idle. Locke is the first to have formulated resolutely and completely this requirement and this rejection. If he was mistaken, or at least if it is not possible to correct his errors while remaining faithful to his principles, then modern democracy, our political regime, reveals itself devoid of a sure foundation, since its legitimacy is founded on a moral and political doctrine that seeks to be rigorous and on a neutrality that is just as rigorous regarding the question of the essence of man. Pressed by this anxiety, let us try to reconstitute the political doctrine of the *Treatises* according to the theory of the *Essay*.[28]

VII

We do not know what man is. We only know that the moral notions that govern the life in common of men are artifacts and thus that society is not natural to man. The starting point of political theory can only be the "idealess" individual, the biological individual separated from his fellows, and without relation to them. Starting with the solitary animal, we do not adopt any moral notions that might be found to be badly constructed. Locke will erect the lofty structure of the liberal and democratic state on the puny base of the solitary animal in search of food.

The only teaching of nature, in any event its only teaching not open to question, is the injunction of animal necessity: survival. If the individual man wants to survive, which is what he wants of necessity, he needs to feed himself. The root of human right, if it is to be as unquestionable as a mathematical proposition, is to be sought in this act without an idea, in this properly animal act. Locke describes the process of taking and ingesting food as an appropriation. This is not going beyond what the phenomena propose. Since it is a matter of drawing out the foundations of right, one inquires into the rapport between this act of appropriation and the idea of right. Or again, under what form should right be considered constructed in order to be able to put it in a necessary rapport with this act? The most immediate and most logical reply seems to be that we should consider right in the first place or essentially as the right to property. In effect, the most traditional and at the same time clearest definition of property is *jus utendi*, the right of usage. Indeed the individual has the right to use what he must necessarily use in order to survive! (Besides, he takes nothing from anyone, since men are few in number and scattered in this age of the beginning of societies.) If he has this right, he is the owner of what he eats. The question now becomes from what time onward he is the owner. The reply is from the moment when edible things have been taken out of the world, from the common domain, to enter into the specific sphere of activity of the one who needs to eat. This activity, according to Locke, is called *labor*, or more precisely *human* labor. The animal, in effect, exercises the same activity: the lion who chases the gazelle to devour it "labors" more than does the savage who bends over to pick up acorns. But we do not use the word labor with reference to animals; and we do not even use it spontaneously to refer to the human activities of gathering or hunting. Locke believes he can use a properly human term to designate an activity within reach and even characteristic of an animal because he sees in *human* consumption the first expression of the specifically human rapport to nature that we call labor. In this quest for the foundations of human right, man is thus always *presupposed*. And we can say here and now that man is the proprietor of what he eats. He appropriates it by his labor, which is thus at the origin of the right to property.

Presented in this way, the argument is not entirely convincing. A link is missing in the deduction. It is not possible to connect directly the owner-ship of things with labor on them. Why would a thing transformed by labor be the property of the one who has so transformed it and not rather, for example, the property of the one who needs it more or even wants it more, now that it is available for use? In order for the laborer to be the owner of the object worked upon, it is also necessary, first, that his labor be truly embodied in the object, and secondly, that it be strictly and truly his own. I shall consider below in section 18 the difficulty contained in the first point. As for the second, the fact that the laborer uses "his" arm or "his" brain is not enough to establish this point; one must be certain that this everyday language can be employed rigorously, that arm and brain are indeed "his"; he must have ownership of himself. Property enters the world through labor because the human individual, being owner of him-self, owns his labor.

Thus, according to Locke, the human individual, considered as abso-lutely separated from his fellows and alone in the face of nature, has in himself the necessary and sufficient foundation of property and, from that starting point, of law in its entirety. Law, which regulates the common life of men, does not have its primary source in the conditions and conse-quences of the common life but in the isolated individual's rapport with nature and with himself. Property, law, and the whole of the human world are contained in the solitary individual just as, one is tempted to say, the human species is contained in the first man.

It has to be acknowledged that this genesis of the legitimate political order from the starting point of the solitary individual obeys a strict necessity. Since, thanks to Locke's starting point that the human substance is an unknown and unknowable "X," law cannot be deduced nor induced from the nature of man as it shows itself in social and political life, it can now be founded only on individual animality in its solitary rapport with external nature and with itself. And yet, as ingenious as it is, Locke's construction is open to a formidable objection. If his reasoning were correct, the animals, who are also biological individualities and who feed themselves with effort, would know of property and law, and thus also of political order; and yet they know nothing of these, proof that this could not have its foundation in the animal operation of eating. In deducing the human world from animality, Locke illegitimately deduces the higher from the lower.

This is, of course, the objection that the representatives of the tradition, particularly the religious tradition, address in general to modern thought. It is ordinarily formulated in the context of a critique of "evolutionism" or "materialism." One can see that the objection, if it has any force, it would obtain just as well in the sphere of moral and political philosophy, where "reductionism," if it must be called by this pejorative term, first appeared. In our attempt here to unscramble Locke's teaching, we arrive at the threshold of a major stake in the history of the mind.

VIII

It is very remarkable that this objection, which is so "evident," had no effect at all on the development of modern thought, which made no attempt to answer it and did not even see it. The "reductionist" movement only spread and penetrated more and more varied domains, ensconcing itself with a growing force and soon with a total sovereignty in the life and viewpoints of modern man. It must thus be admitted that despite its logical or formal correctness, this objection bypasses what is at work and at stake here, and that in the present case it fails to understand Locke's meaning and project.

Locke does not deny that man is different from the animals. He even notes that the "power of abstracting . . . puts a perfect distinction betwixt man and brutes."[29] Only man's substance remains at bottom unknown to us, whereas we know without any doubt that he is also an animal. Moreover, how could we ignore that he is different from the animals, since we

seek to organize adequately, that is to say with justice, precisely the
human world and not animal life? Thus, in all our undertakings, we assume that man is man, but that means for us that "X = X." From this
identity that we acknowledge we cannot deduce or construct anything. It
is the condition or presupposition of our search, but it can in no way direct
it since "X" is unknown and unknowable. If fact, if "X" were to become
explicit *before* us, under the form of properties of human nature from
which we would try to conceive the best political order, it would immediately disrupt our undertaking by presenting to us a confused and contesta-
ble idea of human substance. For example, if we attempted to pursue our
search by taking our bearings from the notion of happiness, surely an
object of the human quest and one that is as unquestionable as nourish-
ment and the other animal goods, we would be stopped from the start by
a slew of questions concerning the definition, the various forms, and the
reality itself of happiness. Before even the first step, we would be assailed
by all the difficulties, which are perhaps impossibilities, of man's knowledge, by the perhaps insoluble conflict of opinions. To unblock the road,
to make the first step possible, then the second, and then the third, the
effects of uncertainty over human essence must be neutralized right away.

This neutral political philosophy can only be worked out after establishing as strictly as possible the line of demarcation between what is uncertain and what is sure in human things. Locke is interested in the human
faculty of understanding only in order to fix the limits of its power, to set
the bounds "between the enlightened and dark Parts of Things."[30] The
enormous undertaking of the *Essay* has this as its principal and almost
sole intent. The notions which gave consistency to the human substance
are one after another systematically weighed and then rejected, and the
principal and almost unique conclusion is that human substance is unknown and unknowable. Joseph de Maistre, who saw himself as an intransigent perpetuator of the Tradition, will have no qualms in reproaching
Locke, in the most spiteful tone, for this disproportion between philosophical effort and its result.[31] He did not understand that this prosaic
and meager conclusion contained an immense promise.

Once the line is drawn between the perfectly clear and the decidedly
obscure, the uncertainty over the nature of "X" no longer impairs our
view. We know that we do not know "X" and that we never will. *Before* us
the space lies open and free for us to construct methodically the human
order that is beyond criticism, the definitive dwelling place of man. We
keep "X" so to speak *behind* us or apart from us, enclosed in itself by its
equality with itself. It is for us a capital from which we would not draw, on
which we would not even set our eyes, for then it would no longer pay the
handsome dividends that put us in a position to arrange the human world
in a rigorously just fashion, without being held to accept any one of the

conceptions of human nature and, inseparably, of divine nature as well, that contend for men's belief; we can live in accord with justice even as we acknowledge that we do not know what we are, as in fact we do not.

It would accordingly not be judicious to characterize Locke and his modern successors as skeptics and in any case their "skepticism" is altogether different from ancient skepticism. Pyrrhon's uncertainty over everything dissuaded him from ever taking a step, or, if in spite of everything he started walking, from avoiding a pitfall.[32] Modern "skepticism" does not invite or constrain us to refrain from or to suspend judgment and action in this way. On the contrary, it makes it possible and even urgent to forge a just society, founded on a demonstrative moral theory, on the rational deduction of rights.

The *Essay Concerning Human Understanding* reveals that moral notions are arbitrary creations of man, which have no foundation or guarantee in nature. The *Second Treatise* lays bare that right, and first of all the right to property, is a creation of the human individual strictly isolated from his fellows and alone face to face with external nature; and that this individual is the exclusive source of right. No higher law or idea of nature or substance intervenes to determine, which is to say impede, this individual creation of right. Since, moreover, this individual right is originally founded on the needs of animal nature, on hunger which brings forth labor, and thus of necessity, it is not open to any reasonable objection or subject to discussion. This right is posited or rather produced by the individual in a solitary, sovereign, and arbitrary fashion and at the same time its begetting is strictly necessary. Thus the theory according to which it unfolds can be compared quite inappropriately to a mathematical demonstration, where it is not necessary to give the numerical value of the unknown. In fact, it is even necessary to abstain from doing so since that would be to bring to an end or to pose an immediate obstacle to the movement of the demonstration and we could no longer arrive at its constructive and wholesome conclusions. The human "X" is the tacit companion of the deduction of rights, or rather, the begetting of right. This "X" which is man, whose "superiority" is not denied, is considered or posited in his animal locus. Far from "reducing the higher to the lower," it is acknowledged that everything that is a part of man, and thus also the animal in him, cannot be anything else than human. In fact, the tradition may be indeed careless in overlooking that the simply "animal" consumption of man is already a human labor. We recall that in his Second *Meditation* Descartes affirms that our sensible perception takes place essentially not through our senses but our mind.[33] The suspicion grows that appearances are deceiving and that perhaps what they offer is contrary to reality. Far from reducing the higher to the lower, Locke and the Moderns on the contrary envelop the lower in the higher and so to speak absorb it.

Man's self-affirmation starts with his animal functions, in them and through them. Animality is in sum the fulcrum point at the heart of the world and of man, on which the human "X" can rest in order to draw clear order from its deepest obscurity, to affirm himself in spite of his indetermination or rather through it to affirm his liberty. Classical thought, which the tradition seeks to preserve, maintains that the human world, that is the city in the first place, should be founded on or, better, guided by what is proper to man, by what sets him apart from the animal, which should be always in the forefront. Modern thought despairs that men will ever agree on what is proper to man, on human substance or ends, and thus it wants to bracket the question of what is proper to man. It seeks to keep man in his efficacious indetermination so that, by taking his bearings from what is not human but animal and thus determined and necessary, he might construct a human world whose order is independent of human opinions, where man can affirm himself without knowing himself, where he can be free.

IX

It is nonetheless difficult to pursue such a line of reasoning to the very end and bracket completely the question of human "substance." This kind of thinking seeks to provide a foundation for right that is independent of any proposition about substance, but it irresistibly gives rise to such propositions and suggests an "anthropology." Thus labor at first seems to signify only the transformation of material nature by human nature and thus to be but one expression of human nature among many loftier ones, but with Locke and in modern philosophy and for modern man generally, it tends to become what one might be forgiven to call the "essential" characteristic of man.[34] As I have already noted, labor is if not the proper, at least the most proper name of man.

Even if one scrupulously refrains from advancing such "essential" propositions, one cannot completely dispense with giving an account of human motives. How can one give a central place to labor and say nothing of the motives that incite man to labor? Is it enough to remark that man cannot do otherwise than to work? How can one consider man to be the creator of moral notions and leave in the dark the motives that animate him in this creation? We have seen in section 5 that "conveniency" only plays a decisive role in this at the price of an extreme formalism and a disturbing equivocation. And it is even more the rule for constructing moral ideas than it is the very goal of man. Locke cannot escape the necessity of at least sketching a description of action, an analysis of human motives. The *Essay* presents this sketch and acknowledges its partial or incomplete character. We need to examine it.

What determines and motivates human actions is uneasiness, a term that denotes at once anxiety and discomfort, let us say ill-being. Human desire is not moved by the good it sees or conceives, but by the ill being it feels. The fundamental formula of Locke's "anthropology" is that "desire is always moved by evil, to fly it."[35] That is saying that the question regarding the *summum bonum*, the supreme good of man, which is the primary question raised by the tradition—and the tradition was divided according to the diverse answers given by the various schools, sects, or religions—is a perfectly idle question for Locke, who observes that one might just as well ask "whether the best Relish were to be found in Apples, Plumbs, or Nuts."[36] Here we need to rise above our indignation over such a vulgar comparison that reduces human inquiry into the good to an arbitrary choice, devoid at that of human interest, among apples, plums, and nuts. We need to rise above our humiliation, or rather acknowledge that it is deserved and thus welcomed. The question of the good is inseparable from the question of human essence and the one is just as vain as the other. The good is what is proper to man, what man is specifically capable of, what perfects and fulfills him in the best part of his nature. I cannot in reality be moved by the good since in reality I do not know what I am. The question of the good and the question of substance are two expressions of the same sterile vanity. By nature the only natural preference is the one that stems from animal nature regarding physical nature: one can prefer apples to plums, or vice versa.

Moreover, the moment a choice is seen as intrinsically arbitrary, there is nothing offensive, no matter what its object, in comparing it to this humble example. When much later modern philosophy and sociology, the ungrateful heirs of the labors and results of the *Essay*, will posit that man is "creator of his values" among which he chooses freely and arbitrarily, they will forget Locke's apples and plums; with Max Weber they will speak emphatically of the "war of the gods." In this way its humble but upright origins are hidden.

X

Hobbes had already affirmed that there is no *summum bonum* and that good and evil only have meaning with reference to the person involved.[37] Locke goes further. The difference between man according to Locke and man according to Hobbes is best expressed in Locke's phrase that "the greatest present uneasiness is the spur to action."[38] For Hobbes, man no longer has any end inscribed in his nature, but he still has a future. He goes beyond the present by his desire for power, which is anxiety and desire for what is to come, desire to master the future, "to assure for ever, the way of his future desire."[39] With Locke, anxiety concerns the present, it is born of the present and deals with it. I do not think there is any description or analysis of human action where man is more the prisoner of the present than Locke's. The mechanization of human action and human behavior is already complete. What in Hobbes is a passionate chase from desire to desire toward ever more power becomes in Locke "a constant succession of uneasinesses," an uninterrupted succession of discomforts. Man can only desire one thing at a time, and thus he always desires above all to free himself from what constrains him, or bothers him, or makes him suffer *now*. And since constraints, bothers, and sufferings do not cease to arise in this world, he never has the time to desire the good for its own sake, whatever meaning one may give to this expression. But also, as soon as present ill-being is eliminated, he is content. This contentment is necessarily of short duration; it lasts the time of transition from one ill-being to another in a never-ending process. Lockean man is as easily troubled as he is easily contented.

Man according to Hobbes has in him the somber weight of Christian concupiscence, lifted up by a glimmer of ancient magnanimity. Forever sinning mightily because he cannot avoid sinning, he is always superior to his circumstances. Neither Christian nor Greek, he is that third man full of force who despairs of the good but not of himself. Whether servant of the king or republican, he will construct the modern state which, like him, has given up seeking the good. Man according to Locke is without either great desire or magnanimity. He too is neither Christian nor Greek, but the tireless laborer and consumer, the man with no ambition who moves and stirs modern society.

It could be objected that this idea of the human impotence to will the good for its own sake, far from being a discovery or an original invention of Locke, is only the reprise of an ancient moral tradition, welcomed and simplified by Christianity, to the effect that, as the poet Ovid puts it, "video meliora proboque deteriora sequor" ("I can see—and I approve the better course, and yet I choose the worse").[40] On this point at least, Locke is both Christian and pagan. He takes it upon himself to correct our misperception. In fact he explicitly adopts this phrase of the one he calls the "unhappy Complainer" only to develop its meaning in the light of his own moral doctrine. Man can desire only one thing at a time. He thus always flees first and foremost the evil he experiences in the present. Present ill-being is always stronger than a future good, and thus the discomfort of vulgar needs and passions is stronger than respect for moral laws or the attraction of noble ends. Locke is careful to remark that his is the only coherent interpretation of this trait of human behavior observed from time immemorial.[41] That is saying, as clearly as it can be said, that the Greek and Christian interpretations are equally false, the one because it does not know the good and the other because of original sin.

Thus, in rejecting the Greek and Christian idea that the life of man is a quest for an uncertain good that is difficult to attain but which alone can fulfill man by making him happy, Locke maintains that the life of man is a flight from evil that makes itself felt in present ill-being, anxiety, or discomfort. According to the twofold tradition, man always seeks the good through a thousand obstacles and illusions; for Locke, man always flees from evil, in spite of a thousand inclinations to the good.

XI

This thought process has brought Locke a good distance from Christianity, but he turns about in a surprisingly brutal way and puts himself in a position to welcome the Christian commandments and counsels into his moral doctrine. Man can desire a good from the moment he can make out that its absence makes him unhappy. He will then flee from the absence of this good, in particular the absence of God, as an evil. When he flees from the absence of this good, everything takes place as if he were seeking the good. By this artifice, Locke very openly preserves the basic tenet of Christian doctrine that God is the supremely desirable supreme good. Furthermore, this very God who moves desire by his absence, acts mainly not by good or promise, but by evil and threat. Far from encouraging us to go forth in loving quest of the Absent One, Locke prefers to take up almost word for word the argument of the wager by which Pascal seeks to reach closed souls:

> he that will not be so far a rational Creature, as to reflect seriously upon infinite Happiness and Misery, must needs condemn himself, as not making that use of his Understanding he should. The Rewards and Punishments of another Life, which the Almighty has established, as the Enforcements of his Law, are of weight enough to determine the Choice, against whatever Pleasure or Pain this life can shew, when the eternal State is considered but in its bare possibility, which no Body can make any doubt of.[42]

This reinstatement *in extremis* no doubt puts at risk the coherence and even simply the attraction of Locke's doctrine. If the fear of the absence of a future good can determine human action just as much as present ill-being, his analysis of human motivation loses its point. Whoever flees from absence will just as quickly perhaps desire presence. In truth, the second movement in the thought process does not carry the same weight as the first. Locke hastily razes the façade of the ancient house after ruining its foundations. This is not only a matter of concern on the part of the "sage" Locke to deal tactfully with authoritative opinions. He cannot do other than to remark that, if he holds rigorously and exclusively to the original version of his moral theory, the man he depicts, however mediocre and puny he be, will be greatly undisciplined; and he will be so on account of his smallness. He will always choose to begin with the action that will deliver him from present discomfort. If he is crossed, he will drink; if he is poor, he will steal. One cannot even discount that fear of the sovereign, even the terrible Leviathan, will hold him to duty, for here fear concerns the future and, in this mechanistic interpretation, man lives only in the present. Moreover, can a drunkard or a lecher be decently hanged? If society is to know a minimum of order, the citizen must be capable of a somewhat broader perspective and not just be subject to immediate solicitations. Locke thus takes into account the Hobbesian concern for the future, but not any longer from the side of action, only from the side of abstention and retention. Thus a policeman God, who distributes the rewards and especially the punishments of the next life, will blessedly consolidate the authority of a limited government.

XII

The fundamental analysis of human action seemed to contradict Locke's need to bracket human nature and to suspend any examination of nature and confine himself to presupposing it, but in fact it does not tarnish or contradict the purity of the algebraic deduction of rights. In fact, if man is always moved by the most urgent ill-being, since what is most urgent in man are animal needs, the first principle of his action will be the uneasiness of the animal in him, which he will strive to appease by his labor. Locke's "psychology," his analysis of human action, does not get us out of the original setting where the human individual, in appropriating to himself the things of nature by his labor, discovers that he has in himself the right to property. The policeman God does not seem to be present in the original setting. In any event he plays no part. Locke suggests rather that as he discovers in labor the uneasiness[43] that frees him from the uneasinesses of the animal in him, the truly rational man will conclude that it is in his power to escape ever more completely his ever-recurring ill-being and satisfy ever more completely his need that will remain indefinite, if he consents to put into his life a discipline whose results correspond broadly to the wishes of morality and religion. The rational organization of labor has the same effects, only more certain and regular than the divine polic-

ing. Of course, there will always be need to be watchful that the idea of a
God who punishes remains clearly present in the mind of those who are
incapable of subjecting themselves to the discipline of the rational transformation of nature.

XIII

At this point, we must attempt to grasp in one sweep the unity, if there is
any, among Locke's fundamental propositions that man fashions his
moral notions, that he has rights, and that he labors. All three are destined to have an impressive career, but in their subsequent history they
will separate and even often oppose one another. The first will give rise to
the idea of "culture" and "values," the second to the idea of the "rights
of man and citizen," the third to the idea of the "laborer" or *homo oeconomicus*. "Culture" and "values" will form an essential element of the
intellectual equipment of thinkers situated on the right or the extreme
right of the political axis. We have already considered Max Weber and we
should also cite the name of Friedrich Nietzsche among others. The
"rights of man and citizen" constitute the rational nucleus of the democratic movement that came to the fore through the American and French
revolutions. The "laborer" must be linked more appropriately to the socialist tradition, particularly the one founded by Marx, even if other
schools or tendencies, some of them hardly socialist, also on occasion
were favorable to him.[44] We observe that these notions, for a long time
mobilized in opposed political and ideological camps, show themselves
today as quite compatible elements of the moral atmosphere of the democracies, which simultaneously appeal to "culture," "values," "rights,"
"labor," and the "economy." Our democracies may be lacking in discernment, but, as we have seen, these three groups of notions in fact have
a common origin: they are already blossoming together in Locke's philosophy, who surely was not lacking in discernment. They are three ways
of saying that the question of human essence has no solution or meaning,
or that man has no ends. They are equally ultimate propositions, which
cannot, it seems, be ranked in order or deduced from one another. Yet
one among them has the advantage that it seems it can not only be
thought, but lived as well. It can not only be formulated by a theoretician,
but in real life man can think it and, thanks to it, become self-conscious.
Which one is this?

As for labor, it is the transformation of the relation between man and
external nature. As such it does not encompass a determined genre of
relation among men nor does it entail a particular political regime or
economic institution. Even when considered as the source and measure of

value, it does not allow it to be measured effectively. There is a price of labor, but no labor of labor. In fact, if we go straight to the truth of the matter, we observe that the regime that claimed with such assurance to found itself on labor and the value of labor, that is, communism, showed itself incapable of establishing any sort of institution, or even any stable relation among men. It can even be feared that where it held sway the longest and most completely, it made men definitively incapable of forging such relations. Labor, as what is proper to man, does not determine the human organization that would correspond to it.

"Culture" or "values" are also of little help in this role. The idea that men are the creators of their moral notions in no way allows, by itself alone, for the ordering of the human world. It can indeed serve to criticize a political organization, or a given moral attitude, by radically ruining its claim to be only conforming to nature or to man's vocation, but since it holds that they are all arbitrary, it cannot legitimate or engender any one in particular. Only a pure spectator can entertain and formulate this idea without contradiction.

Neither labor nor culture can constitute the spontaneous and ordinary identity of Locke's modern man, who nonetheless must be able to say that he is this undetermined "X" equal to itself. If man knows nothing of his nature or if he has no nature, if he transforms himself indefinitely by indefinitely transforming external nature, if he creates himself endlessly by "creating his values," he must at least, in order to think about himself and so to be, be able to identify with this indetermination and to grasp it by reflecting it. It is by defining himself as the one who has rights that man can finally embrace the tautology by which he wants to affirm himself: "X = X." As "laborer" or as "being of culture," man's indetermination escapes him: as laborer because this "X" that he is is absorbed and lost in nonhuman nature, or in the objects produced by it; as a cultural being because his power to determine himself arbitrarily ends and loses itself in each one of his real determinations, his moral ideas. Once a moral idea has been "created" and acted upon, it annuls the power of self-determination that it has actualized. This power cannot be apprehended except in the past, once it has produced its effects and is no longer. But for man to tell himself that he is a being who has rights, is to tell each man, and for each man to say that he is indeed what he is. A sure sign of this is how much other men feel bound to let a man be what he is by "respecting" his rights or even to allow him to appear as all that he already is by according him all that he has a right to "demand." He has no need to know precisely or to will determinedly all that, through his activity and "creativity," he is capable of producing or becoming in all the metamorphoses of his indetermination. He already has it, he already is it, since *he has the right* to have it or to be it.

XIV

The tautology is affirmed so completely that one can ask if there is any space left for the identity of self with self to breathe!

The man who pursues ends that are, or that he believes are, constitutive of his nature fulfills his definition, seizes upon his identity in this very pursuit. It is the distance between his empirical, real being, and the end he pursues—justice, wisdom, truth—a distance that is recognized so as to be eliminated, and yet always invincibly maintained by reason of the "sinful" or simply "intermediary" character of man, that opens a space where he can reflect on himself and recognize himself as man. But for the one who no longer has ends but rights, how shall this indispensable distance be opened, this interior space that allows man to think and speak of himself? For him, there is no longer any differential tension between empirical and completed being, between potency and act, between what is fulfilled and desired. Whether rights are guaranteed or scoffed at, it is in any case the empirical being himself who owns and holds them. The one who seeks justice, wisdom, or truth knows that he does not possess them, but the one who declares his rights and demands that they be respected knows that he possesses them and that nothing he or anyone else does can change anything about this possession. Respected or scoffed at, human rights, whether a man be a scoundrel or a hero, are equally what they are.

One hesitates to go on with this issue. One senses one is approaching uncertain and silent frontiers where the Phenomenon no longer speaks for itself, where one can no longer describe it. One fears being deprived of words oneself or of having to use words too vast to designate, as though through the fog, the great realities or great decisions that the reigning conventions of our age express and conceal. Yet how can one not recognize that the new definition of man as the being who has rights requires that the traditional modalities of being, that venerable polarity of potency and act, be banished, in order to work out a new tautology? Or perhaps it must be said that the definition, to be truly thinkable, requires us to abandon every ontological mode of thinking, every mode of thinking that links man to being, the thought of man to the thought of being?

I am not here presupposing any particular ontology. Even the distinction between potency and act does not refer specifically to Aristotle's ontology. It seeks to designate, in current and so to speak popular usage, the fact that man can find himself in different states or dispositions of his being. We do not necessarily rank these different states in a hierarchy or necessarily associate them to "degrees" of being, but we observe nonetheless that they are linked to one another by the fact that one is the goal and fulfillment of the other. Such is the fabric of human life in its loftiest as well as humblest expressions. At first one is potentially, and later actually, in possession of the truth or the Davis Cup, even if, contrary to widespread opinion today, one of these is harder to win than the other. The point I have in mind here depends so little on Aristotle's ontology that one can find it in marvelously clear terms in Kant's moral philosophy, where man is all the more moral when he obeys the moral law out of a purer respect for it to the exclusion of all other considerations. Here too a tension, a difference of disposition or state projects man toward his inaccessible fulfillment like the arc toward its asymptote. We even find an analogous arrangement when, leaving aside human philosophy, we consider how in theology grace transforms and perfects nature in such a way as to render it capable of its end, which is God himself.

This, then, is the novelty we seek to take stock of. Whether the rights of man be respected or scoffed at changes nothing in the conditions or state of man as possessor of rights. The unemployed have no less right to work, the subjects of a tyranny no less right to liberty, than the employed or the citizens of a democracy. In contrast to natural ends and to law and grace as well, right in this new sense does not modify in any way, whether it is violated or guaranteed, the condition, state, or disposition of man as possessor of rights. It seems that every possible ontology has been left behind, whether it showed itself in terms of the polarity of substance and its teleology, or of being and having-to-be, or human and divine nature.

XV

But no doubt we are on the wrong path here. How can it be said that such a universal proposition as that man is the being who has rights, a proposition conceived and propagated by some of the greatest philosophers and at the foundation of the freest and wealthiest political bodies ever recorded in the annals of human history—how can it be admitted that such a proposition abolishes every ontological perspective, completely separates the thought of man from that of being, that it forgets Being? How can right, which is now what is proper to man, be thought of other than as the chief determinant or primary attribute of man's being?

We have remarked earlier, in sections 3 and 6, that Locke, who introduces us to Vulcan's workshop, the great modern Factory, does not deny that man can have an essence or be a substance; only, this essence or substance is perfectly unknown and only assumed, that is to say, left aside or behind, in its opaque identity with itself: "X = X." Man's being is recognized, but also retained and enclosed in this tautology. Then man can be posited, that is, affirmed without restriction or qualification, not any longer in his being, which necessarily entails the whole of being in which he is rooted, but in what will be called his natural independence, which has no natural limit, or in his rights that are not otherwise defined than as "human rights."

Man is the being that defines himself by the fact of having rights. Whatever being he has can and must be forgotten in the affirmation of his rights, whose reality is sufficiently attested to and their validity confirmed by the very fact that they are "human rights." Man and the rights of man are two poles that refer exclusively to one another. Or perhaps it would be better to say that man and the rights of man form a perfect and self-sufficient circle that contains the promise of an absolutely unprecedented liberation of man, who is now impenetrable to Being.

Before the great instauration, philosophical thinking about man suffered from a harmless but very disabling awkwardness in striving to think simultaneously of both man and being. It strove to think of what is specifically human as a determination of being, to situate what is human on the ladder of the degrees of being. This confusion of ontology and anthropology, or this onto-anthropology, in effect placed thought in an inextricable uncertainty, confining it to an involuntary skepticism. Man could not truly appropriate or acknowledge as his own what is proper to him since it appeared only as a general or a special, which is to say always general, determination of being. Man could not truly recognize himself since he always saw being in general in the mirror. But, on the other hand, the generality of being was irrepressibly linked to what is proper to man and placed at the service of his desires and wishes and thus man always saw himself in the mirror of being. Before the great instauration, anthropology was necessarily ontological or ontocentric, while ontology was necessarily anthropocentric. In order to unravel this chiasm or to break through it, thought about being will have to be strictly separated from thought about man. This is not the place to examine how the possibility of a pure ontology was conceived or its reality posited. The longest digression would not do justice to the subject, since this pure ontology is nothing other than modern science. But we can at least attempt to show precisely how anthropology emancipated itself from ontology.

XVI

Locke is the most explicit and formal witness to the decision to declare man's being unknowable and to condense the whole of onto-anthropology in the tautology "X = X" : whatever man is, man is man. We presuppose the being of man and do not have to think about it any more. This opened the way to a second tautology capable of containing and producing what had never yet been conceived by thinking man: a pure anthropology. This second tautology necessarily takes the general form that, whatever being is, man . . . man. Thus a twofold affirmation of man replaces the affirmation of man and being. One affirms man and man. But what verb links man to man in this new tautology that refuses to use the verb "to be"? We have seen in section 13 that the verbs that were implicit in the notions of "labor" and "culture" did not allow man in real life to articulate his humanity. Man in real life cannot truly or honestly think of himself as produced by his labor or as producer of his culture. Let us dare say it for once that no Tom, Dick, or Harry in his right mind ever honestly thought of himself as the "creator of his values." But Tom, Dick, or Harry can think of himself honestly as having rights that are immediately defined as "human rights." Man has the rights of man. And so one escapes the necessity of the presence, even the fleeting presence, of the verb that affirms and connects. Thus man affirms himself without recourse to any verb. The tautology is complete on its two faces: the whole of man's humanity is contained in his rights and in the fact that he has rights and that these rights are exhaustively defined by the fact that they are human rights. The traditional thinking about man and being that leads to involuntary skepticism gives way to the resolute affirmation of man, reflected and heightened in the declaration of the rights of man. Man can in all honesty forget Being.

XVII

Thus severed from being, the notion of human rights by itself lacks ontological density. It will irresistibly conquer the political and moral realms since, available and unattached, it can easily be tied to the various experiences of man that all appear capable of being looked at in its terms. All the desires of nature, like all the commandments of the law, can, it seems, be looked at without violence or artifice in terms of human rights. If man has a right to life, he also has a right to die, or at least to death with dignity; if he has a right to work, he also has a right to leisure; if he has right to live in his country, he also has the right to travel; if a woman has a right to a child, she also has the right to an abortion; if she has a right to respect, she also has a right to pleasure, even to orgasm; in short, since it is time to stop, there is nothing under the sun or moon that is not susceptible of becoming the occasion and matter of a human right. This verifies the expansive force of the tautology linking man to the rights of man.

According to a way of speaking common to all schools and kinds of philosophy, man is situated along a path between the two poles of passivity and activity such that the more he frees himself from passivity or the more he becomes pure activity, the more he becomes human. The polarity and even reciprocal exclusion of activity and passivity seem to be analytically included in the concepts themselves. The man who has rights is like pure self-contained activity, having no need of an end that would be outside him and containing in his empirical reality all rights, including some yet to be born, which exhaustively define his humanity. But, on the other hand, he is also pure and perfect passivity, having nothing to do in order as a man to be the holder of the totality of these rights that are already explicit or still implicit and that exhaustively define his humanity. *Mirabile dictu*! Man the holder of human rights combines pure activity and pure passivity in his empirical nature.

XVIII

This is not the place to examine the loopholes in the tautology. Human rights can range over the entire field of human experience, but perhaps each and every aspect of this experience can just as well show the flaws in human rights. Doesn't the declaration of the right to experience cast a shadow over the very nature of experience itself? We will also say nothing of the contradictions or incompatibilities that can pit different rights against one another. It is more pressing for us to consider the most serious philosophic critique ever directed against the modern idea of human rights.

As I have noted above, the majestic edifice of the modern state, the system of human rights, rests upon a very fine point: the human individual transforms nature in order to feed himself. This fine point is very hard, rooted in the powerful and universal experience of the hungry animal within us, but perhaps it is just as fragile as it is hard. At least that is the judgment of Locke's great critic, David Hume. Hume is of particular interest to us since he is not concerned with a "reactionary" critique that would pretend arbitrarily to return to an objective, or rather a dogmatic definition of human substance. On the contrary, Hume continues and radicalizes Locke's critique of substance by offering us an internal critique of modern consciousness.

Let us then consider Hume's critique of Locke's conception of property. In Hume's view, Locke confuses the idea of property and the idea of the right to property by assigning the same origin to both: labor. Hume observes that the relation of the individual with the material of his labor cannot be the foundation of the right to property. Hume defeats Locke's reasoning by stating that we cannot strictly speaking say that we join or mix our labor to something else; that is true only in a figurative sense, since, in fact, we only modify or alter this something.[45] For a bond to be established between the individual and the object worked upon, other ideas besides those of the individual must be brought in, such as those of his labor, of what is expected of him, and the loss of his humanity. Labor can found property only if it is accompanied or completed by other elements of the constituted human world that are no less important. This is to say that by itself labor does not suffice to found the right of property, even in its origin.

Unlike Locke, Hume rigorously distinguishes between property—the strict and enduring separation of possessions in a society—and the right of property—the rules by which possessions are assigned and guaranteed to persons. Property in general is founded on the most evident and most urgent interest of society, while the right to property in its innumerable forms "is often determined by very frivolous views and considerations," in effect by "connexions of the imagination."[46] The interest of society is the foundation of the necessity of justice, of which property is an expression or modality. Hume thus tends to invert Locke's theorem on the relations between property and justice.[47] At first one is tempted to think that Hume adopts the classical position on the question of property; that, in distinguishing the necessity and utility of property in general from the contingent and rather arbitrary character of the rules that order it in the different bodies politic, he makes property depend upon *political justice*, as Aristotle did.[48] This is not the case, however. Hume in fact provides a critique of Locke's procedure *from within* by showing that it does not respect the logic of the idiom of "ideas" that is his principal analytical tool. One cannot attach the individual's right to property to an object through the intermediary of *one* idea, in this case the idea of labor, since every idea necessarily entails other ideas that together with it constitute the human world. Whatever one imagines about men at the beginning of history, one cannot in any case conceive of a state of nature of ideas. Locke does not see that ideas take form as a society does, that the right to property in particular is only one idea among all those that constitute the human world and that it maintains with the other ideas necessary, regular, and yet variable relations that are founded on the "imagination."

Locke's error on the right to property is only a particular instance of a general error or contradiction of his philosophy—the philosophy of both human rights and the ideas of human understanding.

Hume essentially accepts Locke's starting point on the activity of the mind in combining simple ideas rooted in external or internal experience.[49] But he considers that Locke is unfaithful to this principle or contradicts it, very specifically in what he writes concerning the notion of power that is fundamental for him, as we have seen in section 3. Locke deduced the simple idea of power from the external experience of movement and above all from the internal experience of the will that moves the members or the understanding. In reality neither experience can give rise to the idea of power or produce it.[50] What Locke ineptly calls power is in fact a necessary connection, which the mind established only by virtue of repetition or habit: "This connexion, therefore, which we feel in the mind, this customary transition of the imagination from the one object to its usual attendant, is the sentiment or impression from which we form the idea of power or necessary connexion. Nothing farther is in the case."[51] Hume seems to say at times that Locke does not give an adequate explanation of the origin of the idea of power,[52] and at other times that this idea simply does not exist.[53] The fact is that Locke's idea of power contains and confuses two ideas: the idea of unknown qualities which, for example, would have it that the movements of invisible corpuscles would produce secondary qualities; and the idea of the necessary connection between an antecedent and a consequent idea.[54] These two notions are perfectly distinct: the first, the idea of cause, is insignificant; only the second, the idea of necessary connection, has meaning. The only power of which we have a clear idea being the necessary connection,[55] the notion of power "belongs entirely to the soul,"[56] and consequently sheds no light whatever on the nature of things.[57]

Thus the modern idea of *power* brings back the impossibilities in the traditional idea of *substance* which Locke had so severely denounced.

Hume rejects Locke's conception of the moral notions or mixed modes for the same reasons. On the one hand, Hume assumes these notions to be produced by the power of the human understanding, with no likeness to external archetypes and thus pure causality; on the other hand, he affirms that they are ordered by a relation of convenience, a necessary connection. Of these two theses, only the second is properly intelligible. In the right to property, there is only a relation of convenience among several ideas, just as in the phenomena of nature there is only a necessary connection between two or among several ideas. Between the idea of labor and the idea of property, there is a relation which, like the notion of necessary connection, "belongs exclusively to the soul," and this necessarily calls into play a certain number of other ideas belonging to it. The idea of a "real" joining or mixing of the person of the laborer and the natural material worked upon is as confused and unintelligible as the idea of a "real" efficacy of a cause in the phenomena of nature, and for the same reason. If we hold rigorously to experience, we will always encounter only connections between ideas that are made necessary by habit or imagination—necessary, therefore, by a *de facto* necessity.

Thus, according to Hume, not only are moral notions in no way founded upon the nature of things or of man, but their cause cannot be brought to light or their scientific deduction worked out. In this sense, they are as absurd as the ideas of superstition, although they are a useful superstition. Founded in the imagination that relates ideas according to their conformities and associations, they formulate the relations necessary to human life. The notion of conveniency . . ., which is already very present in Locke to provide the motive or rule for the arbitrary invention of moral notions, henceforth absorbs this arbitrary causality almost completely. Just as it is useless to seek the cause beyond the necessary connection, it is vain to seek a moral agent beyond the moral ideas he necessarily maintains. There is thus no meaning at all in wanting to attach a "natural" right to the individual.

I had suggested that one can detect a similarity between Locke's dogmatism of rights and his skepticism or rather artificialism of ideas, and more generally a similarity in the modern attitude between the universal affirmation of human rights and the recognition of the diversity of cultures and the arbitrary character of their moral notions. These are two different ways, one from the agent's perspective, the other from observer's, of saying that man has no nature or ends, that he is not an essence or substance. Hume's critique, however, requires us to concede that there is an unbridgeable gap between the idiom of rights and the idiom of ideas. The incoherence of Locke's position lies in the fact that he assumed in fact that the idea of rights—natural rights that reveal themselves in the state of nature—is not an idea like other ideas. It does not obey the laws of conformity and association, the laws of conveniency that regulate all other ideas of the human world, and it is in some way rooted in nature. In Locke, the meaning of the idea of right is not to be found in the analysis of the ideas of right. It is more and something other than a Lockean idea. In rejecting the existence of innate ideas, Locke rejects that ideas, or some among them, have a part in the essence of man. But he preserves the place of this essence—"$X = X$"—and the expression of this absent essence is the rights of man.

In the language of ideas, giving a distinct name to the fact of killing a man rather than a sheep is purely arbitrary. Moreover, calling murder an evil or a crime is just as arbitrary, even if in fact man most often speaks of it that way. In the language of rights, to kill a man is to violate his primordial right to life; to call murder an evil or a crime thus ceases to be arbitrary and on the contrary it becomes necessary to do so. The idiom of ideas allows Locke to define in principle all moral notions as arbitrary, lacking foundation in human nature. The entire domain of ideas and moral valuations, in fact the properly human world as a whole, is thus suspended. On the other hand, the idiom of rights allows him at once to "renaturalize" the elements of traditional morality he wishes to preserve and to "naturalize" the new elements he seeks to promote. One could not imagine a conception of things that offers more convenience and latitude to whoever wishes to change the objects of human esteem. The whole human world, like an open city, will be docile to the will of the reformer.

Hume finds it impossible to countenance this perspective. That some

can claim to hold such an advantageous position, in truth one so contradictory, would rather make him indignant, if anything could trouble his
equanimity. The idea of right could not escape the common fate of ideas.
All ideas "belong exclusively to the soul," such that it is vain and violent
to give to one among them the authority of nature. But if it is arbitrary to
distinguish among ideas one treats as if they were natural, in this case the
idea of the natural rights of man, and other ideas that are simply artificial,
it is also unwise to underline, in an inverse sense, the artificial character of
ideas in general. All ideas belong to the same world, the world of the
"imagination," which is in sum neither natural nor artificial, or at least not
worth considering according to this polarity. It is only appropriate to distinguish between the ideas of the imagination which are "useful" and
those which are simply "superficial."

In Locke, the reformer or modern revolutionary, the skepticism of ideas
is combined with the dogmatism of rights. In Hume, the modern conservative, as we will call him, a yet more radical skepticism, which does not
spare even the notion of rights, leads to a dogmatism of the common oc-
currences of life, whose usual but yet abstract name is "pragmatism" or
"utilitarianism." Yet it would not be exact to say that the only thing that
holds authority in the human world as Hume describes it is what he calls
utility. Hume admits that many of our moral judgments have no relation,
even indirectly, with utility. Their source is simply a sentiment, the moral
sentiment, that has nothing to do with reason, utilitarian or other. For
example, reason sees nothing in incest that is intrinsically condemnable—
reason as such can neither approve nor condemn anything morally—but
it is a fact, a matter of fact that people universally condemn incest. The
source of this moral sentiment is in the frame of our nature which is unknown to us.[58] Thus for Hume the organizing principle of the human
world no longer resides in human rights rooted in the hungry and hard-
working individual's confrontation with nature, but in the moral sentiment that is ever at work in human societies. That is why Hume's more
radical and in some way ultimate skepticism leads, as we stated, to a much
more conservative practical viewpoint than Locke's does.

Hume undoubtedly pushes Locke's critique of ideas to its logical conclusion and he is in that more radical and more coherent than his prede-
cessor. Shall we then say that the modern conservative is the truth of the
modern reformer or revolutionary? In any event the hypothesis is not confirmed by observing the development of modern democratic societies,
where the reformer is ever at work, the principle of human rights always
shines brightly, and the most rebellious and secret parts of our nature are
bent on hearing the good news of human rights, while the conservative is
deservedly condemned to impotent irony, since in seeking to mock the
reformer's projects, he applauds the current state of society, that is, the

results of the prior reform. In reality, the modern conservative's theoretical advantage over the modern reformer conceals a critical weakness.

As I said above, the language of rights is the only language for anyone who wants to organize the human world without positing or accepting *a priori* any idea of human nature or Law by which man is bound to direct his life. The principle of human rights is the only reflexive principle of action of a man who has no ends. To subject human rights to the arbitrary fatality that weighs on all other ideas is to abolish the place of human essence that Locke preserved. Once the idea of human rights becomes an idea like the others, the human world is no more than an endless sky, traversed by ever-changing but at bottom always identical constellations that are perfectly flat, the ordered and arbitrary entities of moral ideas that the observer—the historian, sociologist, anthropologist, journalist—can inventory and describe indefinitely, but among which the real man can find no principle of action. This monotone and flat variety is the world of the philosopher Hume.

But it will be asked whether the "moral sentiment" does not provide an altogether satisfactory principle of action. That would be the case in effect if this principle could be honestly thought through by the man who acts. What he experiences, in his heart or soul, as an imperious sentiment that dictates judgment and action, the philosopher, or the observer, sees in its truth as a pure fact that reason cannot justify. This abyss between practical sentiment and theoretical reason is something more and other than the distance, which in fact cannot be reduced completely, between the passionate engagement of the man who acts—citizen, believer, or lover—and the detached or otherwise passionate viewpoint of the ancient philosopher. There were so many paths that went from one to the other! The desire for justice of the citizen or the religious man, the eros of the lover, were the condition for the possibility and the continuous nurturing flame of philosophy. There is nothing of the sort in the philosophy of the modern conservative, founded on the moral sentiment. There is no common ground between the viewpoint of the observer and that of the agent. From the moment the man who acts strives to reflect, to consider in the light of reason the commandment or evaluation the moral sentiment addresses to him, he sees them as pure facts that could not entail any obligation, validity, or objective meanings. The movement of his moral life, instead of being oriented, corrected, and sustained by the new lights of reason, is instantly deprived of meaning, paralyzed, vaporized. "Why do I do what I do? Because the moral sentiment incites me to, the moral sentiment, that is to say a fact devoid of meaning. What I do, I do then for nothing, or without a valid motive." Real life, under all its forms, is pure superstition. The philosopher, or each one of us when he observes himself or becomes conscious of himself, delivers himself of this superstition, but deliverance does not

give him access to a higher or truer life. It simply allows him to take stock
of the necessary character of the superstition. And this fatal secret he has
pierced he must forget as soon as he returns to life to act, since one cannot
act humanly or reasonably in the conviction that all the motives of our
actions are pure facts that human reason is incapable of justifying. Hume
embodies this moment of precocious twilight where the Enlightenment,
because it has gone to the very limit of its critique of superstition, must at
last fall under its laws, in recognizing that all ideas, not only of the other
world but of this one as well, are equally superstitious. Then the Enlightenment saves its honor, in truth its very reason for being, only by proposing the undoubtedly useful and perhaps superstitious distinction between
a superstition that is useful and a superstition that is simply superstitious.

XIX

In its later development, the European Enlightenment combined the viewpoints of Locke the reformer and Hume the conservative. It adopted the
first viewpoint, the dogmatism of rights, in those societies over which the
Enlightenment reigned, or at least found itself in a position to take action;
and it adopted the second, the absolute skepticism and *de facto* character
of duties and judgments, in those societies which it was able only to contemplate or which it did not really wish to influence. Not leaving a single
stone unturned when it comes to obtaining the recognition and guarantee
of his rights at home, Western man is often marvelously complacent when
he views societies whose ways are foreign to his lifestyle and he even rejects
the right to judge them. Thus again, through different routes, we return to
the observation made in chapter 2, and note once again how liberal dogmatism and sociological or anthropological relativism divide our souls between themselves.

It must be noted also how in the West the skepticism of ideas serves to
reinforce the dogmatism of rights. According to Hume's rigorous doctrine,
this skepticism also takes aim at and attacks the notion of human rights.
But, since this purely theoretical viewpoint is too weak for any honest
attack on the simultaneously active and reflexive viewpoint that affirms
rights, it is made to serve the dogmatism of rights so as to refute, or discredit, the moral ideas that would risk hindering the ever more complete
and extended realization of human rights. Thus the moral ideas inherited
from the tradition are in an untenable situation. Already considered as
antipathetic, even hateful, because certain of the commandments they
contain seem contrary to human rights, they are furthermore deprived of
all solidity by the skepticism that declares them vain and artificial. Dogmatism and skepticism are reconciled and reinforce one another in irre-

sistible hate and spite of the Law, whose commandments seem to have no other content, intention, or meaning than the violation of human rights. And thus while these ruled in an ever more imperious way for the past two centuries in the West, one gets the impression that they have a permanent and truly heroic struggle to wage against a perverse superstition that wants to oppress them and that expresses itself in the impudent pronouncements of the pope. In the most general terms, it is made up of everything that, in the moral and religious tradition emanating from Athens, Rome, and Jerusalem, could not be interpreted according to the strict doctrine of human rights. Fortunately, this superstition is as weak as it is perverse, and thus there is a great number of heroes. Today the doctrine of human rights wages its hottest and most heroic battles in the United States, where it had the fewest obstacles to surmount. It is in the New World that Hume's argument has the smallest chance of spreading, where the least attention is paid to the complex whole of ideas formed on the experience that constitutes the protective and nurturing atmosphere of human life. On the *tabula rasa* of the continent, the appeal to rights gets carried away and loses patience; bursts of strident indignation disperse the already thin topsoil of human tradition; and from one side to the other, all the elements of the human world are attacked in the name of human rights.

XX

The one-sided assertion of rights one finds in the United States is indeed impressive and influential and in some way seals Locke's victory over Hume. However, the modern scheme rests on the tension, which presupposes a certain equilibrium, between the affirmation of rights and the critique of ideas. The conceptual landscape of the Enlightenment is arranged around the two poles of human rights and the ideas of human understanding, which later on receive new names such as "ideology," "values," and "culture." Rights and ideas constitute the twofold determination resulting from the rejection of human essence and produced by the analysis of human substance. Whatever way it was conceived, it encompassed and fashioned the unity of the human phenomenon: it is one and the same thing to be a *substance* and a substance. Substance was a synthesis and the affirmation of the synthesis. Analysis in terms of rights on the one hand, and of ideas on the other, dismantles this synthesis, which is natural inasmuch as it is real: the substance—man, or the nature of man.

This dismantling consists in the division between rights and ideas on the one hand, and in the expansion of rights and ideas on the other. Ideas are indefinite in number because they do not have their model, and thus their limits, in nature, and they are arbitrarily created by the human understanding. Modern man contemplates with a pleasure he finds very vivid what appears to him as the inexhaustible diversity of "values" or "cultures." Rights also are indefinite in number, as their continual multiplication over the last two centuries bears witness. It seems that something prevents one from saying *the* human right, whereas it is, or it was, altogether natural to say *the* nature of man. Human rights nonetheless preserve something more by way of a synthesis than the ideas of human understanding. However immoderate we may be in defining and claiming "new rights," rights are less "indefinite," less "numerous" than ideas. They always preserve some link to what was for the first modern philosophers the fundamental right, the *right* at the source of the other rights: the right to preservation. Even though *right* is irresistibly pluralized in the *rights* of man, it still occupies in some way, as I have noted above, the place of essence or substance. Under the modern regime, the regime of analysis, it is the most synthetic, and thus the strongest entity.

But right is in the place of nature only by taking the place of nature. That is why it is perhaps not very felicitous that, in order to designate the philosophies of human rights, the expression "modern natural right" became accepted. In reality, the substantive here devours the adjective that should qualify it: human rights take the place of human nature. If the language has remained equivocal, it is without doubt due to the manner by which rights replace nature. Rights reveal themselves, and thereby become real, in a situation which the philosophers we are concerned with have called "the state of nature." In this state, "men" have not yet deployed their humanity: they are unaware of religion, politics, society, family, the arts and sciences. But they experience the need to preserve themselves, which they can do by appropriating the fruits of the earth. It is in this prehuman state that their rights, human rights, are revealed: the rights to life, liberty, property. Human rights show themselves and become real when the savage inhabitants of the state of nature do not yet have ideas regarding "man" nor even the idea of "man." Their rights are revealed and become real in the idealess relation of self to self and with external nature, a relation from which will be born, hypothetically, the ideas of rights, of contract, and of man himself. But what name does one give to this idealess relation of self to self that prevails in the state of nature and defines it? How and by what right can one name this relation that is deaf and blind since it is antecedent to the properly human light of the idea? Locke names this relation, which rests on the sentiment of being a self, self-possession. What is proper to man is to possess himself. Or rather, self-possession is the silent and opaque kernel that will blossom in the declaration of rights. Man is he who declares his rights.

The notion of the state of nature occupies an important place in the history of the mind because it reveals and situates at the center of the interpretation of man the possibility of an idealess reflexivity, where the intellect has no part, which both the philosophical and the religious tradition had overlooked. This is the condition for the possibility of the rights of man. In order for the humanity of man to dwell in its rights, man must necessarily be the author of all his ideas and not have ideas "naturally," or, in technical language, have no "innate ideas." If man had ideas of which he was not the author, he would first have to bring to light what they contain or imply of information about himself and his condition. The affirmation of his rights would be subordinated to the recognition of the objective order of his ideas. Man could indeed have rights, within the framework and under the specification of his ideas and what they teach him objectively, but there could be no "human rights."

XXI

In light of the two results of the analysis of substance, that is, "natural" rights and "artificial" ideas, we are forever oscillating between contradiction and affinity when it comes to defining their relation. This is because we are striving to remain faithful to the complexity of the phenomenon. But would it not be possible to arrive at an unambiguous judgment about this relation?

I have underlined several times already the contrast found in the spirit of modern democracies between reforming activism under the banner of universal rights and scientific passivity in the name of cultural diversity. There is without doubt something bizarre, for example, in denouncing the lot given to women in the West in the name of human rights, and accepting the lot of women in the Islamic world in the name of the sovereign particularity of each and every culture. Those who protest that such an attitude encompasses a logical contradiction and a moral fault that are equally inadmissible are assuredly engaged in a salutary work of civic education. But what is clearly shocking in the eyes of the upright citizen loses its clarity in those of the conscientious philosopher. Regretfully, with repugnance, he discerns a point of profound complicity between the two disputed affirmations: man is the being who has rights and man is a cultural being. The vulgar democrat who cries out these two slogans with equal force expresses a truth that he is indeed incapable of understanding.

This complicity goes beyond the other negative one that we have already disclosed. The two propositions equally and simultaneously issue from the rejection of the "substantial" definition of man. Not only do they reject the same thesis, they also affirm the same thesis.

The doctrine of rights and the theory of culture both equally presuppose what the first calls the state of nature. The cultural being that is man, so we are told, presupposes, in order to be able to be specified according to a particular cultural determination, a precultural state which is never actual but which is yet in some way real if acculturation is to take place. In both accounts, man passes from the natural or precultural state, to the civil or cultural state. In fact, what "cultural creation" is there that is more impressive than the social contract? If through the social contract man can be the conscious and sovereign creator of the just regime that respects and protects his rights, this is because implicitly he is also the creator, however poorly enlightened and perhaps corrupt, of less satisfying regimes. As soon as the contract regime and the other regimes are equally the product of such a creative act, then all the regimes that become the diverse cultures that make up the human scene are on an equal footing. The theoreticians of human rights and the social contract assume and posit this creative power of the human will in the name of which man will soon be defined as a being of culture and eventually human rights and the social contract will be attacked. In this context, as we shall see in section 3 of chapter 6, Nietzsche belongs to the same political and spiritual movement as Hobbes, Locke, and Rousseau.

Thus the two propositions that man is the being who has rights and a cultural being both compress the same movement of thought, though specified in different ways. Man is first of all presupposed in his indetermination, his implicit state of humanity or idealess reflexivity; then, on his own he comes out of this indetermination and defines himself and explicitly fashions himself. In the first account, he recognizes and publishes his rights whose protection he arranges; in the second, he gives form to his humanity by placing himself under a particular law which eventually shows little concern for his rights. The law's particularity, no less than the generality or universality of rights, expresses the general power of man over his own humanity and does so the more strikingly inasmuch as it is singular and binding. That is perhaps why the advanced democrats in whom this power arouses a particular enthusiasm and who thus bear with impatience the least constraints of the regimes whose citizens they are, have frequently shown a marked favor for the bloodiest exotic regimes. General Tapioca's consummate cruelty brings home just what is involved in man's creative power over his surroundings that inspires the never-ending claims to ever new rights in the West. Voltaire, who was so indignant at the fate of Calas, could view Japanese tortures with indulgence and even good-naturedly.

Anyone who finds this reference to be unworthy of philosophy can turn to Voltaire's enemy, the most profound philosopher of modern democracy, Jean-Jacques Rousseau, who wants to achieve the most particular body politic possible by means of the most general will possible.

XXII

The two propositions that man is the being who has rights and a being of culture are born of the dissolution of the notion of substance. In return, they condense a movement of thought for which the notion of substance or human nature appears cumbersome and sterile, useless and misleading. This movement is a coming and going from indetermination to determination. When thought descends toward indetermination, toward the state of nature and idealess reflexivity, it sees the notion of human nature as much too complete, rich, and determined and thus it hinders and stops its movement. When thought ascends toward determination, toward specified and guaranteed right and real and therefore particular culture, it sees the notion of human nature as much too vague and undetermined so that here also it hinders and stops its movement. In both directions, then, the recourse to the notion of human nature seems to signify an arbitrary halt in the movement of thought.

This is so because human nature or substance is a real synthesis—in our context, the synthesis of the particular and the general. Nature, which is general, is only real when it is particular. The aspect of particularity coexists intimately and inseparably with the aspect of generality. After the dissolution of substance, these two aspects become two moments that cannot coexist; they are necessarily successive. Moreover, the two moments are not identified with any kind of stability. The state of nature cannot be posited simply as the moment of particularity or generality; the two moments exchange their logical notes, as we have seen earlier in section 5 of chapter 1. If the state of nature is posited as the moment of particularity, the moment of the natural individual, the civil state is determined as the moment of generality, of general law or will. But the state of nature can be defined as the generality of the species and thus the civil state is determined as particularity, for example as this culture. The first line of reasoning belongs to the practical viewpoint, the second to the theoretical.

If we consider the second viewpoint, we can see that the separation of the two moments has major effects on the perception of the human world. In fact, after the dissolution of substance, the mind, in observing the human phenomenon, no longer sees the universal present in the particular. It sees the result of a process that needs to be reconstituted, that is, the linking of causes by which the implicit universal has become the explicit and real particular. This linking is described in different ways by the various human sciences. In chapter 2 we studied the very interesting case of sociology. The sociological viewpoint, which recognizes a process where once a presence was seen, is so pregnant that it can, without scientific apparatus, govern the seemingly most spontaneous reactions of modern man. In the face of an episode or behavior that once prompted one to exclaim, "that's another quirk of human nature!," one says today with smug satisfaction, "it's a social fact!"

To bring in human nature as a foundation and explanation is to short-circuit the coming and going from indetermination to determination. It is to paralyze the analytical thought proper to modern man by placing it before a reality that is always too and too little determined because it joins the universal and the particular in the same presence. Human nature is nothing more than a fact that leaves the human mind stupid and unsatis-fied.[59]

Looking at the notion of human substance in this way is, of course, to see it in the framework of analytical thought about rights and ideas, where its power of synthesis has been deliberately and radically destroyed. Per-haps a reworking of this notion that would rediscover its original meaning would overcome the objections of analytical thought, the obstacles of modern perception, but the fact is that modern philosophy has never re-ally explored this avenue. It rather sought a synthesis in an altogether different direction.

XXIII

I do not have in mind here the philosophy of Kant, which, it is true, is an extraordinarily meticulous reflection on the problem of the "synthesis."[60] It is all in all nothing more than that, one could say. Perhaps for this reason it is difficult to say whether it decisively resolves the problem or aggravates it in dizzying fashion. Doesn't its speculative high point, the introduction of the "transcendental," consist in finding a name for the difficulty it had inherited and then diffusing it in all the articulations of the human self? All the notions Kant inherited and preserved are subordi-nated to the new polarity of the transcendental and the empirical. What had appeared in the poetic and, if I may say, picturesque mode of the polarity between the state of nature and civil state, between the presuppo-sition of humanity and its determination, finds its generalized, radicalized, and displaced expression in the new polarity that appears more rigorous because it touches the imagination less. Seeking salvation in depth, the notion of the transcendental overcomes the inherited difficulty of the dual-ity by condensing the two moments of presupposition and determination and thus allowing the empirical to emerge, the pure fact deprived of any meaning since it is incapable of true universality.[61] As we have seen, early modern philosophy replaced the real simultaneous presence of the partic-ular and the universal in the substance with the two successive moments of presupposition and determination. To the "metaphysical" search for the cause of substance, Kant now substitutes the investigation of the conditions for the possibility of experience. Modern man, who is no longer "naturally" man, must act "as if" he were citizen; more generally and radically he must act "as if" he had a real experience. He is not truly citizen since his citizenship, far from being an expression or end of his nature, is only an instrument, a means to guarantee the human rights he has discovered as his own in the state of nature. His "real" experiences hold no genuine interest, since henceforth the only truly interesting and genuine experience would be the experience of the conditions for the possibility of experience, which is just as impossible and even more impossible than the return to the state of nature. Or could one consider the possibility of an experience of the totality of the conditions for the possibility of experience, an experience not of the totality of the cosmos, which, as "successive synthesis," is indefinite,[62] but nevertheless an objective synthesis: the experience of the world? It is not surprising that a thoroughgoing reflection on Kant accompanied the "synthetic" movement of thought that for some time was called "existentialism" and that I wish to consider here.

I can only propose a very sketchy review of the last great movement of modern thought. Modern philosophy was uneasy over the necessity and the impossibility of the "return to the state of nature." In its prime, existentialism seeks to disclose the common root of both. It begins by confirming the duality and tension between presupposition and determination, between implicit and explicit humanity. It begins, if one wishes, with the acquisitions of modern philosophy. But where its predecessors stumbled, existentialism finds a firm footing and takes flight. Man is enjoined to understand that this process is what makes him be what he is, or better, that he truly "exists" when he is conscious of this process, when he identifies himself with this process that has become conscious. The modern scheme presupposes man's humanity; but this presupposed humanity is never present to itself. It is only active through the mediation and under the form of rights that are proclaimed, of culture that is theorized, or of the hidden causalities that the human sciences uncover. It acts only under one of these three definitions that presuppose but do not present it and even prevent it from being present to itself. Always present and dormant, the hidden character of humanity conceals itself even more behind the façade of refined civilization. In order to be free and powerful and wise, modern humanity is organized on the active forgetting of itself. Defining himself as being-having-rights or as being-of-culture, modern man is the parasite of his hidden double, of he who is capable of making culture, the unique source of the diversity of rights, the one who, deprived of essence, occupies the place of essence and deploys its efficacy. It is just this implicit and dormant double that existentialism wants to bring to light. Since he presupposes himself rather than posit and affirm himself, or since he only affirms himself in presupposing himself, modern man lives with a built-in bad faith, a constitutive inauthenticity. As actor or as observer, citizen or scholar, he mobilizes the empathetic objectivity of "human rights," of "culture," of "social" or "psychological causes"—of "society" or of the "unconscious"—so many parasitic propositions, so many masks of the only affirmation that would be truthful! To affirm himself where he presupposed himself, the implicit and dormant double must take a resolute hold on himself, and, freed of his past, his present, and his motives, project himself toward the future.

It certainly would not be a question of returning to good old "human nature." It too is part of the bundle of interested illusions. What must be mobilized for an affirmation that is finally truthful, would not be the old essence or substance. Any honest thought on the matter is ruled out by the equivocation of early modern philosophy, which did not know clearly whether it posited the nonexistence or only the unknowability of human nature. Human essence or nature is simultaneously cast out and recalled, and it can then be no more than pure fact deprived of meaning, an opaque and mute frame, a vague cause, and therefore dear to academicians, one more among the precise causes which the human sciences investigate. Human essence must be resolutely rejected, along with human rights and culture. The implicit and dormant hearth, of which human nature—maintained under the residual and mutilated form of "psychology"—human rights, and culture are only deceiving objectifications, must at last become explicit, and be expressed and made present.

Modern consciousness—it seems to me that I have written this book only to make this point—comes into itself in the two moments of the presupposition of "X" and the objectification of "X." The existentialist project emerges in the abrupt awakening to this duality or duplicity. Its task is to reduce duality to unity, duplicity to sincerity or authenticity by the perfectly resolute affirmation of "X" which, this time, finally, will not be deceptively confused with essence, rights, or culture. Of course, existentialism cannot be a humanism, since "X" is an *absconditus* or *absconditum* (a hidden person or thing) for whom or which being human is in sum only the most plausible and thereby the most misleading objectification. Moreover, when the existentialist writers deal with what is central to their theme and concern, they do not speak of man but of the *pour-soi*, or of liberty, or *Dasein*. To be sure, for some among them, for whom the old man remains still frisky beneath the shroud, the *pour-soi* is just one more odd fellow, a prickly weed sprung up on the sidewalk of the old boulevard. But the most serious of these authors understood that if man must be able one day at last to be, there must precisely be no "man," but *Dasein* must exist in its genuine or authentic relation to the world, a relation that is the true synthesis. Existentialism has access to the synthesis by elaborating the notions of *Dasein* and world, the notions of being-in-the-world and transcendence-of-the-world.[63] Common sense today is quick to mock these notions and terms. The effort toward unity always appears comical to a contented plurality. But in these notions and the scholarly pursuits linked to them, modern consciousness makes its most heroic efforts at overcoming its own duplicity. Therein resides the greatness of Martin Heidegger.

CHAPTER V

The Triumph of the Will

THE READER may be surprised to find that our attempt at describing modern consciousness has devoted only one paragraph to the subject of liberty, in section II of chapter 2. Liberty seems to constitute the link between common consciousness and political life on the one hand and philosophical work on the other. Is not modern history the history of the acquisition of liberty and is not modern philosophy in its very different versions always a philosophy of liberty? Does not modern philosophy lead one to see and understand the passage from man defined as "nature" to man defined as "liberty"? The broad meanings of the word, its diverse nuances, and the intense feelings it arouses are treasures one would be ill-advised to do without, simply to mark one's disdain or lassitude over a term that in other contexts has become hackneyed. However, a more serious motive keeps us from placing this notion at the center of our study.

At the very moment the notion of liberty comes to the forefront of political philosophy and life, it undergoes a sort of internal rupture. Up to the seventeenth century, it was inseparable from one account or the other of free will. With the thinkers who founded modern liberty, the theoreticians of political liberalism, the notion of liberty severs itself from that of the free will and even turns against it. Hobbes and Locke, no less than Spinoza, assert the necessary character of human acts.[1] It would not be giving an inexact description of what took place if it were said that the philosophers refuted and denied liberty at the very moment they offered liberty to man, or claimed it for him. How can one interpret such a singular phenomenon?

Beginning at a certain date, and for reasons we shall need to make clear, the idea of free will (free choice of the will) began to seem beset with an internal contradiction. It characterizes man as provided with a free nature; and it characterizes his nature as endowed with or capable of liberty. In such a conception, nature is the substantive or the substance, while liberty is a quality or power[2] of the substance or a predicate of the substantive. Nature envelops liberty and is stronger than liberty and thus negates it. Modern philosophy, by denying free will, negates this negation and liberates liberty.

The doctrine of free will indeed affirms human liberty, but only up to a certain point. Man is free within the framework and by means of his nature; he does not have a choice of his ends, which are inscribed in this nature.[3] That is saying, in an inverted way, that his nature comes between man and liberty. The proposal of liberating liberty leads to extenuating nature, dismantling substance, and abolishing essence.

But is it the discovery of the contradiction contained in the idea of nature that induces the modern project or is it not rather the modern project that makes this contradiction emerge and, in brief, invents it? Furthermore, just what kind of liberation is this since it begins with the affirmation of the necessity of human acts?

The tradition already made a counter-distinction, in certain contexts, between nature and liberty, under its twofold aspect of will and reason.[4] One could say that this crack, as it grew larger, led to the fall of the majestic edifice. At least this distinction rendered possible that attack that would come. But in the premodern context, this fissure could not grow larger to the point of rupture. Something stronger than nature or liberty held the two together. Free nature as well as unfree nature were two modalities of the same condition of creatureliness. It was thus not nature that rubbed against liberty, but on the contrary supernature, that is, God, the Sovereign dispenser of grace. It is in the context of its connections to grace that the meaning of liberty was then investigated. Moreover, in its confrontation with the Almighty, liberty grew stronger. A theologian might say that in its long wrestling match with grace, liberty came out too strong for nature. But that is how theologians think.

Whatever the case may be, even if the ultimate causes of the break between liberty and nature escapes us, we can attempt to describe what took place. We can, in particular, try to understand why the affirmation of human liberty began with the affirmation of the necessity of human acts.

Once, in accord with his nature, man has left nature or creation, his liberty derives its motives from nature. From the point of view of liberty, nature is the whole or the sum of possible motives. Liberty, then, depends so much on the world for its exercise that one cannot see how it could emancipate itself from the world, how it could elevate itself above nature; it lives in tune with nature. But in every body the joints are relatively the weakest parts, and in the great body of the human order the articulation between liberty and nature is also a point of relative weakness. This articulation, considered *sub specie naturae*, is the end or rather the ends of man; considered *sub specie libertatis*, it is the motives of human liberty.

Modern philosophy aims its guns at these two faces of the juncture. It is well known how many crushing regulations, what devastating sarcasms modern philosophy has directed against the idea of end or finality. Less apparent, but no less important, is the rejection of the idea of motive. Now motive is removed, whether human action is interpreted as mechanical behavior deprived of motive, or the effect of motive is considered necessary. To affirm the necessity of human acts, "motivated" or not, is to abolish by that very fact the role of the motive in human action; it is to emancipate it from its motives that limited it just as it activated it; it is to prepare a liberty more free, a liberty without limits. To affirm the necessity of human acts is the make possible the affirmation of pure liberty; and that is simply to affirm without motives.

This could be stated in another way. The idea of a free nature connotes an exquisite equilibrium between nature and liberty, each one determining the other. Liberty amplifies nature, nature gives being and life to liberty. The one and the other are both finite. This equilibrium is by itself difficult to preserve. Any occasion which solicits liberty or disturbs nature could break it. Such a situation could make this rupture definitive and irreparable. As soon as the two elements no longer limit one another by determining one another, they go beyond their borders and they become extremes: nature becomes infinite substance and liberty becomes infinite freedom.

Something else needs to be noted. The tradition tacitly equated free (choice of the) will and will. It is the same faculty, the same *potentia*.[5] But this same faculty does not do the same thing: free will chooses or elects, the will wills. Willing is not exactly choosing; willing is stronger than choosing, since one continues to will after choosing. And choosing never takes good hold of itself; one is always before or after the choice; the instant, if it is an instant, of choosing evades us. Willing knows itself very well and can express itself at every instant. Unless, unaware of itself, it is a blind will; but then, stronger than the liberty of free will, it includes necessity. In any event, whoever wills to does not choose, or no longer chooses. Free will needs the world wherein are its motives. The will is willingly tautological: the will wills and it will itself. It can will to go without the world.

Liberty as free will got along nicely with nature, but liberty as will is too strong for nature and will dissolve its union with nature, which grace had both blessed and cursed.

III

It is certainly very difficult to judge and to understand fully the import and meaning of this emancipation of the will, this liberation of liberty. If one judges by the tone of early modern political philosophy, a tone of ambition, provocation, and prophecy, it held infinite promise. By disengaging the will from nature, his will from his nature, man promises himself something unheard of. What? And for what? Once again, it is very difficult to describe precisely. But the following remark may put us on the right track.

Greek philosophy had no greater praise to give a political regime than to say that it was "according to nature," even if and precisely because it was in practice impossible for a real regime to be completely or perfectly "according to nature." Aristotle as well as Plato would have deemed it absurd or unintelligible to say of a political regime that it was "nature itself and for itself," or that it was "nature actualized." But let us read what Hegel writes in the opening lines of paragraph 258 of *The Principles of the Philosophy of Right*:

> The state is absolutely rational inasmuch as it is the actuality of the substantial will which it possesses in the particular self-consciousness once that consciousness has been raised to consciousness of its universality. This substantial unity is an absolute unmoved end in itself, in which freedom comes into its supreme right. On the other hand this final end has supreme right against the individual, whose supreme duty is to be a member of the state.[6]

What makes this text so extraordinary, and so important for our inquiry, is that what Hegel calls the state reconciles in itself all the oppositions that traditionally constitute the human world—the particular and the general, right and duty, thing and consciousness, movement and rest—and that it achieves this reconciliation inasmuch as it is the realization of the will. Nature, which is the norm or model, is never "realized," since it is the nature of nature to be beyond human grasp. Whoever seeks nature strays from himself. It is this distance and height of nature that open up to man the space between his reality and his finality, and thus the possibility of willing. But if I consider willing in its reality, as willing something and also necessarily willing to will, if I consider the will separate from "nature" or the "world," then the words of Hegel we have just cited are less astonishing, less exorbitant than they appeared at first. They only say, though with the exhaustiveness that is Hegel's strength, what the will says of itself, what it wills from itself, and, first of all, what it wills for itself. They articulate the infinite promise that the reality of the will contains. The will cannot do otherwise than will its realization, and, in the measure that it realizes itself and becomes reality, it does not cease to will it, thus accomplishing the unity of motion and rest. What the will realizes is necessarily rational, since the only thing that can be truly willed by one will is what can be willed by another, what can be universalized and in its realized form, universal. And the "state" is necessarily all that, since it is nothing other than the framework and the consequence of the will's activity. It is what the will wills in order to be able to realize itself. All of modern politi-

cal philosophy, which founds legitimate political order on the will of the
human individual, thinks as Hegel does. Or rather Hegel, in conformity
with the interpretation he himself gives of his work, articulates thoroughly
the meaning of modern political philosophy, what it means in the twofold
sense of the expression.

Once the human will as the reasonable will of each man is genuinely
engaged and inscribed in the workings of political institutions—the critical accomplishment of the French revolution—the political order is from
that point onward intrinsically satisfying, as Hegel also emphasized.
There may be a divergence of appreciation, and thus a difference of satisfaction, between those who consider that what the reasonable will wills is
here and now achieved—the party of order or the *status quo*, the right—
and those who esteem that this is as yet only realized imperfectly and
important reforms are needed, even a revolution that would be the last
effort in the realization—the party of movement and progress, the left; but
for the essentials, if he considers the institutions of modern democracy
inasmuch as they realize the principle of the reasonable will, modern man,
at least a reasonable modern man, is necessarily satisfied. Politically, he
desires nothing else but what he has. Indeed, what can one desire other
than what he wills? Since modern democracy is the regime founded on the
human will, how can the will will anything other than this democracy? In
willing democracy, the will wills itself.

IV

In terms that differ greatly from Hegel's, Tocqueville introduces us to similar thoughts when he unfolds before our eyes how democracy is irresistible. This characterization had a twofold aspect. It signifies on the one
hand that modern peoples, democratic peoples, will never consent to any
other social regime than the one founded on the equality of individuals
and that any return to "aristocracy" is henceforth impossible. No difference in condition can survive for long, even less be revived, once it is generally admitted that there is no legitimate obedience other than one to
which consent has been previously given. And once the principle of the
will or consent has been isolated and identified, how can one consent to a
regime that is not founded on consent? How can one consent not to consent? How can one at once will and not will? But irresistibility means on
the other hand that democracy is destined to spread its power indefinitely
over democratic man: more and more actions, feelings, thoughts, "contents of life" irresistibly come under the sovereignty of democracy. As is
well known, it is in America that Tocqueville discovered the import of the
democratic idea, that is, the democratic will. "Thus in the United States

the creative principle underlying the republic is the same as that which
controls the greater part of human actions."[7] The principle of consent, set
in motion by the will of the individual, penetrates and rearranges the relations that appeared up to then invariably inscribed in the eternal order of
human nature and above all the relations between parents and children,
and man and woman, or in the eternal order of the world, especially those
which constitute religion.

Consequently, for Tocqueville, unlike the Greek philosophers, democracy and aristocracy are not two political regimes always and equally possible in the framework of a natural order that encompasses still other regimes that are as legitimate, or more so; it is rather a matter of the two
great successive regimes of human life, about which he says, "they are like
two distinct kinds of humanity."[8] The regime of the human will triumphs
over and replaces all other regimes. It seems to be, then, something more
and other than a novel political regime, however satisfying it may be: it
brings forth, Tocqueville tells us, a "new humanity."

Once liberty is severed from free will, once the will emancipates itself
from nature, nature evidently no longer can have value as the comprehen-
sive framework in which one dwells and interprets human things. The
appearance of the regime of the will rejects all other regimes in a movement forward that can be considered from a decisively superior perspective. Whether this "advance" is conceived as an order of nature and force,
or again as an order of tradition and religion, it designates the epoch when
humanity was still "immature." Indeed, when the Greek philosophers isolated the idea of "nature" or *phusis*, and thereby constituted philosophy
itself, they severed themselves and us from the rule of tradition and religion, which were consigned to the plane of "convention" and the rule of
nomos. *Phusis* and *nomos* are clearly two opposite poles, but once the will
emancipated itself, this polarity was toned down. Nature and tradition, or
convention, came to resemble one another as two orders wherein the
human will is equally, though differently, subjected. The world of classical
philosophy, the world of "hierarchical nature" and thus of inequality and
force, and the various traditional worlds now form a single "ancient
world."

This ancient world can be characterized according to one or the other of
the poles it brings together and appears to reconcile or to confuse. It can be
designated as the world of nature or substance, which is succeeded by the
world of the will or subject. But, in a contrary sense, it can be maintained
that the apparently universal idea of nature, and thus of philosophy, is at
bottom only an expression of the particularity of the Greeks, one of their
"singular institutions," the *logos* an expression of their *muthos*, the idea of
phusis a consequence of their *nomos*. In practice, the two theses are often
found together in the same account without the author showing the least

embarrassment. The new opposition has deprived the first of any force and has therefore made the two poles interchangeable. The appearance of the will causes the liberating prestige of ancient nature to fade and thereby obscures the original meaning of philosophy.

Whatever the case may be, once these two "distinct humanities," "aristocracy" and "democracy," are seen or made to appear, the need arises for a link or common element that holds them together in some fashion. The element that penetrates both humanities and moves from one to the other, the one element in which man can still live and think once his will has raised itself above his nature, we take to be History. Man is a "historical being" because, or if, his will is stronger than his nature.

In this way we discover again in another context what we were saying in the first chapter, that the idea of History finds its motive and foundation in a polarity between the New and the Old, which the old nature is no longer strong enough to reduce. But it is not yet time to join the threads of the two developments. Let us simply note once again that the question of the classification of political regimes is in no way a formal question, but one that gives access to the essential. And just as the lack of a place for the English regime in Montesquieu's new classification had provided the impetus to our first investigations, we can here begin our inquiry concerning the modern regime of the will by basing ourselves on the powerfully significant fact that, whereas ancient democracy enters into a classification of political regimes, modern democracy does not.

V

To begin to make ourselves aware of the significance of this difference, let us listen in turn to Aristotle and Rousseau. Aristotle writes:

> Now the reason for there being a number of regimes is that there are a number of parts in any city (households, the well off and the poor, different occupations, differences based on family and virtue). . . . It is evident, therefore, that there must necessarily be a number of regimes differing from one another in kind, since these parts differ from one another in kind.[9]

One could not be more obliging with regard to the plurality and diversity of elements within the city, as well as the consequent plurality and diversity of political regimes among which several are legitimate. Without going back on this generous appreciation, Aristotle next remarks, as if it were a meteorological fact, that this diversity tends to crystallize into two great tendencies:

> [T]here are held to be two sorts of regimes particularly: just as in the case of winds some are called northern and others southern and the others deviations

from these, so [many hold there are] two sorts of regimes, [rule by] the people and oligarchy.[10]

For Aristotle, the political problem is naturally susceptible of several good, albeit unequally good, solutions. Rousseau gives us an inkling of the intransigent and unambiguous character of modern democracy by the way he characterizes the act of the will that is the social contract, the principle and source of this democracy: "The clauses of this contract are so completely determined by the nature of the act that the slightest modification would render them null and void."[11]

Thus, for Rousseau, there is only one good solution to the political problem: the will can only will, and it can will only what it wills.

Aristotle's motley list of the city's constitutive elements, and thus of Greek democracy, proves that the city, and thus Greek democracy, is basically pluralistic. On the other hand, as Rousseau's formulas demonstrate, modern democracy is and wills itself to be monistic, since it recognizes as legitimate but one constitutive element, the individual will. The intensity and strangeness of the contrast are underlined by the fact that the only element retained by Rousseau is absent from Aristotle's listing. How can two philosophers, both of whom are esteemed to be supremely competent, formulate the political problem in such different terms? Aristotle's line of reasoning needs to be looked at more closely.

VI

To the question, what is the city or what constitutes the identity of the city, Aristotle answers that it is its constitution or government, its political regime or *politeia*. But just what is a political regime? It is a particular understanding of justice, the conclusion of a debate that is both explicit and implicit and that takes place or could take place within the city on the subject of what is just and what is unjust. Practically, as the passage cited above shows, in an actual city the debate takes place between the oligarch and the democrat. Instead of constructing political legitimacy, political justice, starting from a prepolitical "state of nature" as will the modern doctrines of the social contract, Aristotle's inquiry starts from the opinions on justice as they are formulated in the real city, in the public square: it takes seriously the citizen's viewpoint on politics.[12] I cannot here follow the thread of Aristotle's subtle analysis as it unfolds in book 3 of *Politics* and must limit myself to a few remarks.

Aristotle writes that "all fasten on a certain sort of justice, but proceed only to a certain point, and do not speak of the whole of justice in its authoritative sense."[13] Thus both parties have a real and positive rapport with justice, but neither party grasps the whole of justice. Every opinion about justice is necessarily an opinion on the nature and end of the city, or its raison d'être. Every opinion regarding politics is a political opinion: it concerns the Whole, it puts the citizen is an emotional and intellectual rapport with the Whole. One could say that the citizen cannot refrain from thinking and from thinking politically. Thus the oligarchs, basing their rights to govern on their superiority in wealth, assume or imply that the city is a sort of commercial society with limited responsibility, a joint-stock company one could say, where the political privileges of each are proportionate to his fortune: to each according to his capital. The democrats who invoke the equal liberty of all citizens and rest content with this purely formal principle deprive the city of every substantial goal and reduce it to a sort of defensive alliance against every injustice.[14] To be a citizen comes down to not being oppressed. In reality, according to Aristotle's correction of both understandings, the city's raison d'être is "to make the citizens good and just."[15]

To be sure, everyone, even those most intent on following Aristotle, smiles at these last words. But a moment's reflection erases this patronizing smile that greets every mention of virtue.[16] If one wishes to be able to judge regarding what is just in the city and thus what a just city is—and who would not want to, if it were only to know whether or not it is hampered by the actual organization of the regime in which he lives?—it is necessary to know the city's raison d'être. What other end could the city have but to produce, which is to say educate, citizens who are "good and just" and by that very fact happy? Would one want the city to prefer that they be wicked, unjust, and unhappy? The nature of this goodness and happiness still remains indeterminate here, but we begin to have the inkling, and thus the desire, of a justice that is devoid of any partisan partiality.

If the true end of the city is happiness and virtue, it must be governed by those who contribute the most to these goals, by the virtuous, those who engage in "noble actions."[17] But in that case it will exclude from its honors, and then, in fact, from itself, the great mass of citizens.[18] The city will no longer be but a small part of itself: the *true* city will be but a small part of the *real* city. If the city is governed exclusively according to its end, then it is no longer the city that is so governed. It is in this context, it seems to me, that the problem of democracy arises for Aristotle. The demands of the many, the poor, are no more founded than those of the rich, and they are certainly less so than those of the virtuous. But if the city they demand is not truly a city, neither is the one that excludes them truly a city. For the city to be truly a city, the great number must have a part in the city, that is to say in certain magistracies, in particular the judiciary. In order to resolve this problem of the composition of the whole and the parts, Aristotle advances or confirms democratic arguments. To summarize both the neatness and the limits of the democratic moment in the thought of Aristotle, one might say that the demands of the multitude are justified in the measure that they are satisfied, that is, in the measure that the multitude really participates in the wealth and virtue of the city.

But to form a complete idea of the problem of justice, we must take into account not only the opinion of the democrats, but also that of the oligarchs. We will then say that the just is both a kind of equality (according to the opinion of the democrats) and a kind of inequality (as the oligarchs see it). Now, what sort of equality or what sort of inequality is a proper qualification to participate in political power? Aristotle emphasizes with a certain solemnity that "this involves a question, and political philosophy."[19]

If political offices, at least the eminent ones, must be distributed according to a certain superiority or inequality, the question is superiority or inequality in what? It cannot be any sort of superiority. In effect, the best flute would not be given to the one who is most well-born or richest, but to the one who plays this instrument the best. To give the best flute to the richest, for example, would be to suppose that any good whatever is comparable or commensurate with any other good, which is impossible.[20] Thus, "it is clear that in political matters too it is reasonable for them not to dispute over offices on the basis of every inequality. . . . The dispute necessarily occurs in respect to those things that constitute a city."[21]

We know that these elements are, for example, birth, liberty, wealth, virtue, military valor. Thus nobles, freemen, and the wealthy legitimately claim a share of the honors, as do the just and courageous. But we have become alert to the problem of the commensurability of goods. How can the goods that are simply necessary to the life of the city, riches and liberty for example, be compared and find a common measure with the goods that contribute directly and positively to the end of the city, as does virtue? A superiority in riches or in virtue calls for a corresponding superiority in the political order, for riches and virtue are elements of the political order. But what does "corresponding" mean? How much virtue equals how much wealth?[22] One is tempted to say that wealth is no more commensurable with virtue than with the art of the flute, except in the sense that wealth and virtue, unlike the flutist's art, are both properly political elements of the city.

The problem is insoluble theoretically. Yet it must be resolved if the city is to exist and it is in practice resolved since cities do exist. What does that mean?

Aristotle advances two propositions simultaneously. On the one hand, "there is a question affecting all of those who dispute over political honors";[23] and on the other hand, "the judgment as to who should rule is not disputed under each (regime)."[24] Thus a political regime is defined by the way it gives a practical and authoritative answer to the question—the "aporia" or stumbling block which theory cannot resolve—of the justice of political honors. The political problem is thus defined by the tension, which can never be completely overcome, between the unquestionable judgment or decision—the *krisis*, the active characteristic and the very form of every real regime, and the insoluble aporia that is the question of the just or the good.

Every political regime, as a particular regime, imposes a solution to an insoluble problem. It authoritatively puts an end to the interminable dialogue about justice, about the commensurability or incommensurability of goods. It mandates a certain equivalence between virtue, wealth, and liberty, a certain relative value, if one wishes, to the different elements of the city. In this sense, political justice, because it is constrained to impose or to accept comparisons or equivalences that are admittedly approximate between goods, and accomplishes what political theory is incapable of conceiving since it necessarily uncovers the impossibility of such comparisons. But this superiority of practice over theory in Aristotle's political doctrine must not be interpreted as a manifestation of the philosopher's "empiricism." Contrary to modern political science, for which reality is what it is exactly and precisely while science is "approximate," in the best of cases "asymptotic," for Aristotelian political science, science is exact and reality is approximate, since it is a labor of approximation.

There is thus here a real indetermination which no science can abolish. And whoever wishes to compose a political order or influence its composition is constrained in order to master this indetermination as much as it can be mastered, to say and to do more than he knows, or something other than what he knows. Pathetically interpreted, this situation makes man appear as the "arbitrary creator of his values." But in truth, why imagine man facing the abyss, Caspar Friedrich? No need to cry out, Zarathustra! Indetermination is not an abyss, but the complexity that holds out the promise of the good. Political man resembles rather a painter who has placed his easel by the pleasure gardens and asks himself how he will harmonize the acid green of the grass with the ravishing red of the skirt.

Just how does Aristotle teach political men the art of composition? How does he teach real cities the art of achieving the impossible and necessary commensuration in the least inexact way possible?

Since excessive claims which are unjust and founded on one particular element of the city cannot be refuted by appealing to another element—the diverse elements, or goods have no common measure—each claim will be subject to critique by itself. For example, the oligarchs who found their political claims on their superiority in wealth will be told that they can be surpassed in riches either by a multibillionaire or by the multitude itself.

The virtuous are exposed to an objection of the same type. The democrats, who will take into account only the status of the free man, will be told that the argument of "free birth" is an argument founded on "birth" no less than on "liberty," and that this is, after all, comparable to the argument of the well born:[25] the poor, too, take the pain to be born.

Thus, if all the claims founded on the possession of a constitutive element of the city are in some way justified, they are all no less equally susceptible of being refuted by the very principles they invoke. Every claimant then is led by prudence and, at bottom, by logic, to moderate his claims. In advancing his claim, each proposes a certain equivalence between his own good and the goods of others, a certain relative measure of the goods that constitute the city, which is generally not unfavorable to it. Faced with having to acknowledge that this equivalence is less certain than it seemed to him at first, he moderates his claim and lowers the relative measure of his own good. The result is the practical commensuration of the theoretically incommensurable goods.

The compromises that prudence concedes have only the name in common with those that cowardice lets itself submit to. The latter come from a feeble heart; the former are born of a judgment of the intellect. In the act of true prudence, I honestly put in doubt the first approximation, the first equivalence I had advanced. The criticism, perhaps the opposition, I aroused make me reconsider what at first seemed to be the best composition of the political good. I had conceived for my party, my children, or myself, the place that corresponded to the truth of its principles, the illustrious character of their lineage, or the extent of my merits; I recognize now that the truth of this first composition is not certain, in any case it cannot be proven and I need to revise my judgment. It will be said that in most compromises, even the honorable ones, the motive for the new moderation is necessity or conveniency and rarely, if ever, an intellectual change. That is perhaps true in the ordinary compromises that are made so to speak without thinking about the matter, like letting the driver coming from the left go first at an intersection. As soon as the stakes are important, the compromise needs to be worked out at a more thoughtful level and concludes in a judgment that requires thought. Besides, neither conveniency nor even necessity are easily recognized. Whether in a given compromise it is a matter of my party, my family, or myself, I reduce my claims so that our or my good will be more compatible with the good of others, which is to say with the other goods. Thanks to this moderation, the sum of the goods in which my party, my family, or I myself will share will be increased. To conceive a compromise is first of all to resolve intellectually a difficult problem of composition by working out and then proposing a new equivalence that measures a smaller part of a greater sum of goods.

We can see now how the human significance of political power took shape.

Thanks to political power, every good can exist, endure, and affirm itself in the human world, and at the same time communicate and "live together" with the other goods. One needs to pause to reflect on these two apparently contradictory characteristics which nonetheless, when taken together, constitute the secret of power. The true secret of power, the *arcanum imperii*, is that political power makes it possible for the different goods to be at home together in the human world and at the same time for each good to be measured against other goods without detriment to its own worth. The first aspect, the "open" or "offensive" aspect, enlarges the human world and expresses itself above all in outright military conquest. The second aspect, the "closed or "defensive" one, provides a protective cover for the good and acts as closed doors and high cypress walls.

Power is eminently dangerous because the task of deciding *aporia* and exercising *krisis* brings with it the temptation to impose such uneven equivalences, preferring goods so meager and lowly that the whole structure of the human good collapses and the ideological satisfaction of a handful of fanatics becomes the equivalent of the life of races or classes of men. But power is also eminently beneficent since, thanks to the participation of the different goods in one and the same organization of power, regime, or city, man can find all the human goods near to hand around him and be self-sufficient in tune with the specific composition of his regime or city.[26]

The statesman thus has a particularly noble and delicate task. He must give each good its due, in conformity with the intrinsic dignity of this good as he judges it. In making this judgment, he applies a principle of personal and private appreciation, for example, of a philosophical or religious sort. But he must do it in such a way as to assure the integration of all the goods in the unity of the same city. Here he acts in his specifically political role of statesman whose task is to preserve and promote the common good.[27]

The common good is not a good that can be isolated from the different goods and elements that constitute the city. Nor is it a sort of common denominator, unlike the good of self-preservation which for the modern philosophers will be the foundation of human rights. It is both the supreme good and the good which binds the different goods together that can have no direct rapport with one another because they are incommensurable. It is the good without which the other goods could not coexist, that is, could not be present at all in the human world.

One sees why the individual with his will does not appear as such as a theme in Aristotle's *Politics*. The true elements of the city are the goals or motives of action of the individuals, that is, their goods. Aristotle's "pluralism," or, if one wishes, his "liberalism" does not lie in the recognition of

the equal rights of free individuals, but in his affirmation of the simultaneous presence of diverse and unequal goods in the same city and his
recommendation that the groups particularly attached to these various
goods and thus particularly apt to produce or at least preserve them ought
to take part, in unequal ways to be sure, in the government or magistracies.

The city's constitutive element is not the will but the different goods
that the will is able to will.

VII

As I have underlined, Aristotle always takes the political claim seriously.
He speaks of human groups and their goods and deals with "spiritual
masses" and "contents of life." Now if we leap over the centuries and turn
to Aristotle's great modern critic, we observe that Thomas Hobbes, on the
contrary, treats the political claim with derision, as an expression of individual vanity. This difference gives us access to the difference which characterizes modern politics.

For Aristotle, I recall, the various political claims are both founded and
open to question, since the human good is complex, uncertain, and diverse; it is because they are both that their partisans can coexist in the
same city. For Hobbes, on the contrary, the fact that all the claims are
exposed to objections is the sign that none of them is justified. Where Aristotle discerns the beginnings of a dialogue on justice worthy of the philosopher's serious attention, Hobbes sees a comic scene where each candidate
for power throws out his chest and vaunts his merit without equal. Perhaps one should say it is a tragicomedy since the weakest can always kill
the strongest through trickery or alliance with others, thereby refuting his
own pretensions to superiority. In every political debate, it is ultimately a
matter of vanity, the vainglory of one man that there is no reason to prefer
to another man's.[28] Hobbes "individualizes" and "psychologizes" political claims. Where the Greeks esteemed the citizen's public voice, the Englishman unmasks the individual's private passion.

Why does Hobbes treat every political claim to power and every affirmation of superiority with such disdain, to the point of seeing Aristotle's
broad statements on human inequality as manifestations of the personal
vanity of Alexander's wise preceptor? Why does he interrupt, before it has
even begun, the dialogue on the just or the good that Aristotle described so
carefully and analyzed so subtly in book 3 of the *Politics*, and which he
saw as the wellspring of both common life and political philosophy? This
brutality heralds the deliberate coarseness of Locke in reducing the question of the sovereign good to a choice among apples, plums, and oranges,

as we saw in section 9 of chapter 4. Why does modern philosophy fling such sarcasm on the very question of philosophy, the question that is philosophy itself?

It must be admitted that there is something, in the eyes of Hobbes and his successors, that makes this dialogue on justice simply impossible. I was saying above that the statesman's task was to assure the best possible commensuration and integration of the different goods in the unity of the same city. But what does one do once the city itself becomes divided, when there is no longer one but two cities, the human city and the city of God? The political and philosophical dialogue on justice is interrupted and in fact prohibited by the eruption of religious claims, or certain religious claims. The pretensions of the Catholic church and those of different Protestant sects that, emulating the Catholics, proclaim themselves the holiest or the only holy ones, are by definition absolutely incommensurable with any other claim, just as eternal salvation is incommensurable with temporal salvation and eternity is incommensurable with time.

Aristotle had foreseen the case of an absolutely disproportionate superiority, the case of the family or person "so outstanding in virtue that this virtue is more preeminent than that of all the rest."[29] He then proposed, as the only solution in conformity with justice, to grant him all power, but not without first giving serious consideration to the solution of ostracism.[30] The Middle Ages, when Aristotle came to the fore again, will naturally countenance, if I dare say, these two solutions. The Catholic church, in keeping with the idea it held of itself, its virtue, and its mission, judged itself founded to benefit from the first solution and staked its claim, as *vera perfectaque respublica*, if not to all power, at least to the *plenitudo potestatis*. The adversaries of its temporal power, such as Dante, employed all the resources of their imagination to work out the most honorable and rigorous form of ostracism by setting up the whole human world as a self-sufficient universal body politic under the power of the emperor. Aristotle was of no help in this, or worse, the resources were not at hand to solve a problem when the principle of the solution can yield two strictly contradictory solutions with equal plausibility and legitimacy. It appeared necessary to break completely with Aristotle. By radically changing the terms of the problem, Hobbes was to find the simple and unambiguous solution by which we still live today.

Since among the candidates for power in the Christian world there is at least one who is always so to speak outside the game, a player who always has the trump card in hand, an interlocutor whose speech comes from God himself, the configuration of power can no longer arise, as in Aristotle's city, from the natural play of the political community, the spontaneous and then developed dialogue on justice and the good. Power must be created wholly from scratch, it must be fabricated artificially, that is, voluntarily, by the purely voluntary act that is the contract. Henceforth power, or the state, and society will be two realms apart from one another, or at least separated one from the other.

In order for this astonishing scheme to be conceived and put into practice, first all claims to power, and not only those of a religious origin, must be radically disqualified. All will be, including those of a religious origin, if, that is, a power is set up that does not entail any vested interest, without social or religious foundations, a pure power with no other content but itself nor any other cause but pure will. The power created by the contract neither expresses nor serves the claims of the priests, nor those of the nobles, the rich, the mighty, or the wise; it results from the will of every man as man, from the purity and universality of that will. In this way alone can it be sovereign or absolute. Its title is without common measure, strictly incommensurable with all other political claims since its law of construction makes it the only power that is properly willed, that is to say, *authorized*.

But can a power be willed purely, solely for itself? Isn't the contract set in motion by motives that have nothing "pure" in them? The will that wills the absolute or sovereign power of the modern state expects that the state will protect the life of all. More precisely, each will is set in motion by each individual's desire for protection. In this sense this will wills something more than the power of the state, it wills a good that is not the common good, but which is the common denominator and condition for the possibility of all the goods that individuals can desire: the preservation of life and the integrity of its members. Every individual desires this good and wills the means to protects it. The good is particular, but the means is of necessity general: every individual is protected only if all are. Willing this general means the will, unlike the desire that moves it, is general, or disinterested, or pure. Pure power is indeed the work of the pure will.

For all that, this creation is voluntary, it is not fortuitous or arbitrary. The will is naturally motivated by the unbearable situation that prevails in the state of nature, that is in society deprived of a sovereign state. The war of all claims and of all opinions, in short the war of every man against every man, is in the eyes of Hobbes the truth regarding the dialogue about justice and the good. At this point, a digression is in order.

VIII

The difference we are seeking to pin down between the political viewpoints of Hobbes and Aristotle is at bottom the one that in general separates modern man from ancient philosophy, the one which separates, for example, the approach or rather the method of Descartes from that of Aristotle or Plato.

Descartes, Aristotle, and Plato all have the same starting point established by Socrates, that all human opinions need to be examined and for that reason are open to question or doubt.[31] But the Greek philosophers considered that, as uncertain as they may be, opinions are the only means we have to move toward the truth. Through the dialogue of opinions, or dialectics, one can rise above what each opinion has in it that is incomplete and, to that extent, false. Aristotle offers us an admirable example of this approach in book 3 of the *Politics*, as we saw in section 6.[32] Descartes, on the contrary, maintains that, since all opinions are doubtful, one has to go all the way to the end of this doubt and even beyond it and posit or "imagine" that all opinions are false: "I thought it necessary . . . that I reject as absolutely false everything in which I could imagine the least doubt, as to see whether, after this process, anything in my set of beliefs remains that is entirely indubitable."[33]

As is well known, Descartes's "cogito ergo sum" provides the first "entirely indubitable" proposition, the starting point from which the edifice of rigorously true knowledge can be built.

The gesture with which Hobbes derisively reduces to so many displays of vainglory the claims to superiority that are open to question, as all of them are, needs to be set next to Descartes's "hyperbolic" doubt that rejects all doubtful opinions, as all of them are, as absolutely false. In both cases, the will of the philosopher, cutting short what would have been for Aristotle a long and complex dialectical debate, comes to the fore in an abrupt way. In what appeared as a *chiaroscuro*, he opts to see only darkness, and in what is poorly ordered, he chooses to see only chaos.[34]

As we have already suggested, what Hobbes calls the "war of every man against every man" is in sum the "hyperbolical" depiction of the confrontation of opinions. The negative experience of war or darkness leads in both cases to the first positive experience, which is in both cases that of the simple life or existence: of the brute fact of existence, with the consequences it contains implicitly. That is the point of departure of the affirmation and construction of the new order of certain knowledge and absolute sovereignty.

As decisive and foundational as Hobbes's approach is for the development of modern politics, Descartes has the honor of being the hero of modern thought, and is thus the modern hero par excellence.[35] He is himself the subject matter of his book and the object of his experience. Without needing to, he places himself in an extreme situation, the worst possible for the human mind, that of general and absolute doubt. One recalls the impressive comparisons he uses to describe it: he is henceforth "like a man who walks alone and in the shadows";[36] it is, he says anxiously in the first person, "as if I had suddenly fallen into a deep whirlpool."[37] He chooses to place himself, without needing to, in what political men call the "state of emergency" or "state of exception," to which they generally have recourse only under pressure of necessity. Now, in the words of Carl Schmitt, the great theoretician of the state of exception who also considered himself a disciple of Hobbes, "the sovereign decides regarding the state of exception."[38] Descartes is the sovereign, the absolute sovereign of his experience of doubt.

I know of no text whose author shows such a sense of his own assurance and certainty than Descartes's account of his experience of total doubt:

> Thus I will suppose not a supremely good God, the source of truth, but rather an evil genius, as clever and deceitful as he is powerful, who has directed his entire effort to misleading me. I will regard the heavens, the air, the earth, colors, shapes, sounds, and all external things as nothing but the deceptive games of my dreams, with which he lays snares for my credulity. I will regard myself as having no hands, no eyes, no flesh, no blood, no senses, but as nevertheless falsely believing that I possess all these things. I will remain resolutely fixed in this meditation, and, even if it be out of my power to know anything true, certainly it is within my power to take care resolutely to withhold my assent to what is false, lest this deceiver, powerful and clever as he is, have an effect on me.[39]

The experience of voluntary doubt is not primarily that of the search for truth, for a first truth, although it is that too; it is above all the experience of the sovereignty of the will over the conditions of human experience. Every extension of doubt is an extension of the empire of the will, to the point where the will is capable of conquering an "evil genius," that is, to prevent it from leading the judgment astray. Nothing in human experience, whether real or even only possible, is capable of having an effect on the will, which is absolutely sovereign. Moreover, the exercise of the will in doubt becomes the decisive experience for man.

It will be said that all this is as old as philosophy, as old in any case as skepticism. But this is not at all a matter of skepticism. On the contrary, the philosopher of hyperbolic doubt is the least skeptical of philosophers.

If it were only a matter of "rightly conducting one's reason" and "seeking the truth," one could simply start from the idea of God which, in Descartes's technical language, contains so much "objective reality" that "no idea is truer in its own right, and there is no idea in which less suspicion of falsity is to be found," to the point that "although such a being can perhaps be imagined not to exist, it nevertheless cannot be imagined that this idea shows me nothing real." With the idea of God it is impossible to "imagine"; "of all those that are in me, the idea that I have of him is the most true, the most clear, and the most distinct."[40]

Descartes doubts, or "imagines" to doubt, what common sense takes to be most evident, such as the existence of the body itself—of this hand which is writing the word "hand"—and considers the existence of God as almost evident,[41] to the point of putting in doubt one's own doubt and the possibility, here, of the "imagined" doubt: the idea that stands for the richest reality—the idea of God—is also for us the clearest idea. The conjunction of the sovereignty of the human will and the accessibility of the idea of God defines Descartes's position and in effect makes him the true father of the Enlightenment. By this conjunction he places man in a position of never encountering anything obscure. Every aspect of experience that isn't perfectly transparent is suspended as doubtful, and then illuminated as certain; every object is reduced to its share of clarity. Natural light, of which the will disposes, becomes coextensive with human experience. Or rather there now remains only one experience, which is the substitute of all the others, even and above all of doubt, the experience that the mind has by its own light.

Before we stray any further, let us return to our subject and establish this point firmly: the inquiry pursued by Descartes and Hobbes follows a rhythm unknown to classical philosophy. By starting resolutely with negation, the will gives itself an advantage that it will never again lose.

IX

To return more specifically to Hobbes, it seems to make sense that if all political claims are equally illegitimate, they are thus only claims to power. If to claim power, or some power, in the name of religion or virtue or wealth or liberty comes down in each case to a display of vainglory, then the appeal to religion, virtue, wealth, or liberty is a vain appearance, a disguise of the desire for power. What they really want, all just as they are, is not power to . . ., or the power of . . ., but power for the sake of power. This conclusion, in turn, springs from its premises and reinforces them: if all want only power for power's sake, then their avowed motives show their worth, which is nil. In brief, the wellspring of human life is the desire for power. As we have seen in section 2 of chapter 4, every man is a quantum of power.

It would be idle to seek to compare this "conception of power" with Aristotle's, for whom there is no "power," neither as an institution nor a passion. As I tried to show above in analyzing certain aspects of book 3 of Aristotle's *Politics*, what we call power is in his eyes an articulation of the human world that overcomes and preserves the incommensurability of the diversity of goods and thus the perilous and generous indetermination of the good. The manner in which this is accomplished is in each instance what the Greeks call the regime or *politeia*. Hence their conceptual tool for thinking about politics is not power but regime. Once power becomes a passion of the individual, the passion to be first and to acquire the means to satisfy his future desires, whatever they may be, power finds its name but loses its breadth and noble ambiguity. This terrible simplification makes it a very convenient principle for explaining human behavior, and thus a very promising principle for constructing new institutions. After all, the most satisfying political forms are not necessarily those which best reflect the starry skies above.

When what was an articulation of the world becomes a passion of the soul, a matter of "psychology," a twofold process is occurring, or rather two successive processes are unfolding. First, the finesse of the psychological analysis paradoxically undergoes a marked diminution. As marvelously human as Hobbes is, his understanding of our nature is not well served by his reduction of human desires to the desire for power. From simplification to simplification, from Hobbes to Locke then to the utilitarians, the explanation of human behavior will be increasingly abstract and mechanical. Such a degradation and obscuring of the image of man and his self-consciousness, ended up evoking a reaction among sensitive natures who, like Rousseau or Nietzsche, will strive to recover the lost human complexity. Allan Bloom has shed valuable light on the very interesting case of Rousseau.[42] For his part, Nietzsche, the prisoner of the polemical and reactive logic he otherwise unmasked so well, corrected Hobbes by exaggerating and generalizing him. The ungrateful Nietzsche was never lacking in sarcastic remarks about "English ideas," but it was under the heading of the "will to power" that he sought to grasp anew the breadth and nuances of the human world.

The example of Nietzsche helps to explain the intellectual disorder so peculiar to the nineteenth century and why it was "the epoch of world-conceptions." The broad Greek phenomenology that was taken up, confirmed, critiqued, modified, and obscured by the Christian tradition had in the end been reduced by the Enlightenment to the kind of psychology we call English psychology, which, for the reasons we have just given, was untenable. But it was also extraordinarily difficult to replace, since the whole ethical history of the West, with its complex affinities and opposition, culminated in this puniness. In order to escape its hold, it would have been necessary at least to unscramble its exact genealogy with great care and effort and above all impartiality. But the route starting from the back was not taken and instead, filled with hope, sights were set to looking ahead. Psychology might be abstract, but the century had seen the outpouring of the inexhaustible source of the concrete: World-History, *die Weltgeschichte*. Without mincing, the high road was taken and the history of the world was made to enter into this psychology. Marx, the optimistic Englishman, made no attempt to revise it: history is a gigantomachy of interests. Nietzsche, it is true, proposed a genealogy, or rather several. Unfortunately, he neglected the genealogy of the "historical viewpoint" to which he was as subject as any man of his time. He refused to deal with the difficulty and thus extended the abstract Hobbesian psychology of power over all aspects of the concrete human phenomenon, over the "historical" diversity of "cultures" and religions. His genius drew some flashes from this exercise against nature, but it could not be relied on. Despite the intricate details and varied shading, it was always a matter of connecting one with the other, and even to make coincide, an abstract psychological scheme, residue of many centuries of contradictory distillations and the whole of the human phenomenon, compressed and reduced to History. The two things were yet without rapport, since they did not belong to a Whole that was common to both, being each a residue or distillation of the human Whole. Being able always to make a rapport between two things without rapport, whatever they may be, that is precisely in what a "worldview" consists. Now, in the element of Cartesian light, everything can be put into rapport with everything since, regardless of its being, this is always a matter of thought. The master of suspicion, Descartes, still relied on the least skeptical of philosophers whom, ever the ingrate, he deemed "superficial."

But what evil genius has led us to a new digression? We have to come back to the Hobbesian conception of power, which holds one of the great secrets of the physiognomy and trajectory of modern politics.

Once the claims to power have been subjected to the greatest power men can imagine, the only legitimate absolute power, the Sovereign, they undergo a remarkable mutation: they are all justified. General accusation and reprobation give way to no less general excuse and approbation. To define man as desire for power is simultaneously to accuse and to justify him. Let us take a closer look at this political and moral mystery that is the key to so many things.

If man is naturally, and thus necessarily, avid for power, the warrant of superiority he invokes is necessarily moot and worthless, and cannot legitimate any power; but once pure power, legitimate power, the power of the impartial state, is founded, then the desires for power are free and justified—within the limits authorized by the sovereign power—precisely because they are necessary. Men will continue—who could reproach them for doing so?—to want to be the wealthiest, most virtuous, most learned, and in this sense the most powerful, but the sovereign is there to see to it that their ambitions have no direct political effects. For example, contrary to what Aristotle thought, being wealthy is no longer in itself a warrant to a share in power: the wealthy man is just as subject to the sovereign as the poor man. But the wealthy man is now freer than ever to become ever wealthier.

The Aristotelian or classical solution, of the political problem repeats in some way the terms of the problem: each part of the Whole must participate in the Whole. Since the political problem is a problem of arranging "contents of life" no less than groups, several solutions are conceivable and legitimate. It could be said that there are several legitimate regimes because the problem is "bigger" than its solutions. The problem of the commensuration of goods is "bigger" than man, at least in his political capacity. The Aristotelian or classical solution repeats the problem because Aristotle maintains his heroically moderate position against all temptations: all political opinions are simultaneously and inseparably justified and open to challenge. The Hobbesian solution, we could say the modern solution, consists in radically separating these two aspects of affirmation and negation and attributing to each a different "moment." Being radically separated, negation and affirmation no longer moderate one another and are no longer reconcilable at a higher level of complete political justice. Instead, each makes of itself an extreme in such a way that all human claims, after being seen in the first moment as absolutely unjustified inasmuch as they were claims to power, in the second moment find themselves all justified as liberties or claims to liberty. This separation and ascent to the extremes of negation and affirmation imply and underlie the separation between state and society.

The attentive reader may have noted the lack of certainty over the number of "moments." There are in reality three moments: first, the unlimited affirmation of claims to power in the "state of nature"; next, the absolute negation of these claims by the sovereign; and finally, the affirmation of each man's liberty with no intrinsic limit. The second and third moments are visible and institutionalized in the state and society, respectively; the first, the moment of nature, although it conditions the other two, remains on the whole invisible since it is mixed and fused with the third.

XI

The state makes the will's sovereignty real and efficacious. The will accedes to sovereignty in and through the separation and succession of the two moments of general prohibition and general authorization identified by Hobbes. The first consists in eliminating all human goods, all "contents of life" from the political, that is the public, domain; the second consists in giving them a free and inviolable space designated as "private." The separation of state and society that is the powerful engine of modern liberty hangs on this twofold act of the will. More than any other, the modern regime is *cosa mentale.*

XII

The thinker who sensed more than any other the strange character of this spiritual decision of negation-affirmation that gave rise to and sustained the separation of state and society is commonly referred to as "the young Marx." Because Marx was the most naturally Aristotelian of modern philosophers, he understood better than the others the upheaval implied in the privatization of what he called "the material and cultural elements which formed the life experience" of individuals.[43] He saw that the political elevation of man—"die politische Erhebung"—above his life experience both "annihilated" and "presupposed" religion, birth, social rank, education, occupation—in brief, the parts of the body politic according to Aristotle, to which was now added religion.[44] He saw the political emancipation characteristic of modern democracy as a considerable advance; but the definitive liberation, total human emancipation, would entail the reuniting of the sovereign will and the contents of life. Of course, the perspective of such a reunion was a "revolutionary illusion" on Marx's part since the sovereignty of the will, which is the condition of human emancipation as well of as of political elevation, presupposes just this separation. But one could just as well say that in this very illusion Marx was faithful to the spirit of classical philosophy and to that extent was a "conservative," since he did not imagine that this separation could hold or last. He did not imagine that the will could live indefinitely separated from its motives, that is, the "world": it was going to create for itself a new social world after annihilating the ancient world of the motives that alienated it. Marx casts himself into a contradiction in order to escape the contradiction into which he sees, better than anyone, we find ourselves cast.

Or wouldn't Marx's revolutionary illusion reside not in the project of overcoming such a contradiction, but in the very sense he had of perceiving it? After all, contrary to what he foresaw, but in keeping with what Tocqueville foresaw, the political device of the separation turned out to be very lasting, one might say even irresistible, as I noted at the beginning of this chapter. One might maintain that man cannot renounce the sovereignty of his will once he has come to institutionalize it in a viable political form, or that he cannot cease to will. But if this form is viable and powerful, is it not because social nature and democratic will are not as contradictory as Marx or the reactionary authors think, though in very different ways, and that it is natural for democracy to have become natural for us? Not at all! We will not get out of this so easily, by the easy route of common sense, since Tocqueville himself perceives and describes the life of democracy as a continual revolution and indefinite operation on human nature. The democratic hypothesis of the sovereignty of the will induces its own

verification in the continual and indefinite recomposition of all the contents of life of ancient man, who as each day proceeds becomes ever more
a democratic man.

XIII

Before the separation of state and society, human goods occupied a distinctive place in political life: they had their expression in the law that
ordained what was good. After the separation, these goods ceased to have
any part in the law, which is now limited in principle to guaranteeing
liberty; they become the matter of rights: men have the right to seek them
freely. For example, religious liberty or freedom of conscience replaces
"authoritarian" religion, whose dogmas and commandments were a part
of political law. The early Moderns separated the law from the good because they had come to the conclusion that it was no longer possible for the
ends of man to have a place in the law. Men had ideas about ends that were
too incompatible; these disagreements easily degenerated; what mattered
was above all to avoid civil war, which is the greatest of evils. Moreover,
giving human ends a place in the law was not desirable, for a good cannot
be a good for man if it is not found and so in the first place freely sought.
The new law, the liberal law, instead of leading man authoritatively toward the good, allows him to seek his good freely; it guarantees his right
to the "pursuit of happiness" by forbidding anyone to prescribe the form
of this pursuit and thereby to hinder this liberty.

At least some of the early Moderns, such as Milton in his *Areopagitica*,
hoped that men would obtain more and more what they recognized as
each other's right, that the pursuit of the good and the true, which is eternal since it is natural, would be all the more fervent in that it could be in
the end perfectly sincere. Lessing still expressed this noble hope with elo-
quence in *The Education of the Human Race*.[45] Has the outcome lived up
to their expectation? What was and is the effect of liberty on the contents
of life that were liberated in this way? This is a delicate question, but one
that assuredly deserves to be examined. As early as the second half of the
eighteenth century, Rousseau, who can hardly be suspected of being sympathetic to the old regime, frets over the effects of the "philosophic spirit"
on the tonality of the souls this spirit is in the process of modifying.[46] At
the beginning of the nineteenth century, Tocqueville anxiously details the
transformations in moral and intellectual life wrought by democracy.[47]
Two generations later, Nietzsche sketches the lugubrious portrait of the
"last man" who thinks he has "invented happiness."[48] Each one of us has
his own observations to make; I will confine myself to just one remark.

Modern democratic man has the very acute sense that no one has the right to prevent him from seeking his good according to the idea he himself forms of it in sovereign fashion. At the same time he sincerely thinks that he has no right to compel his neighbor to engage in this search in the way he does himself, to evaluate the things of the world as he does, or to think as he does. My neighbor is as free as I am myself; I will his liberty by the same movement I will my own. Thus in this way my neighbor becomes my equal and we recognize each other as equally human. This mutual recognition makes less urgent the knowledge of the good—if it even exists—common to the two liberties which in this way recognize and respect one another. The subjective demand of my equal claim puts the objective claim of the good in second place, if it does not do away with it completely. By this I mean the call that the good—whatever it may be and if it even exists to begin with—addresses to every man as man. The more we recognize and affirm the equality and likeness of men, the more my equal's liberty acquires authority in my eyes. From that point on, if my good cannot be law for him, will there remain any truly commanding demand for me? There is more precisely only my good. Why would I not abandon or at least treat lightly what my neighbor, my equal, has the right to dismiss? Each one's right to pursue his good becomes the right, that is the authorization, not to seek it. By subtle and indirect routes, yet in an irresistible way, so to speak, this authorization resembles more and more a suggestion, and before long an injunction, whose effects in any case it bears. The new law at first allows for indifference toward all goods that are the object of human searching, even truth, which is the chief good; then little by little it commands indifference: how can one think that what the law, which is naturally majestic, authorizes can be truly damaging or bad for man?

It seems that the modern or liberal understanding of law is here defective. Let us at least attempt to circumscribe the difficulty by considering for a moment the Greek conception of law.

In the Greek view, law was not separated from nature. Indeed, Greek philosophy had brought to light the notion of nature by bringing out the polarity and thus in some way the mutual exclusion on nature and law. But if nature were the sole object of the philosopher in his own work and continued to guide him as an impartial counselor or critic of the city, it never appeared of itself as a given in the human world, but only with the aid and modification of the law. The law, the expression of the regime, formulated in authoritarian fashion, as *krisis*, the relative worth of the goods naturally desired by man. To use once again the analogy with painting and to explain imitation with the help of imitation, we could say that the city is an imitation of nature and the artist is law, as we saw in section 6. Whatever the regime, the citizen lives under a law that fulfills his nature while modifying it: he lives under a certain confusion of nature and law.

It will be said that, once the notion of nature is isolated in its purity, it ought to awaken the impatient desire for a political regime that would be wholly "according to nature" or nothing but "nature," and thus of a law capable of bringing into being nature in its integrity and purity. But philosophy itself, which had uncovered the distinction between nature and law, persuasively counseled, through the voice of Plato and Aristotle, consent to their confusion, at least within certain limits, for the good of human nature. Nevertheless, beginning at a certain date, this voice ceased to be persuasive, either because men were no longer capable of hearing or understanding—but then their nature itself would have had to change—or rather because it was covered over by another voice, the powerful and seductive voice of modern philosophy which, faced with an unprecedented situation, worked obstinately to disentangle completely this confusion. In previous chapters, I have indicated the elements of the new situation that incited the ever more vigorous separation of nature and law. Pure nature then ceased to be the secret of the philosopher to which the vulgar had no access, in order to become the horizon of a collective quest. In order for nature and law to be free from one another, the understanding of nature changed: henceforth, it would not concern itself with ends; it would be a nature without finality. This new nature entailed and presupposed a new law, detached from human nature and sovereign and artificial to the extent that it leaves nature altogether free to be itself and nothing but itself, without any modification.

Nevertheless, the experience of modern democracy, the appearance of a democratic man characterized by an unprecedented taming of his nature, suggests that this perspective was not confirmed by experience, at least not by what has been experienced up to our time. Law is always active; from the moment the law's place is occupied, its effect must be fulfilled, which is to modify nature. The law which authorizes produces no fewer effects than the law which prohibits, even if the effects are not the same. In this sense, authorization too is authoritarian.

XIV

The experience of modern democracy puts before us a strange contradiction: democratic man is the freest man to have ever lived and at the same time the most domesticated. It will be said that the difficulty is quickly clarified: he can only be granted, he can only give himself, so much liberty because he is so domesticated. One has to ask how, since the dog whose contentment the wolf envies is not unaware of the collar to which it is tethered, modern man is so sure of being ever more free if in reality he is ever more subjected?

It seems that here the paradoxes are intertwined, that we are forever going back and forth, with no possibility of arriving at a firm appreciation of the modern condition. On the one hand, in effect, the will, in order to leave nature completely free, has to raise itself above all natural determinations, and thus to define and affirm itself again and again as pure will. But then, it is proper to man that the will determines him and thus his nature all the more. Without any doubt, the more the will liberates itself from nature and liberates nature itself, the more it subjects it. But if voluntary determination is now to this extent stronger than natural determination, it is not judicious to speak of domestication since the humanity of man resides much more in his will than in his nature. If we say, as we can, that man attains his humanity by overcoming his nature, do we not find again the immemorial notion of the moral progress of man, joining the Ancients and the Moderns across the centuries?

In reality, the classical notion of the pursuit of moral perfection assumes the victory of the higher part of human nature over its lower part, the instauration or restoration of the natural order of the soul.[49] With the moderns, it is a matter of the victory of law, or will, or liberty, over nature as such, both lofty and base, and thus as well over free will as a natural faculty of man.

Formerly, the complexity of the human phenomenon was uncovered and mastered by the exploration and affirmation of the soul, the all-encompassing substance of a natural order. From now on, phenomenological precision has become blurred and its very possibility grown dim. It is less a matter of describing and analyzing the moral world than of conceiving the possibility of a pure law, so completely detached from both the higher and lower nature of man that the internal articulation of such a law loses a good deal of its interest: the new law views nature from as far above it as the absolute sovereign views the relations of his subjects among themselves, as long as they render him homage.

CHAPTER VI

The End of Nature

I

Iɴ ᴛʜᴇ ʙᴇɢɪɴɴɪɴɢ, the world was without form and void, without laws, arts, or sciences, and the spirit of man moved over the darkness.

Such, in brief, are the first words man speaks to himself when, rejecting alike both Christian law and pagan nature, he decides to receive his humanity only from himself and undertakes to be the author of his own genesis. Hobbes, Locke, and Rousseau give us three synoptic versions of this genesis that all proclaim the same good news.

In his original state, man—let us call him by the name we are accustomed to—is essentially undetermined, a perfectible unknown quantity bent on self-preservation; an embodied individual, a quantity of force, whose primordial impulse is the desire for preservation, as the principle of inertia is for brute matter. Such an atom can only be animated by the most entrenched egoism. Yet reality is made up of many atoms forever colliding against one another by chance as much as by necessity; every egoism is the enemy of all the others and consequently its own enemy as well. In order to overcome the misery or war in which it is thrown, it must construct an artifice to protect itself and all the others equally. The most selfish desire can only satisfy itself by the most disinterested means of the impartial state and the general will, as we have seen in section 7 of chapter 5.

Man invents generality in order to save his particularity. He creates his moral being to preserve his physical being.[1] In traditional terms, one would say that the means, humanity properly speaking, is infinitely greater in dignity than the end, animal survival. In any case, the undefined unknown only wants to avoid perishing and to that end invents labor, property, law, the arts and sciences. It is then he discovers that he has become a man.

His moral being consists chiefly of the general law or will, an authority that has no other author or addressee than man. It is the interior word by which man defines himself and a command man addresses to himself; he is at once sovereign or lawgiver and subject. He becomes the man he is by giving himself the law which he obeys, and by obeying the law he gives himself. The human world takes a human form because man gives himself his own law and he sees or believes that this is good.

Such an idea is incomprehensible to both Christians and Jews, for whom God is the sole author of the law. It would have been incomprehensible to the Greeks as well. In Greek democracy, every citizen can be, in turn, the one commanding and the one commanded, *archon* and *archomenos*, but he could not be both at the same time.[2] Even as resolute a champion of the modern state as Bodin recoils from the possibility that a man could be his own commander and rejects it explicitly. Because one cannot command oneself, the sovereignty of the republic must be vested in a monarch.[3]

It will be said that there is nothing earth-shattering in this idea, which is simple, plausible, and even necessary. When the body politic, through whatever institution, enacts and promulgates the laws its members are to obey, it can be said that man is more or less commanding himself, depending on the regime. Is this so certain? Without a doubt, through the political institution man governs himself: he is his own shepherd, even if, for a long time, the memories of the rule of the gods and the divine prohibitions hindered the liberty and prudence of human government, as the fate of the Athenian generals at Arginusae testifies.[4] Hence, it will be said, politics is the truth of the human order, democracy the truth of the political man, and obedience to the law one has given to oneself the truth of democracy. But are we well advised to lower in this way the threshold of plausibility?

Following the indications of Aristotle, let us admit that the Greek city, particularly in its democratic form, actualized and thus revealed man's aptitude to make human goods present and available by his own powers and to live in self-sufficiency. It thereby revealed human autonomy. By the same stroke it revealed both the ends of nature and the limits of the human as well as the divine commandment. In manifesting the articulations of the human order, it revealed itself as a natural city. Philosophy revealed it to be such. What the philosopher seeks, what Socrates sought, escapes the commandment: what is the nature of the diverse classes of things or beings? The essential, which is the essence, escapes the command because the essential or essence does not change. Philosophy therefore teaches the limits of the human and divine law, the limits of the political order which is inconceivable without law.

Of course, law and command are not the same thing. Law is necessarily command, but the converse is not true.[5] The first cause of the command resides in a twofold difference within nature, between the higher and lower parts of the soul and between men made to command and those who are by nature slaves.[6] This twofold difference is the condition for the possibility of law.

In this way obedience of oneself to oneself, the very form of modern

democracy, is not in continuity with Greek understanding of self-sufficiency. It presupposes a breadth and meaning of the law's command that
the Greeks had excluded, its so to speak miraculous character; in short it
presupposes a reversal of the Greek viewpoint. The first cause, the truth,
and the legitimacy of the commandment reside not in nature but in the
law. If on this score we compare Rousseau's *Social Contract*, Hobbes's
Leviathan, and Locke's *Second Treatise* on the one hand with Aristotle's
Politics on the other, we can say that the Moderns bring back the mytho-
logical age of the founding wills.

II

This mythology, like all others, is marked by a strange, even monstrous
disproportion between the elements of human action, in particular, as we
saw at the beginning of this chapter, between the end and the means. From
this there results a great uncertainty about the motives of the actors. The
wildest moral imagination cannot conceive what goes on in the mind of the
contracting party. As the bearer of the general will, each nonetheless
thinks only of himself.[7] The individual has and ought to have no idea of
the Whole that he is forming along with the other individuals, whose
minds are as virgin as his.

   One can say, of course, that since the "social contract" does not sketch
a "real" process, its descriptive or phenomenological incoherence is of little importance; that its three synoptic versions each have their strengths
and weaknesses, their plausible and unlikely aspects; that the essential is
the stylized, symbolic, even allegorical presentation of consent as the principle of modern legitimacy. After all, is not the massive fact of history in
the past two centuries the development of democratic institutions which,
if they do not correspond exactly to any of the three versions of the contract, do embody their common intent.

   Such a reading is surely comforting. But can modern legitimacy, that
claims to be founded essentially and even exclusively on reason, be content
with such approximations? In fact, we have come up against a singular
chiasmus that reverses all our ideas of what is appropriate or plausible.
Aristotle's "best regime" no doubt cannot be realized, but it can be
thought: thought surpasses reality, but both are on the same plane of
Being. It is the regime founded on nature that does not exist. The legitimate modern regime does indeed exist, since our societies are in effect
"founded on the contract," but it cannot be thought; modern political philosophy cannot strictly speaking think what is at the center of what it
affirms; more precisely, the founding contract cannot be thought, since
one cannot become part of the whole without thinking this whole, without

having the idea of this whole, and such an idea is the negation of the contract. The regime that cannot be thought of is the regime founded on reason.

The fact will appear less significant if we learn to distinguish the two elements whose confusion makes for the strength and solidity of modern legitimacy.

The first element, the constitutive and essential part of the contract doctrine, is the idea of the general law or command that is radically superior to nature. As we have seen at the very beginning of our inquiry, this idea is not an arbitrary invention of modern philosophy, but rather, as worked out by it, the sum and the product of what is most central and fatal in all our history: this law is the secret wellspring of the "ascetic planet" we inhabit.

As for the notion of contract properly speaking, which is as old as humanity, or in any event Roman law, it is by itself altogether distinct; its specifically modern founding and creative breadth is due exclusively to the fact that it amalgamates itself with the notion of the general law, which is born of the reciprocal action and usury of the city and the church.

It should be noted that once Rousseau had pushed it to its farthest limits by compressing into it extreme generality and extreme particularity, political philosophy abandoned the notion of contract. No other mind after him dared or was able to embrace such a contradiction. The way out could be sought in two directions: either from the side of pure particularity that would perhaps allow the will and nature to be reconciled in an unprecedented way; or from the side of pure generality, which would necessitate at least a rupture of law with nature, even if the attachment had been tenuous and reluctant. The first is the path chosen by Nietzsche.

III

Nietzsche's critique of the contract can be summarized in the following way. If modern man wants to found the political order on the will, as he does, he then assumes or implies that man is at bottom will, that man's "nature" is to be will. If man is at bottom will and the nature of man is to be will, then all that he has been up to the present, all that he is today, all that he will be tomorrow is an effect or a result of his will.

It is obvious that man has been very different things: Greek, Jewish, Christian, Buddhist. It is thus also obvious that the will can will very different things and that there is in the will a prodigiously broad and complex principle of creation and differentiation. Since, therefore, the will appears to be so profound and mysterious, it is ridiculously superficial simply to say, as do modern democrats, that the political order shall be founded on the reasonable will of each person.

Moreover, the democrats contradict themselves or do not know what they want or how to will truly, since they most often champion a representative regime. What does it mean in fact to construct a representative regime if not to give one's will the crutch of another will? One wants to will something, but on condition that the majority of the people want to also! And the leaders themselves, the members of the "representative government," hide behind the "will of the people"! They will nothing by themselves; their sole desire, their only will is to translate, to serve, to express, to represent, and to realize the will of the people. Therefore, while modern humanity is caught in the representative circle, where only the will matters, but always the will of another, and no one has the courage to will by himself alone, what solace, what satisfaction, what contentment when at last a true master appears, that is, a man who knows how to will alone:

> [T]he appearance of one who commands unconditionally strikes these herd-animal Europeans as an immense comfort and salvation from a gradually intolerable pressure, as was last attested in a major way by the effect of Napoleon's appearance. The history of Napoleon's reception is almost the history of the higher happiness attained by this whole century in its most valuable human beings and moments.[8]

Nietzsche and the democrat share in some way the view that man is will, but the democrat concludes that each will must make itself compatible with all the others, that is, must generalize or universalize itself, and that all wills must be equal or at least at the foundation of equal rights. Nietzsche on the contrary concludes that inequality is desirable. There are all kinds of will, all kinds of intensities and qualities of will, in particular—and here nature returns to Nietzsche's thought with a vengeance—the noble will and the base will, or resentment. Like the command it exercises, the will is particular. It is all told the *most particular* thing there is.

IV

One might object that our chronology is off and that reference to the social contract did not disappear with Rousseau and was even preserved by as weighty an author as Kant. In reality, the notion of the social contract loses all essential value with Kant. It is now only an allegory and vaguely utilitarian. It incites legislators to respect the general will, or what can pass for it.[9]

Moreover, how would the social contract have a real part to play in Kant's fundamental thought, since it confuses in a forceful way precisely what his work succeeds for the first time to rigorously distinguish and separate?

As I noted above, the founding and creative role of the social contract has to do with the fact that it confused extreme particularity and extreme generality, making the former spring from the latter. Man created himself only by realizing the impossible: he formed a new whole by thinking only of himself. Kant overcomes these contradictions by liberating generality from any attachment to particularity. Man can again think of the other man when he thinks of himself. He even has to do so, since the true Whole of which he is a part is no longer an arbitrary or contingent circumscription, but the totality of men, or rather of "reasonable natures."

In the view of Montesquieu and Rousseau, the Law preserved a paradoxical anchorage in nature. According to Montesquieu's epigram, we recall, it is the very frustration of their nature that makes monks love the rule that oppresses them, that is the only thing left for them to love. As we have seen, in section II of chapter I, Rousseau oscillated between horror over the cruelty of the law and a kind of celebration of that cruelty. Neither Montesquieu nor Rousseau succeeded in answering clearly and plausibly the question of how man can find in his nature a motive for obeying a law that is hostile to his nature. Kant answers the question by rising above the oscillations and paradoxes of his great predecessors to a height from which one dominates over them because he understands them.

Kant's solution is luminous and moving: the law can be, in and by itself, a motive of human action; it is even the motive par excellence. There is no need to be ingenious and put nature in contradiction with itself. The Law, separated from nature and precisely because it is separated from it, is the pure motive of human action and gives rise in man to a feeling that is distinct from all others, *respect*:

> Respect for the moral law, therefore, is a feeling produced by an intellectual cause and this feeling is the only one which we can know completely a priori and the necessity of which we can discern. . . . This feeling, under the name of moral feeling, is therefore produced solely by reason. It does not serve for an estimation of actions or as a basis of the objective moral law itself but only as an incentive to make this law itself a maxim. By what name better than moral feeling could we call this singular feeling which cannot be compared with any pathological feeling? It is of such a peculiar kind that it seems to be at the disposal only of reason, and indeed only of the pure practical reason.[10]

The feeling of respect overcomes the inclinations of nature because it combines the two tendencies that define and order nature. By nature, men are attracted by certain things, good things, and the Ancients interpreted the human world in the light of this desire. But also by nature, men are repelled by other things, those which are bad, and the Moderns analyze human action as a flight from or a fear of evil. Respect is the singular feeling that combines and merges the naturally contrary inclinations of attraction and fear.

Only the phenomenon of the Law and the respect associated with it can give meaning and content to the modern notion of the creation of oneself by oneself that the social contract theories imply so irresistibly and formulate in such a contradictory way. It is only because he can obey the Law by pure respect for the Law that man is the free cause of his actions and thus enjoys autonomy. The autonomy of the will, Kant says, is the unique principle of all the moral laws and duties that are in conformity with it.[11] Only the phenomenon of the Law and the respect associated with it establishes, manifests, and demonstrates the fact that pure reason suffices by itself to determine the will. In this way the Law brings out something in us that is comparable to a divine power of creation: "For, in fact, the moral law transfers us into a nature in which reason would bring forth the highest good were it accompanied by sufficient physical capacities. . . ."[12]

Kant examines the phenomenon that the mythology of the Enlightenment interpreted and obscured under the light of reason and reveals it to be reason.

V

The social contract theorists made generality issue form particularity and disinterestedness issue from thoroughgoing selfishness, and the impartial state or general will from the individual's desire for self-preservation. Kant shows that the phenomenon of the moral life presupposes or implies an immediate rapport with generality or universality and that in fact it consists in such a rapport. In doing so he makes social contract theory appear to be confused, violent, and untenable. One is tempted to say that with Kant's moral philosophy, modern man has achieved clarity on what he had been seeking since the beginning of the modern movement. At last he can think what until that time he could only will: he can now think that he is neither a creature of God nor a part of Nature, that he is in short born of himself, the child of his own liberty. In being able to apprehend exactly the phenomenon of the Law and respect, modern man is equally removed from Christian salvation and pagan happiness. He has arrived at clear and definitive self-consciousness.

A difficulty remains, however. The particular whole—the city—which the individual of the social contract at first had to overlook if his disinterested selfishness was to produce the general will, is also misunderstood by the moral conscience that Kant clarified. In order to act morally, man must act in such a way that he can will that the maxim of his action become a universal law, and in this way become the maxim of reasonable beings.[13] As a moral conscience, he does not simply distinguish the particular body politic to which he belongs. The same law commands the same respect on both sides of the Pyrenees and both shores of the Rhine. It is hard to see how one could show a positive connection between the pure generality of the law and the pure particularity of the body politic without having recourse to arbitrary complementary hypotheses. Just as the social contract theorists went from the individual to the body politic by an arbitrary leap, so, it seems, Kant can only pass from the universality of reasonable nature to the particularity of the body politic by an equally arbitrary leap in the opposite direction.

This difficulty regarding the extension of the law is simply the expression of a difficulty regarding the proper understanding of the law that leads us to the heart of Kant's moral doctrine.

As is well known, Kant seriously countenances the possibility that no perfect act of obedience to the law through pure respect for the law was ever accomplished; there has never been a perfect act of good will. But, if man has respect—one can almost say naturally[14]—for the law, why is it that he does not always respect it? Precisely because freedom, and with it the law, are radically separated from nature, it is hard to conceive what power nature could exercise over liberty and law that would prevent man from obeying them regularly and perfectly. Moral failure cannot be seen the way ancient moral philosophy sees it, as a rebellion of the baser parts of nature against the nobler, a rebellion fomented by a clouding of the intellect. This is also the view of Catholic moral theology, which in addition speaks of the "wound" inflicted on our nature by original sin. Nature cannot provide the link between the two conflicting terms, since it is one, and only one, of the terms.

Kant strives to resolve the difficulty by appealing to what he calls "radical evil." This consists above all in a reversal of the proper order of motives. Instead of conforming strictly with the law as the sufficient motive of his actions, man seeks other motives drawn from self-love and lets the law fall to the level of a means.[15] This failure, which resides in and is the doing of reason, is extremely difficult to understand:

> But the rational origin of this perversion of our will whereby it makes lower incentives supreme among its maxims, that is, of the propensity to evil, remains inscrutable to us, because this propensity itself must be set down to our account and because, as a result, that ultimate ground of all maxims would in turn involve the adoption of an evil maxim [as its basis]. Evil could have sprung only from the morally evil (not from mere limitations in our nature); and yet the original predisposition (which no one other than man himself could have corrupted, if he is to be held responsible for this corruption) is a predisposition to good; there is then for us no conceivable ground from which the moral evil in us could originally have come.[16]

Radical evil is unfathomable, we are led to understand, because it issues from a free act and since it comes first, one cannot explain it because it is what explains. But once again, why would pure practical reason turn away from the only motive that is sufficient for it?

After the passage we have just cited, Kant adds that this incomprehensibility is "expressed" in the characters of the biblical account of the fall. Must Kant, who has revealed the rational meaning of the mythology of the Enlightenment, return to Christian dogma in order to find the coherence of his moral philosophy? As we know, the Bible here is by no means seen in a dogmatic perspective as the objectively revealed divine Word, but simply as a repertoire of "stories" filled with suggestive and edifying images whose only significance lies in its practical meaning, or its capacity to make us better. According to Kant, the account of the fall makes the character of moral evil more transparent, but it is his doctrine of radical evil that gives the account its true and rational meaning.

Have we made any progress here? If the rational explanation is incomprehensible, if reason does not understand itself, it is hard to see what help can be expected from a religion whose superrational authority has been rejected from the start. Instead of reason and religion clarifying one another, perhaps we have only the sterile juxtaposition of a religion that has renounced truth and a reason that is incapable of clarity.

One can then ask if the Christian dogma or mystery of sin, either original or actual sin, is not paradoxically clearer than Kant's doctrine of radical evil. Whatever interpretation authoritative theologians or adventurous laymen may give to this mystery, it necessarily presupposes a certain human situation: sin is located in the human action par excellence, which consists in deliberating about one's own self. The complex and undetermined good that is sought because it is desired and that is the subject of deliberation becomes simplified and crystallized into two opposed goods between which one must choose when one makes his first decision,[17] the decision, if I can put it this way, that is decisive for all other decisions. Everyone—Satan, Adam, each individual—in the beginning as at every instant of his action, has to choose between a lesser good that is finite yet infinitely close by, himself, and an infinite but distant good, namely, God made present in His law and His grace. It would be out of place here to say anything that would take away from the just horror one should have for sin, but, all told, faced with such a choice, one can be allowed to hesitate, at least in the sense that if there is to be any deliberation, there is something over which to deliberate. Moreover, God can only forbid those actions—for example, eating the fruit of the tree of knowledge—that our nature makes it possible for us and even invites us to engage in; otherwise there would be no point to the prohibition. It is as attracted and perplexed natures that we live our lives, deliberate, and err regarding the good. Man is a rational animal, and sin is a reasoning process that has come to a bad conclusion.

But Kantian reason does not deliberate; it legislates. In giving itself law, it recognizes nothing above itself, or else it would not be autonomous. Its sufficient motive, respect, has no rapport with the motives that move nature that is beneath it. How could it ever prefer those over this one?

In a curious note in *Religion Within the Limits of Reason Alone*, Kant seeks to make traditional moral philosophy acknowledge the incomprehensibility that his new doctrine recognizes:

> "It is a very common assumption of moral philosophy that the existence of moral evil in man may easily be explained by the power of the motivating springs of his sensuous nature on the one hand, and the impotence of his rational impulses (his respect for the law) on the other, that is, by *weakness*. But then the moral goodness in him (his moral predisposition) would have to allow of a still easier explanation, for to comprehend the one apart from comprehending the other is quite unthinkable. Now reason's ability to master all opposing motivating forces through the bare idea of a law is utterly inexplicable; it is also inconceivable, therefore, how the motivating forces of the sensuous nature should be able to gain the ascendancy over a reason which commands with such authority. For if all the world were to proceed in conformity with the precepts of the law, we should say that everything came to pass according to natural order, and no one would think of so much as inquiring after cause."[18]

It is strange to see how Kant seems to retract the heart of his moral doctrine and pretend not to understand how reason has the power to command, whereas his whole philosophy has no other aim than to establish that fact. But he declares that the legislative power of reason which he has shown to be supremely intelligible is unintelligible, only to be able to declare equally unintelligible what in terms of his philosophy and for the first time in the history of thought it is strictly impossible to conceive: the power of selfish or natural motives over reason. The ingeniously naive last sentence of the note acknowledges that it would never enter into anyone's mind to question even the cause of the general obedience to the general law, because everyone would perceive the legislative power of reason which Kant is the first man to have established.

VI

Nevertheless, would not the effective realization of the law mean the realization of its contrary, since the law has value as law only when it is separated from every reality or "nature"? Hegel has analyzed profoundly how, in what he calls the moral vision of the world, each moment transforms itself into its contrary.[19] It is not my concern here to go back to or confirm Hegel's critique of Kant or even less to be foolish enough to propose a new

critique. But the preceding remarks prompt us to raise the question in a
more pressing way: does Kant succeed in thinking about the human phenomenon by articulating it around a pure law radically separated from
nature? And if he does not, does not the whole self-conscious modern regime contain something essentially unthinkable or at least not yet thought
of?

If the preceding paragraph has any validity, one is tempted to conclude
that the phenomenon of respect does not suffice to account for the human
phenomenon, that "something" brings together nature and law and allows
for their rapport within each individual, and that in this way one is
brought back to one or the other version the traditional definition of man
as a substance, which would be the only way to make the power of "nature" over "liberty" intelligible. Yet such a conclusion appears hasty and
weak. It carries weight only if we are willing to superimpose the phenomenon of respect, and more generally Kant's doctrine of the moral law, on the
traditional boundaries of our experience, rather than be taken up with the
imperious motive for taking the risk to refurbish these boundaries.

Kant himself seems to take the lazy route. To make the new understanding of man compatible with the natural or traditional frameworks of
experience, he invokes the indefinite progress of the individual toward the
holiness of the will, of the body politic toward the republican regime, and
of the international order toward perpetual peace. He even goes so far as
to evoke the irresistible progress of nature toward the rule of law.![20] The
notion of indefinite progress pushes back the limits of traditional ontology
only to confirm and subvert its principle, since it preserves and confirms
the scale of goodness while depriving the good of its primordial role in the
human world. Kant has recourse to this sterile hybrid, one might dare to
say, only because he pulls back from the ultimate endeavor that his work
has made possible. For if reason is truly legislative, if through it humanity
gives itself the law, then without doubt the Law will in effect be obeyed
and reason realized, provided only that one give oneself an adequate
framework to interpret the human phenomenon. But which framework? It
is now clear that neither the individual, nor the body politic, nor the sum
of bodies politic, nor even humanity in their indefinite progress within
history are adequate. If reason and law are essentially distinct from nature, they cannot become effective by "ameliorating" nature, by making
man "more reasonable" or "more moral"; that would be to "ameliorate"
the state of human substance and thus to reinstate substance. All of modern philosophy's labor then would be lost. But if neither the individual nor
the city nor humanity is an adequate framework, then putting into effect
the phenomenon identified by Kant takes us out of the world that is nor-
mally recognizable as human. As we have noted, existentialism engaged in
an impressive and serious search to find man's new name as liberty effect-

ing itself. Hegel preferred to observe or to decide that this world, as the state, was already the realization itself. In short Hegel reproached Kant the same way Montesquieu had reproached another old republican with seeking reason without understanding it and building Chalcedon while the coast of Byzantium was before his eyes. In both cases man's respect for the law disappears.

It seems that if Kant identified the phenomenon of modern experience, the phenomenon requires us to leave the world where it is possible to have this experience.

VII

At the point to which we have arrived, we find there is no path before us. We need to stop and take in the scene our inquiry has gone over.

It would only be repeating what it says of itself if modern man's self-consciousness is characterized by the will to discover and to speak the "effectual truth" about man and the world, the "realist" will it opposes victoriously to the "idealist" desire that inspires the construction of "imaginary principalities" in "backward worlds." The idealist desire finds its noble expression in the "good regimes" conceived by the Greek philosophers, in particular in Plato's "Republic," and its base expression in religion, in particular in the Christian religion, "Platonism for the people." The Christian religion is essentially corrupting in that it divides man by adding to rational or natural motives—to properly human motives—other motives that claim to be supernatural or superior to reason. Man is thus compelled to "see double" and no loner knows how to orient himself rationally in the world.[21] In short, "two worlds are too many, only one was needed."[22]

The critique of religion is easily persuasive since there will always be "unpleasing priests."[23] But how can the unity of the human world be recaptured or reconstructed, how can the reunited city be built, where man, now that he has attained maturity, will find his motives only in himself, that is, in his own reason? It is Kant's extraordinary merit to have succeeded in showing how and under what conditions such an achievement was possible, not by arbitrarily inventing an imaginary man—the complacent inhabitant of the state of nature who founds the social state once the philosopher is willing to recognize its necessity, or the "new man" whom the future will bring—but by analyzing the moral phenomenon, that is, man's rapport with the moral law. Now, by a strange reversal and a vexing irony, at the very instant when, thanks to Kant, we attain our maturity, we undergo by that very fact a more rigorous and insuperable division than any man had undergone up to that point. It is now our nature and our liberty that are implacably separated, with no conceivable human link to reunite them or even to bring them closer together. Human reason or liberty itself now becomes an "imaginary principality" without rapport with the needs and desires of human nature, with the "effectual truth" of our condition. The law of reason is more radically and more haughtily separated from our nature than was divine grace in the old theology. In fact, it is more difficult for a man to enter into Kant's kingdom than for a camel to pass through the eye of a needle!

It will be said that Kant, after separating nature and law, strives very sincerely and seriously to bring them closer together, either by drawing consoling conclusions from the empirical observation of empirical history,[24] or more profoundly by identifying the "postulates of practical reason," in particular of the existence of God. Since it is a duty for us to assume the possibility of an ultimate harmony between nature and law, between happiness and morality, it is also our duty to acknowledge the existence of God. This harmony is in fact only possible under the condition that God exists.[25]

But if we can and must hope for the reconciliation of nature and law and of happiness and virtue in and by God, then it seems that faith and hope in God and not respect before the law becomes the primary motive of pure practical reason. As everyone knows, Kant rejects this conclusion.[26] In introducing the distinction between subjective and objective moral necessity, he even goes so far as to write, after underlining that "it is morally necessary to assume the existence of God," that "there cannot be any duty to assume the existence of a thing, because such a supposition concerns only the theoretical use of reason."[27] This allusion to the *Critique of Pure Reason* reminds us that to refute Kant's moral philosophy would entail a refutation of his philosophy as a whole, and in particular his *Critique of Pure Reason*! Foolish presumption should be rejected, but we cannot renounce using our reason. Kant affirms here that it is a duty for us to believe in the existence of a thing whose existence we are forbidden to affirm. He commands an act of our mind from which he removes the first condition, which is also its expression. He enjoins on us as a duty to be very strictly dishonest. Not only does the separation of nature and liberty not deliver us from the division between this world and the other, but the division penetrates to the heart of the most elementary act of human reason—regarding the existence of a thing—and the highest act of human reason—since in this case the thing is God.

VIII

The moral law according to Kant is purely formal. It has value for each man only if it carries weight for all men, and it is defined by this generality or capacity to be generalized. One would not hesitate to say that, reduced in this way to the kernel of the command that can be universalized, it isolates and consolidates the universal form of morality by separating it from its particular and changing contents and that it defines the first and only truly universal, rational, and human morality. One cannot say that all men thus find themselves in the situation of Montesquieu's monks and love the law only in the measure that it oppresses their nature, since they love the law for its own sake, or rather, they respect it without loving it because it is not lovable. No inclination arising form their nature binds them to this law that is completely detached from nature.

But if the moral law in and by itself is completely detached from nature, nature makes its presence recognized when the law is at work in the actual moral act. When the moral agent generalizes the maxim of his action in order to see if it conforms with the universal law, he performs a mental experiment in which he formulates a hypothesis about the real behavior of other men, based on the characteristics of their nature, and of course taking into consideration what he knows of his own nature. Kant exposes it candidly and in detail in the second section of the *Foundations of the Metaphysics of Morals*. After articulating the imperative of duty in the most formal and most universal terms,[28] he cites four examples in which he makes the universal law operative in some way. As commentators have often pointed out, in each instance he justifies the law thorough wholly empirical considerations regarding the constitution of human nature, which are sometimes more narrowly and opaquely empirical than those that traditional morality ordinarily puts forth. For example, regarding the prohibition of suicide, where traditional morality asserted that what was given by God could only be taken back by God, Kant invokes "the feeling whose special office is to impel the improvement of life."[29] And to the man who prefers amusing idleness to the exercise of his natural gifts, Kant objects that "as a rational being, he necessarily wills that all his faculties should be developed, inasmuch as they are given to him for all sorts of possible purposes."[30] This is just about what the Greeks said, and, more generally, the moralists of the period of man's "minority."

At the same time, this universal moral law, which has no effectiveness nor any plausibility except by a natural reality about which it wants to know nothing, runs counter to all morality when this reality would require it to concede an exception to its rule: I must tell the truth even if in doing so I deliver an innocent man into the hands of a tyrant's police.[31] In order to affirm and justify the general law in its practical implementation, Kant sometimes relies on man's natural tendencies (contrary to the principle of law) and sometimes brutally refuses to take them into account (and thus does violence to the spontaneous sense of morality). This remark is critical, for it signals that Kant's analysis of morality, like Montesquieu's construction of the idea of virtue and the social contract theorists' descriptions of the state of nature, includes an essential artifice: it gives access to the phenomenon under its aspect of law and withholds it under its aspect of nature, and it does so with a sovereign arbitrariness whose sole purpose is to elaborate fully the pure idea of law.

But if the idea of law is such an artifice, then respect for the law could not be this pure phenomenon that we were seeing in it. What Kant calls respect does not overcome, through a synthesis that is radically original and superior to its constitutive elements, the two fundamental tendencies of attraction and repulsion, of "pursuit" and "flight,"[32] that divide and order nature and even define its relation to man. Respect for law is not a pure motive effectively detached from nature; it is an artifact elaborated by Kant, the most ingenious, plausible, and noble ever conceived by the human mind, to persuade man that he can be and already is the offspring of his own reason, untainted by any contact with pagan nature.

One can say, of course, that the charge of artifice is very unjust and that Kant is simply putting into effect a possibility inherent in the definition of man as rational nature, or better, that he brings the definition to its logical conclusion. In fact, if man is defined in this way, then reason is by nature the first principle of human acts;[33] and man commands his actions by his practical reason.[34] It seems natural, based on these observations, to draw out the decisive propositions: the rule of human acts is the reason that commands them and reason commands them according to a law defined as the pure command of reason. Kantian morality in this sense is only drawing out the consequences of the definition of man worked out by the Greeks and confirmed by the Christians, without adding any adventitious hypothesis. More precisely, it arbitrarily excludes from its consideration complementary elements without which moral phenomena cannot be faithfully described. We can willingly take the equation of man and reason as a starting point, but how shall we ever prove that practical reason can be pure and can determine the will by itself, if we define practical reason precisely by this capacity, that is, if we presuppose that there is such a thing as pure practical reason? Because we come to know liberty through the law? But what if the law is our artifact, and not a fact of reason? In reality, this equation is obscure and confused. Practical reason immediately sets before us this impure determination: it considers all things, above all human actions, in relation to the good and its contrary, such that the precepts of reason, whatever they might be, must be founded on this natural principle of "pursuit" and "flight": one must do good (or, the good is what one must do); one must avoid evil (or, evil is what one must avoid).[35] In a note Kant underlines the ambiguity of the good, only to lament it.[36] But this twofold ambiguity is the primary human phenomenon that characterizes the human experience of the moral phenomenon. Perhaps the task of reason is to explore this complexity, instead of constructing an artifact that excludes the two ambiguities and overcomes the division of the human tendency, instead of elaborating and positing a law that compresses the whole of morality and casts the world of goods and evils where we nonetheless have life and being into the outer and inner darkness of "nature" or "love of self" or "one's own happiness."[37]

In truth, human reason is no less deliberative than it is legislative or imperative. It commands actions only because it deliberates in and over a world it considers "sub ratione boni," under the aspect of the good.

The world of the good, the world of goods and evils, is certainly rich with uncertainties and complexities. In particular, the properly human goods are subject to the greater claim of the superhuman goods promised by religion, an uneven match that intimidates reason and crushes the will and is always pushing man back to the condition of immaturity that he wants to leave behind. But to strive, as Kant does with more passion and rigor than any other modern philosopher before him, to neutralize this claim and ban this uneven match, that is, to tear human life from the element and the question of the good, is to sunder man from the properly human world. In his immaturity, man lived between two worlds and at times he thought there was one too many. Thanks to the labors of modern philosophy, he has arrived at autonomy and banished the other world, but he has lost this one.

IX

The reader who has followed me thus far may be ready to admit that Kant's description of the human world can be challenged, but he will no doubt reject the idea that the moral law would at bottom be an artifact without sufficient support in the human phenomenon and that Kant worked out this artifact within the framework of a project that had a vested interest and could not be confused with the quest for the truth.

Few men were as devoted to the search for the truth as Kant; fewer still had mental powers comparable to his. The feeling we have that he strayed from the truth and leads us away from it and that he went astray in proportion to his moral fervor and intellectual ability, evokes in us the deep desire to understand this going astray. Or do we have it in ourselves to note as a brute fact that "Kant was mistaken" and go on our way as though it were nothing?

If we go back over the path we have traveled and take stock of our reflection, we find once again the support and illumination of Nietzsche's formulation that modern consciousness interprets the Earth we live on as the "ascetic planet." This is the best definition, for it contains the ambiguity that pushes us onward and designates the propelling force that makes

our history comparable to "a river that wants to reach the end."[38] The
harsh law that makes this planet go round, is on the one hand what modern man wants to flee: it is what is common to both pagan and Christian
virtue, the form and fatality of the past that leaves behind it the progress
of modern, English liberty touted by Montesquieu. But this harsh law is
also what modern man wants in the end to realize, the virgin birth of
oneself by oneself proclaimed by Kant, reason emancipated from nature as
from God; this law that man gives to himself is the instrument itself of his
new liberty. The central place of Rousseau in modern consciousness is
rooted above all in the fact that he embraces the two faces of the law and
the two inclinations it gives rise to: he flees it and seeks it with almost equal
passion. The law has gone crazy.

I devoted considerable attention in sections 8 to 11 of chapter 1 to the
way Montesquieu identified the notion of "virtue" and also how his analysis continued and refined the implicit elaboration achieved by the spiritual
and political masses of Christian Europe who were worn away as they
turned on one another. The frank and open conflict between the secular
body politic and the church, between civic magnanimity and Christian
humility, gradually gave way to the elaboration of a sort of common denominator to the two types of virtue that incorporates and confirms the
critique each makes of the other: "virtue" is then separated from its specific civic or Christian motive.

It seems to me that Kantian law is another elaboration or result of this
dialectical process of the two spritual masses. Or perhaps it is the same
result seen in a different way: the law is regarded with respect. The virtuous man according to Kant is in a sense perfectly humble: his respect for
the law "strikes down self-conceit"[39] by which everyone tends to be satisfied with himself and to want to satisfy his desires; at the same time, like
the magnanimous man, he is perfectly above his conditions of existence,
his "circumstances," and is dependent only on his reason. In respecting
the law whose author he is, Kantian man is in one sense inferior to this
liberty, but he is decisively superior to its nature. He acknowledges his
own sovereignty with humility—with respect.

What Kant has wrought on the two movements or virtues of the human
soul differs from Montesquieu's. However ingenious or thoughtful the latter, he produces the figure of "virtue" by means of a sort of geometric
superposition or arithmetic calculation (we have seen how it is a matter of
identifying a sort of common denominator): it is a caricature destined to
produce an impression of inhuman strangeness and susceptible of being
summed up in an epigram. On the other hand, Kant in effect invents a new
moral notion by reinterpreting human experience or certain aspects of it.
One can even say that "Kant's morality" is the only new moral doctrine
since the Greeks and Christians. He has entered into the intimate metabo-

lism produced by the encounter of the two virtues with a depth and sincerity that were inaccessible to Montesquieu, since Montesquieu sided clearly, if not frankly, with the magnanimity of Epaminondas. Rousseau opened Kant's eyes to the dignity of humble lives.

In what does pagan magnanimity consist? The magnanimous man knows he is capable of the greatest actions and the greatest honors, about which he nonetheless shows little concern because he is above the honors he deserves. Moderate in triumph, he is not discouraged in misfortune: he is superior to fate. He easily forgets any services done to him since they bring out his dependence, but he is a willing benefactor, even though he despises most men and employs irony in his dealings with them in order to veil his superiority. These traits I have taken from the portrait sketched by Aristotle[40] are bound together by the fact that the magnanimous man is essentially self-sufficient: he needs no one. The Christian critique obviously focuses on this point. One can remark that St. Thomas Aquinas interprets the various traits brought out by Aristotle with what one could call Christian generosity if not magnanimity and that at one point he emphasizes how "magnanimity and humility are not contrary to one another, although they seem to tend in contrary directions because they proceed according to different considerations."[41] Not long after, however, he says more precisely, after recalling that according to Aristotle the magnanimous man has no need of anyone, that man is essentially a needy or destitute being and that every man needs above all the help of God and that of other men as well.[42] In reality, Christian humility cuts diagonally across ancient magnanimity, since it consists in recognizing the essential human dependence: every man needs to know clearly and to feel intensely that he has received and continues to receive his life and being from someone other than himself. One can imagine all sorts of honorable compromise formulas between the two virtues, or, more broadly, between the two moralities or directions of the heart that the two virtues epitomize—Thomas Aquinas's proposal is at once the most modest and most generous—but no combination can preserve what is proper to each or the main point of each one. Accordingly, their relation, although it is not a war, is essentially a turning on one another, from which come some of the great and perhaps the greatest phenomena of the modern European consciousness, as diverse as, for example, the figure of Hamlet and thus Kant's morality.

The magnanimous man points to and embodies the lofty power of nature and this is what makes his behavior so strange and shocking in the eyes of Christians or in our modern eyes. He realizes a certain possibility, the loftiest possibility of the human soul; the disdain he experiences for the multitude, with the irony that veils it, is in sum a necessary consequence of this natural fact. By nature—at least if one isn't telling himself stories— the man who is truly superior necessarily and legitimately disdains the man who truly is his inferior.

For the pagans the Gospels tell just such "stories." For the Christians, they teach that the world in which nature displays these characteristics— let us admit it—is just "the world" or "this world,"[43] whose prince is Satan, and that there is another world where unequal souls are equally creatures of God who wishes to save them all and are equally worthy of being loved for the love of God. They even teach that God, by an irony that confounds the irony of the magnanimous man, has distributed the gifts of grace without concerning himself to maintain the least proportion with the gifts of nature and has revealed to the foolish and the weak what he has hidden from the wise and the strong.[44] Consequently, humility equally becomes all men who are all equally subject to God, since they are his creatures.[45]

Once the story of God's salutary or saving interventions spread and was accepted in faith by the whole world with extraordinary authority,[46] men found themselves caught between the conflicting authorities of nature and magnanimity on the one hand and grace and humility on the other. Some again found or strove to recover the Greek understanding of the human world and, in seeking to be magnanimous, publicly or secretly waged a struggle against the lowering of humanity by the "Galilean." We call them Greeks or pagans. Others were "meek and humble of heart,"[47] humble to the point of considering themselves the vilest of men, the most wretched of sinners: among those who call themselves Christians, these are the saints. As time went on and the two parties or camps kept turning on one another, the reciprocal erosion I spoke of earlier was becoming more serious and deeper and the number of those who did not want to choose or could no longer do so was growing. They sought a third term, another virtue that overcomes, envelops, or erases the opposition between Athens and the Gospel, between magnanimity and humility. They sought the unprece- dented combination that would allow man to erect a "new world" to in- habit, neither "this world" nor "the other world," but a third world or third city that is neither natural like the city of the Greeks nor supernatu- ral like the city of the Christians, but simply and purely human: the city of man. This third party, which became more and more numerous and ended up subjecting or absorbing the two original camps almost completely, is the party of the Moderns.

Modern man is the man who does not know how to be either magnani- mous or humble. He is defined by this twofold negation. He overlooks and rejects these two virtues that correspond to the two principal directions of the human soul and that equally rebuff and even make him indignant. The equal refusal of these two virtues, the effort to flee them both equally, gives the modern mind its extraordinary irritability and energy.

When one becomes seriously concerned to open up this third way, one must at the same time and in the same affirmation deny magnanimity, without reinstating humility or lending it support—and deny humility, without reestablishing magnanimity or lending it support. Now this seems to be an extremely complex problem of moral geometry, but it will turn out to be at bottom strangely simple; or, at least, the effort toward the solution, the calculation of the parallelogram of forces, if I can speak of it that way, will express itself in a moving force of strangely constant direction and intensity. Modern man, or rather man in the process of becoming modern, is engaged in a combat on two fronts and in the process he uncovers more and more what is common to the two enemies. Their common and unique root soon becomes clear to him.

In his polemic against grace, modern man feels like and wants to be natural man and to make himself equal to his nature. But at the same time, in his polemic against nature, he finds a secret ally in grace that has revealed to him possibilities unknown to nature, in particular possibilities of equality. Thus, just as grace is a burden for the natural man he still is, so also nature appears as an obstacle to the new man he is becoming. The bonds of this dialectical knot get tighter at the same time and with the same force. The more grace seems to him to be a burden, the more he feels like a natural man and the more nature is an obstacle he wants to evade or an enemy he wants to subject. Rousseau sought both to rediscover "natural man" and to "denature man," and in so doing he tightened the dialectical knot in the most rigorous fashion; or it was he who revealed with the greatest clarity the extent to which this knot is implacably tightened.

The reciprocal turning of the two adversaries on one another in the end reduces and even destroys and abolishes their incompatible aspects, allowing only the compatible elements to remain and thus to become common to both. Man in the process of becoming modern discovers that nature and grace both entail his obedience and that, strangely, nature does so no less than grace. If the life of the Christian is to obey the grace of God who created him, the magnanimous man also only obeys the nature that he did not make, when he becomes aware of his natural superiority and expresses it with his disdain and irony. Indeed, this was not unknown to the Greeks, for whom the "good life" was life lived in obedience to nature, "according to nature." Since nature was at that time counter-distinguished from "law" or "convention"—from *nomos*—life according to nature appeared to be much more a liberation than a matter of obedience. Grace, however, is opposed to nature in a very different way than is law. Whereas law appeared narrower and more particular than nature—nature encompassed and dominated law and gave it its measure—grace appeared to be something broader than nature. Whether one believes grace to be real or a fiction, it is a fact that it claims to overcome or reduce to pettiness the most basic natural differences—for grace, there is neither master nor slave, neither male nor female, neither strong nor weak[48]—and at least it has the power to make this claim accepted by a countless multitude. One can attempt to interpret grace as only a new modality of ancient "law" or "convention" and unleash against it all the disdain and irony of which nature is capable, but it is nonetheless the case that grace makes nature appear narrow and particular, as the principle of particularization which, in the ancient world, signified the universal vis-à-vis the *nomos*. Obedience to nature, which was liberation and liberty among the pagans, comes to resemble obedience. Since the authority attained by grace entails a certain obedience of nature to grace, the experience of nature's obedience to grace has made man sensitive in a new way to his obedience to nature.

Whatever the case may be, caught in the conflict between magnanimity and humility, humble or magnanimous, man obeys something which is not himself: he is a prey to what Kant calls heteronomy. And, in a certain way, the heteronomy of nature is more radical, more substantial, more essential than the heteronomy of grace. In the first place, nature is the pivotal point on which every heteronomy must necessarily articulate itself in order to reach man. In particular, man only receives grace because his nature is capable of receiving it.[49] Then, as even the most authoritative theologians agree, nature is more essential to man than grace, since its "mode of being" as a "substance" is nobler than the mode of being of grace, which is an "accident."[50] Thus, to open the third way, to bring to an end the endless battle between magnanimity and humility and nature and grace, one must first of all and above all keep nature at a distance and even subject it since it is the key to the scheme of heteronomy. The definitive artifice needs to be elaborated, the pitchfork that would make it impossible for nature to return.[51]

Kant, unlike Rousseau, found himself in the situation of man in the process of becoming modern without having chosen it; but, very much unlike Rousseau in this, Kant accepted his situation with remarkable docility; one can even say that his own greatness in this context resides in the fidelity of obedience with which he deferred to the demands of the speculative situation I have attempted to describe.

X

We are now in a position to state precisely the intellectual content or internal articulation of the figure of the consciousness that provided the point of departure of this inquiry and where we saw the first determination of modern man.

Modern man lives in History; he understands and defines himself as a "historical being." Taken seriously as it ought to be, this definition signifies that a new element has been discovered that envelops and dominates the traditional articulations of human experience. To recognize this new element and to act and think in accord with it—with History and not any longer with Nature or Law—is the duty and privilege of modern man inasmuch as he is modern.

If our inquiry has not been an aimless rambling, it leads us to impose a rigorous restraint on the import of these affirmations. Once we put aside the pride and intoxication that accompanied the enthronement of History and Historical Man, we see that this discovery is rather an invention and that, far from revealing an unheard of third element or essence, it simply displaces man's relations to nature and law. That is no mean thing, of course!

We have attempted to establish that modern man, as modern, both flees from and seeks out law. He flees the law that is given to him and seeks the law he gives himself. He flees the law given to him by nature, by God, or that he gave himself yesterday and that today weighs on him like the law of another. He seeks the law he gives himself and without which he would be but the plaything of nature, of God, or of his own past. The law he seeks ceaselessly and continually becomes the law he flees. In flight and in pursuit, with the difference of the two laws always before him, modern man proceeds in this way to the continual creation of what he calls History.

In this enterprise, the nature of man is his principal enemy. It is the mother of all heteronomies, the ever available base of grace that perhaps is always possible, and as such nature preserves, through memory and by habit, the law of the past, the dead letter. Nature is the condition and summation of all that one must flee. Modern man thus affirms the difference between the law he seeks and the law he flees by ever more completely fleeing and subjecting nature, including his own nature. He subjects nature to his "liberty," his "autonomy," to the law that is always new and of which he is forever the author. This is to say that he subjects nature to the continual affirmation of the difference itself.

Of course, it is not nature in all its aspects and expressions that he flees and seeks to subject in this way. On many sides, the life of modern man, democratic life, is much more "natural" than the life of earlier regimes. Or would one say that wearing a wig and kissing the hand are more natural than the brush cut and the handshake? But he flees or seeks to subject so to speak the "naturality" itself of nature. However one may understand it precisely, nature manifests itself in what is common to diverse human individuals; it is what one man awakens in another man; it is the bond between them of which no one can ever be completely the author nor the master. As we have noted, this unbreakable and undetermined bond that for these *two* reasons needs to be instituted and that for the Greeks took the form of either the equality of friends or the inequality of the magnanimous man and the slave, was decisively extended or complicated by the Christian proposition that the man who, for his own natural good ought to serve and who could not be a friend by nature, now has his master wash

his feet and serve him. The master and the slave are now more than
friends; they have become brothers. What am I now? Master, servant,
friend, or brother? Shall I remain forever caught in the suspense of this
overwhelming uncertainty like an "embittered prince along the shore," a
"lord who cannot become what he is meant to be"?[52] No, I ran toward the
resolution by casting into the past all the natural and supernatural
bonds—still natural for all that—as a dead weight, so that I could at last
be sovereign over myself: every uncertainty will be overcome when I shall
be the sole author of all my bonds. Of course, at any moment in time—I
know it well, as "progressivist" as I am, and the "reactionaries" could
spare hitting me with it as one those "first truths" they cherish—at any
moment in the future, I will not be in full command of my nature, but, by
ascribing the difference of the two laws to the articulation of the differences in times, I do exercise a kind of continual sovereignty, which I exercise according to History. For me to stop for a second would be to fall back
into the well of the centuries, and that is why the "reactionaries" and even
the "conservatives" horrify me so sincerely. In this sense, too, I am truly a
"historical being."

Becoming conscious of himself and defining himself as a "historical
being," modern man resolutely blinds himself to the very thing he is in the
process of doing. He pretends to take from History the difference between
the two modalities of the law he is forever producing. By perceiving a
voluntary, deliberate, and arbitrary perspective on his own action as
though it were an objective element and even the supreme element of reality and at the same time the very element of his sovereignty, modern man
surrenders to the most bombastic illusion that has ever enslaved the thinking species. Compared with his self-consciousness, there was a good deal
more sobriety and modesty in the soul of Xerxes.

XI

It is difficult for us to acknowledge that the historical point of view which
is ours is a methodical illusion. We find it hard to believe that we try so
hard to deceive ourselves. Our sense of History is surely a sincere feeling
that merges irresistibly with our sense of time. Let us attempt to conceive
the modern enterprise in traditional and poetic terms as a new empire that
extends over time rather than space. Thanks to the backward and forward
perspectives of the historical viewpoint, all of humanity is gathered under
our gaze, which is to say that humanity gazes on itself in a kind of conquest of itself by itself. This empire in continual expansion toward both
the past and the future does not come up against the limits of other empires: its boundaries are forever being extended with the flow of time.

There is no more natural or noble idea than that of empire, of the gathering of the human race under one sole governor who is the instrument and symbol of its unity. Once man defines himself as a historical being who lives essentially in the element of history, he gives this idea the greatest conceivable extension by integrating the succession of generations into a unified whole. As human energy embraces temporal succession, time itself provides the principle of order. Humanity gathered in this way no longer needs any visible head: with no emperor, it is the truly universal empire.

One can sense nonetheless that in thus going beyond the boundaries of space and invading time itself, humanity absolutely breaks out of its natural limits and condition. It is man's nature to realize himself within the framework and under the conditions of space. No matter how long an empire may last, what defines it is that it holds together the entire human species, or at least it aims at doing so, in the present time. The empire gathers in the present time and in the presence of its emperor; it gives presence and visibility to the principle of unity.

Machiavelli remarks that after the end of the Roman Empire this gathering in the present of human energy could not be realized again.[53] A thousand "historical reasons" no doubt explain why this supreme effort of human magnanimity had no real successor. But, apart from these thousand reasons, there is one reason that suffices. From inside this empire, or, at least, within it, there arose a new empire, or a new kind of empire, one more vast in extent since it encompasses all men in space and time and more vast in understanding since the virtue that gathers it is not magnanimity, which makes masters visible and sets them apart, but rather humility, which does not recognize persons and, being invisible, opens the invisible space of hearts. The emperor of the visible empire, "sol invictus," the invincible sun, has as his opponent and successor the vicar of the invisible empire, "servus servorum Dei," the servant of the servants of God.

Some other time we shall study the cause that resides in the separation of the two Romes. We must prepare for a second and altogether different crossing. We never understand more than the half of things when we neglect the science of Rome.

INTRODUCTION

THE QUESTION OF MAN

1. Immanuel Kant, *An Answer to the Question: What Is Enlightenment?*, in *prin.*, in *Perpetual Peace and Other Essays*, trans. Ted Humphrey (Indianapolis, 1982), 41–46.

2. "Dasein is never to be taken ontologically as an instance or special case of some genus of entities as things that are present-at-hand." Martin Heidegger, *Being and Time*, Introduction, par. 9, trans. John Macquarrie and Edward Robinson (New York, 1962), 67–68.

3. See Raymond Aron, *Introduction to the Philosophy of History*, sec. 6, pt. 3; and Martin Heidegger, *Being and Time*, Introduction, par. 6, *in prin.*, and par. 7, *in fine*, as well as his letter to Karl Jaspers of June 27, 1922, in *Martin Heidegger/ Karl Jaspers. Briefwechsel 1920–1963* (Frankfurt am Main, 1990), 27.

CHAPTER I

THE AUTHORITY OF HISTORY

1. See the author's Foreword to *The Spirit of the Laws* and the epigraph from Ovid: "Prolem sine matre creatum." *Metamorphoses*, II, 553.

2. James Harrington, *Oceana*, ed. J.G.A. Pocock (Cambridge, 1977), 161.

3. See Montesquieu, *The Spirit of the Laws*, bk. 14, chap. 3; bk. 18, chap. 23; and especially bk. 30, chap. 19.

4. Niccolo Machiavelli, *The Prince*, chap. 15, trans. Harvey C. Mansfield (Chicago, 1985), 61.

5. Montesquieu, *The Spirit of the Laws*, trans. Anne M. Cohler, Basia Carolyn Miller, and Harold Samuel Stone (Cambridge, 1989), bk. 3, chap. 3.

6. After noting that the "true political man" is concerned above all with virtue, Aristotle proposes as "paradigms" of this proper preoccupation the lawgivers of Crete and Sparta, who certainly did not live "under popular government." See Aristotle, *Nicomachean Ethics*, 1027ff.

7. Montesquieu notes elsewhere that "Plato was indignant of the tyranny of the people of Athens." *The Spirit of the Laws*, bk. 29, chap. 19.

8. See Plato, *Republic*, 562 b–c.

9. Thomas Hobbes, *Leviathan*, chap. 11, *in prin.*; and chap. 15, *in fine*.

10. Hobbes, *Leviathan*, chap. 12. It should be noted that Hobbes is capable of lying no less boldly than Montesquieu about the content of Greek political philoso-

phy: "From Aristotle's civil philosophy, they have learned, to call all manner of commonwealths but the popular (such as was at that time the state of Athens), tyranny." *Leviathan*, chap. 46.

11. Montesquieu, *The Spirit of the Laws*, bk. V, chap. 2.

12. As early as *The Persian Letters*, one finds the following in the story of Aphéridon and Astarté: "'What!' I said, utterly overcome. 'So, my sister, you believe that religion to be the true one?'

"'Alas,' said she, 'how much better for me were it not! I am making for its sake too great a sacrifice to be able not to believe it'. . . ." Letter 67, op. cit., trans. J. Robert Loy (Cleveland, 1961), 143.

13. Chapter 6 of book 4 already compared Lycurgus to William Penn and the Jesuits in Paraguay. In a note to chapter 5 of bk. 3 Montesquieu produces this denial: "I speak here about political virtue, which is moral virtue in the sense that it points toward the general good, very little about individual moral virtues, and not at all about that virtue which relates to revealed truths. This will be seen in book V, chapter 2." Yet, as we have seen, in bk. 4, chap. 5, the individual virtues "are only" the preference for the general interest over the particular, which is the very life of democracy. And we have also just read in bk. 5, chap. 2, the passage to which Montesquieu refers in this note, that there is a very strong likeness between the political virtue of citizens of democracies and the ascetic virtue of monks, which surely cannot but "relate to revealed truths." The denial of bk. 3, chap. 5 draws attention to and confirms the affirmation of bk. V, chap. 2.

14. Montesquieu, *The Spirit of the Laws*, bk. 4, chaps. 6 and 7; bk. 19, chap. 16.

15. Montesquieu, *The Spirit of the Laws*, bk. 4, chap. 8.

16. Montesquieu, *The Spirit of the Laws*, bk. 5, chaps. 2 and 3.

17. See Aristotle, *Nicomachean Ethics*, 1101a14, 1102l5, 1176b7; and *Politics*, 1295a37.

18. Montesquieu, *The Spirit of the Laws*, bk. 5, chap. 3.

19. Benjamin Constant, *The Spirit of Conquest and Usurpation and Their Relation to European Civilization*, pt. 2, chap. 7, in *Political Writings*, trans. Biancamaria Fontana (Cambridge, 1988), 108.

20. Nietzsche writes on this matter: "Up until now *this* has been the only great war, there has been no more decisive interrogation than that conducted by the Renaissance . . .; I behold a spectacle at once so meaningful and so strangely paradoxical it would have given all the gods of Olympus an opportunity for an immortal roar of laughter—*Cesare Borgia as Pope*? . . . Am I understood? . . . Very well, that would have been a victory of the only sort I desire today—: Christianity would thereby have been *abolished*!—What happened? A German monk, Luther, went to Rome. This monk . . . fulminated in Rome *against* the Renaissance. . . . Instead of grasping with profound gratitude the tremendous event which had taken place, the overcoming of Christianity in its very *seat*—his hatred grasped only how to nourish itself on this spectacle." Friedrich Nietzsche, *Anti-Christ*, trans. R. J. Hollingdale (Hammondsworth, 1972), 184–85.

21. See Machiavelli, *The Prince*, chap. 11.

22. See Augustine, *The City of God*, bk. 4, chap. 4.

23. See Thomas Aquinas, *Summa Theologiae*, I, q. 8, a. 8, ad 2.

24. See Montesquieu, *The Spirit of the Laws*, bk. IV, chap. 4.

25. See, for example, what Montesquieu writes in his *Pensées*: "The Two Worlds. One spoils the other and other spoils the one. Two are too many. Only one was needed." *Pensées*, 1176.

26. "A Spartan woman had five sons in the army and was awaiting news of the battle. A Helot arrives; trembling, she asks him for news. 'Your sons were killed.' 'Base slave, did I ask you that?'

" 'We won the victory.' The mother runs to the temple and gives thanks to the gods. This is the female citizen." Jean-Jacques Rousseau, *Émile*, bk. 1, trans. Allan Bloom (New York, 1979), 40.

27. Montesquieu, *The Spirit of the Laws*, bk. 25, chap. 4.

28. Rousseau, *Discourse on the Origin and Foundations of Inequality among Men*, in *The First and Second Discourses*, trans. Roger D. and Judith R. Masters (New York, 1964) 136–37; *Rousseau juge de Jean-Jacques*, Premier Dialogue and Deuxième Dialogue, in *Oeuvres complètes* (Paris, 1959), vol. 1, 670 and 823ff.; *Lettre à Christophe de Beaumont*, in *Oeuvres complètes*, vol. 4, 970, note.

29. See Rousseau, *On the Social Contract*, bk. 1, chaps. 6 and 8.

30. See Plato, *Republic*, 443d–e; St. Paul, Romans 6.17–18; and Thomas Aquinas, *Summa Theologiae*, I, q. 77, a. 4.

31. Rousseau, *On the Social Contract*, bk. 2, chap. 7; and *Émile*, 41.

32. See Hobbes, *Leviathan*, chaps. 21, 32, and 44.

33. Friedrich Nietzsche, *The Genealogy of Morals*, bk. 3, no. 11, trans. Walter Kaufmann (New York, 1969), 117.

34. Rousseau rails against these very criteria in his *Discourse on the Arts and Sciences*. In the debate between "Plato" and "us" Rousseau takes the side of Plato. What he says in the preface to *Narcisse* is the exact opposite of Montesquieu's position: "Everything that facilitates communication among nations brings with it other nations' crimes, not their virtues, and alters in every nation the mores that are proper to their climate and the constitution of their government." *Oeuvres complètes* (Paris, 1961), vol. 2, 964, note 2. With exquisite critical finesse Rousseau gathers in one sentence his adversary's two great theses of practical politics and makes us ask ourselves whether they are not contradictory. Whether commerce does not tend precisely to dissolve this "general spirit" that according to Montesquieu a good legislator must above all respect. See Montesquieu, *The Spirit of the Laws*, bk. 19, chap. 5.

35. Montesquieu, *The Spirit of the Laws*, bk. 20, chap. 2.

36. Constant, *The Spirit of Conquest and Usurpation*, pt. 1, chap. 2, in *Political Writings*, 53.

37. See Adam Smith, *An Inquiry into the Nature and Causes of the Wealth of Nations*, bk. 1, chap. 2, *in prin.*; and see below, sec. 3 of chap. 3.

38. Montesquieu, *The Spirit of the Laws*, bk. 7, chap. 2. One should recall what Montesquieu says of the virtue of monks in chap. 2 of bk. 5: "what remains, therefore, is the passion for the very rule that afflicts them."

39. See Aristotle, *Politics*, 1252b.

40. See below, secs. 6 to 10 of chap. 5.

41. Montesquieu, *The Spirit of the Laws*, bk. 22, chap. 21.

42. Montesquieu, *The Spirit of the Laws*, bk. 21, chap. 20.

43. Montesquieu writes in his *Pensées*: "It is striking that men invented the letters of exchange only recently, since nothing in the world is so useful." *Pensées*, 77.

44. Montesquieu, *The Spirit of the Laws*, bk. 21, chap. 20.

45. In his *Replies and Explanations Given to the Faculty of Theology*, Montesquieu writes: "The law of Basilius thus prohibited receiving interest indefinitely and in all cases. The emperor Leo made another law, in which he exalts the beauty and sublimity of his father's law; but he says that it has caused the greatest evils, that lending has ceased everywhere, and that the empire has suffered so greatly that he is obliged to revoke this sublime law and to rest content with reducing usury from 12% to 4% *per annum*." Montesquieu, *Oeuvres complètes*, ed. R. Caillois (Paris, 1951), vol. 2, 1186–87.

46. Montesquieu, *The Spirit of the Laws*, bk. 21, chap. 20.

47. Machiavelli, *The Prince*, chap. 7; and see Harvey C. Mansfield, *The Taming of the Prince* (New York, 1989), 121–49.

48. Machiavelli, *The Prince*, chap. 15.

49. Machiavelli, *The Prince*, chap. 18.

50. See sec. 1 of chap. 3 below.

51. Montesquieu, *The Spirit of the Laws*, bk. 25, chap. 12.

52. Montesquieu, *The Spirit of the Laws*, bk. 14, chap. 13; and bk. 19, chap. 27.

53. Montesquieu, *The Spirit of the Laws*, bk. 14, chap. 13; bk. 19, chap. 27; bk. 8, chap. 8; bk. 23, chap. 11; bk. 5, chap. 11; bk. 13, chap. 17; bk. 20, chap.2.

54. The lover of the Law speaks to the Lawgiver in these terms:

> I will delight in Thy statues;
> I will not forget Thy word.
> Deal bountifully with Thy servant,
> that I may live and observe Thy word.
> Open my eyes, that I may behold
> wondrous things out of Thy law.
> I am a sojourner on earth;
> hide not Thy commandments from me!
> My soul is consumed with longing
> for Thy ordinances at all times.

　　　　　　　　　　　　　Psalm 118.16–20 (Revised Standard Version)

CHAPTER II
THE SOCIOLOGICAL VIEWPOINT

1. Alphonse de Lamartine, *Voyage en Orient* (Paris, 1859), 271.

2. Adam Smith in some way provides the mediating link when he praises the merits of commercial society, as we shall see in chapter 3.

3. Montesquieu, *The Spirit of the Laws*, bk. 20, chap. 7.

4. As is well known, the "reactionary" political attitude is born of the "reaction" to the French Revolution. The so-called "reactionary" or "retrograde" school (Maistre, Bonald) holds that the revolution, by an unprecedented and properly

Satanic arrogance, has foolishly and moreover vainly placed the will of man above
the necessities of the social order.

5. *Quid Secundatus politicae scientiae instituendae contulerit.* "Montesquieu's
Contribution to the Rise of Social Science," in Émile Durkheim, *Montesquieu and
Rousseau: Forerunners of Sociology*, trans. Ralph Mannheim (Ann Arbor, Mich.,
1965), 1–64.

6. Durkheim, *Montesquieu and Rousseau*, 3–4.

7. See Aristotle, *Nicomachean Ethics*, 1094–95.

8. See Durkheim, *Montesquieu and Rousseau*, 9.

9. See Durkheim, *Montesquieu and Rousseau*, 11–13.

10. Durkheim, *Montesquieu and Rousseau*, 12.

11. Durkheim, *Montesquieu and Rousseau*, 18–23. See also in *The Rules of Sociological Method*, the second part of chapter 5 devoted to "the explanation of
social facts." Trans. S. A. Solovay and J. H. Mueller, ed. G. Catlin (New York,
1966), 97–112.

12. See Philippe Reynaud, *Max Weber et les dilemmes de la raison moderne*
(Paris, 1987), sec. 2, chap. 2.

13. Durkheim, *Montesquieu and Rousseau*, 10. See section 3 above.

14. This was already the judgment of Auguste Comte: "What characterizes the
principal strength of this memorable work (*The Spirit of the Laws*), such as to
attest unimpeachably to the eminent superiority of its illustrious author over all
contemporary philosophers, is the preponderant tendency one senses throughout
to conceive henceforth of political phenomena as necessarily subject to invariable
natural laws in the same way as all other phenomena whatever. This disposition is
clearly articulated from the outset by this admirable preliminary chapter where for
the first time since the dawn of human reason the general idea of law is at last
correctly defined with regard to all possible subjects, even political subjects."
Cours de philosophie positive, 47e leçon.

15. "[Montesquieu] seeks out the causes upon which the form of society itself
depends and, among these causes, the one that plays the major role, that is, the
volume of the society. . . . So close is the relationship between the nature of a
society and its volume that the principle peculiar to each type ceases to operate if
the population increases or diminishes excessively." Durkheim, *Montesquieu and
Rousseau*, 37–38. According to Durkheim's mature thought, volume is only deter-
minative in relation to the dynamic density of society. See *Rules of Sociological
Method*, 113–16.

16. In a work written prior to *The Spirit of the Laws*, Montesquieu writes: "It
is not chance that rules the world. Ask the Romans, who had a continuous sequence of successes when they were guided by a certain plan, and an uninterrupted
sequence of reverses when they followed another. There are general causes, moral
and physical, which act in every monarchy, elevating it, maintaining it, or hurling
it to the ground. All accidents are controlled by these causes. And if the chance of
one battle—that is, a particular cause—has brought a state to ruin, some general
cause made it necessary for that state to perish from a single battle. In a word, the
main trend draws with it all particular accidents." *Considerations on the Greatness and Decadence of the Romans*, trans. D. Lowenthal (Ithaca, N.Y., 1968), 169.
Durkheim pushes the idea to its limit: "In consequence of the society's particular

situation, communal life must necessarily assume a certain definite form. This form is expressed by the laws, which thus result with the same inevitability from the efficient causes. To deny this is to assume that most social phenomena, particularly the most important, have no cause whatsoever." *Montesquieu and Rousseau*, 43.

17. Durkheim, *Montesquieu and Rousseau*, 43.

18. See the end of the Durkheim passage cited in section 3.

19. Durkheim's first and most fundamental rule for the observation of social facts is: "Consider social facts as things." *Rules of Sociological Method*, 14.

20. See Philippe Reynaud, *Max Weber et les dilemmes de la raison moderne*, 31.

21. "He [Montesquieu] understood with a wonderful lucidity that the nature of societies is no less stable and consistent than that of man and that it is no easier to modify the type of a society than the species of an animal." Durkheim, *Montesquieu and Rousseau*, 21.

22. See in the transcendental dialectic, the Introduction and the opening of book 2 of *The Critique of Pure Reason*.

23. Parmenides, fragment 3, in *The Presocratic Philosophers*, ed. G. S. Kirk and J. E. Raven (Cambridge, 1957), no. 344.

24. See Max Weber, *The Protestant Ethic and the Spirit of Capitalism*, trans. Talcott Parsons (New York, 1958), 109–12.

25. "Accordingly, to the question of how the individual can be certain of his own election, he has at bottom only the answer that we should be content with the knowledge that God has chosen and depend further only on that implicit trust in Christ which is the result of true faith. He rejects in principle the assumption that one can learn from the conduct of others whether they are chosen or damned. It is an unjustifiable attempt to free God's secrets. The elect differ externally in this in no way from the damned. . . . Quite naturally this attitude was impossible for his followers as early as Beza, and, above all, for the broad mass of ordinary men." Weber, *The Protestant Ethic and the Spirit of Capitalism*, 110.

26. See R. H. Tawney, *Religion and the Rise of Capitalism* (London, 1964), 319–21.

27. See Weber, *The Protestant Ethic and the Spirit of Capitalism*, 183.

28. In an otherwise very incisive commentary on the thought of Max Weber to which I have already referred, Philippe Raynaud writes: "Weber was in no way concerned to assign to religion the role that Marx gave to economics, but on the contrary to explain certain traits of Western capitalist development that are unique to it and that cannot be deduced *a priori*." *Max Weber et les dilemmes de la raison moderne*, 31. I do not understand this "on the contrary." "In addition" would be more appropriate, it seems to me. The explanation of an individual case presupposes a general proposition and moreover its application to the case under consideration, which is only rarely a deduction. One cannot see how Protestantism could have acted upon the capitalist development of the West without "religion" acting upon the "economy." Perhaps Raynaud means to say only that the fact that religion is in this case in the position of a cause or of particularly marked influence does not prove that it is always in this causal role. Indeed, but Weber precisely rejects such an affirmation of eminent causality *in this case*. See Weber, *The Protestant Ethic and the Spirit of Capitalism*, 183.

29. Weber, *The Protestant Ethic and the Spirit of Capitalism*, 183.

30. Weber, *The Protestant Ethic and the Spirit of Capitalism*, 227–28.

31. Weber, *The Protestant Ethic and the Spirit of Capitalism*, 181.

32. This clause excludes from the benefit of axiological neutrality those societies that are subject to a massively criminal regime and that therefore are inclined to self-destruct. This exclusion is itself axiologically neutral, since it matters only that a society be truly a society. There remains, of course, the difficulty that certain criminal regimes are terribly durable.

33. Montesquieu, *The Spirit of the Laws*, bk. 19, chap. 14.

34. See Montesquieu, *The Spirit of the Laws*, bk. 14, chap. 5.

35. Raymond Aron has described very well the circular character of sociological analysis: "Let us consider the first meaning, society as the social milieu which determines other phenomena. Durkheim rightly insists that various institutions— family, crime, education, politics, morality, religion—are conditioned by the organization of society; each type of society has its type of family, its type of education, its type of state, its type of morality. But he has a tendency to 'realize' the social milieu—i.e., to take it for a total reality—and to forget that it is an analytical category and not a final cause. *For what is* social milieu as cause in relation to a particular institution is from another point of view merely all the institutions which social milieu is *supposed to explain.*" *Main Currents in Sociological Thought,* trans. Richard Howard and Helen Weaver (New York 1989), vol. 2, 102–3 (emphasis added).

36. Montesquieu, *The Spirit of the Laws*, bk. 19, chap. 21.

37. Montesquieu, *The Spirit of the Laws*, bk. 24, chap. 7.

38. "Be perfect, therefore, as your heavenly Father is perfect." Matthew 5:48. See also 1 Peter 1:15–16 and James 1:4.

39. Adam Ferguson, *An Essay on the History of Civil Society* (Edinburgh, 1966), 183.

40. See Montesquieu, *The Spirit of the Laws*, bk. 5, chap. 11; bk. 5, chap. 14; bk. 8, chaps. 6, 7, 8; and bk. 23, chap. 11.

41. See Montesquieu, *The Spirit of the Laws*, bk. 2, chap. 4.

42. Ibid..

43. I have given the broad lines of Montesquieu's interpretation in *An Intellectual History of Liberalism*, trans. Rebecca Balinski (Princeton, 1994), 53–64.

44. See Montesquieu, *The Spirit of the Laws*, bk. 19, chap. 16.

CHAPTER III

THE ECONOMIC SYSTEM

1. Smith's complacency prompted Walter Bagehot's summary of *The Wealth of Nations*: "How, being a savage, man rose to be a Scotsman."

2. Adam Smith, *An Inquiry into the Nature and Causes of the Wealth of Nations*, ed. Edwin Canaan (Chicago, 1976), bk. III, chap. 3.

3. Smith, *The Wealth of Nations*, bk. 2, chap. 3.

4. Ibid.

5. Ibid.

6. See, for example, what Smith says about China in *The Wealth of Nations*, bk. I, chap. 9.

7. David Hume, "Of Civil Liberty," in *Essays Moral, Political, and Literary* (Oxford, 1963), 94; Montesquieu, *Pensées*, 32, and *The Spirit of the Laws*, bk. 20, chap. 4.

8. Smith, *The Wealth of Nations*, bk. 2, chap. 3.

9. Hobbes, *Leviathan*, chap. 11.

10. Hobbes, *Leviathan*, chap. 13.

11. Smith, *Wealth of Nations*, bk. 1, chap. 5.

12. Adam Smith, *The Theory of Moral Sentiments* (Indianapolis, 1976), part 1, sec. 3, chap. 2.

13. Smith, *The Wealth of Nations*, bk. 2, chap. 3.

14. Ibid.

15. Ibid.

16. Ibid.

17. Smith, *Wealth of Nations*, bk. 1, chap. 2.

18. Smith, *Theory of Moral Sentiments*, part 4, chap. 1.

19. Ibid.

20. Smith, *Wealth of Nations*, bk. 4, chap. 2.

21. Smith, *Wealth of Nations*, bk. 3, chap. 4.

22. The epigram is even repeated two pages later: "Having sold their birthright, not like Esau for a mess of pottage in time of hunger and necessity, but in the wantonness of plenty, for trinkets and baubles, fitter to be the play-things of children than the serious pursuits of men, they became as insignificant as any substantial burgher or tradesman in a city." Smith, *Wealth of Nations*, bk. 3, chap. 4.

23. Smith, *Wealth of Nations*, bk. 3, chap. 4.

24. Smith, *Theory of Moral Sentiments*, part 4, chap. 1.

25. Ibid.

26. Ibid.

27. Ibid.

28. Ibid.

29. Ibid.

30. "His self-existence is, therefore, inherently universal, and self-interest is merely a supposition that cannot get the length of making concrete and actual what it means or supposes, viz. to do something that is not to further the good of all." G.W.F. Hegel, *The Phenomenology of the Mind*, VI,B,1a, trans. J. B. Baillie (New York, 1967), 520.

31. See Smith, *Wealth of Nations*, bk. 1, chap. 5.

32. I admit that I feel directly addressed by the following remark of Schumpeter commenting on Smith's texts on value: "To this day, it has remained difficult to make the philosophy-minded see that all this is completely irrelevant for a theory of value—considered not as a profession of faith or as an argument in social ethics, but as a tool of analysis of economic reality." Joseph Schumpeter, *History of Economic Analysis* (Oxford, 1954), 311. Schumpeter contends that Smith did not really work out a theory of value-labor. See *History of Economic Analysis*, 188–89 and 309–11.

33. Curiously, Marx, who saw the first point so well, remained blind to the

second. It can indeed be said that, logically, the source of all value cannot of itself have any value; but practically, in order to be able to produce its effects, it has to obey the law it gives.

34. Smith, *The Wealth of Nations*, bk. 1, chap. 6.

35. Smith, *The Wealth of Nations*, bk. 3, chap. 4.

36. See Karl Marx, *Capital*, ed. Frederick Engels (New York, 1967), vol. 1, 235–37 and 535–42.

CHAPTER IV
THE HIDDEN MAN

1. See Hobbes, *Leviathan*, chap. 46.

2. Blaise Pascal, *Pensées*, trans W. F. Trotter, #137 (Brunschvicg).

3. Hobbes, *Leviathan*, chap. 8.

4. See Hobbes, *Leviathan*, chaps. 3 and 5.

5. Carl Schmitt, *The Concept of the Political*, trans. George Schwab (Chicago, 1996), 65.

6. John Locke, *An Essay Concerning Human Understanding*, ed. Peter H. Nidditch (Oxford, 1982), bk. 2 chap. 21.

7. See Locke, *An Essay Concerning Human Understanding*, bk. 2, chap. 8; bk. 2, chap. 21 and chap. 23.

8. See Locke, *An Essay Concerning Human Understanding*, bk. 2, chap. 21, par. 17 to 19.

9. See Locke, *An Essay Concerning Human Understanding*, bk. 3, chap. 10.

10. See Hobbes, *Leviathan*, chaps. 4, 5, and 46.

11. See Aristotle, *Posterior Analytics*, 46a; *Nicomachean Ethics*, 1140a; *Metaphysics*, 981a–b, 1074b; and Plato, *Laws* 888–89.

12. See Locke, *An Essay Concerning Human Understanding*, bk. 2, chaps. 2 and 12.

13. Locke, *An Essay Concerning Human Understanding*, bk. 1, chap. 2, par. 10; and *The Second Treatise on Civil Government*, chap. 5, par. 3.

14. See Locke, *Second Treatise*, chap. 5, par. 40.

15. See Locke, *An Essay Concerning Human Understanding*, bk. 2, chaps. 12 and 22, par. 9.

16. See Locke, *An Essay Concerning Human Understanding*, bk. 3, chap. 5.

17. See Locke, *An Essay Concerning Human Understanding*, bk. 3, chap. 5, par. 6.

18. Ibid.

19. See Locke, *An Essay Concerning Human Understanding*, bk. 3, chap. 9, par. 7.

20. See Locke, *An Essay Concerning Human Understanding*, bk. 2, chap. 22.

21. Hobbes, *Leviathan*, chaps. 6 and 42.

22. Montesquieu, *The Spirit of the Laws*, bk. 1, chap. 2.

23. Jean-Jacques Rousseau, *Discourse on the Origin and Foundations of Inequality among Men*, in *The First and Second Discourses*, trans. Roger D. and Judith R. Masters (New York, 1964), 138–39.

24. Locke, *An Essay Concerning Human Understanding*, bk. 3, chap. 5, par. 7.

25. Locke, *An Essay Concerning Human Understanding*, bk. 1, chap. 3, par. 1; and bk. 4, chap. 4, par. 7.

26. Locke, *An Essay Concerning Human Understanding*, bk. 2, chap. 25, par. 8.

27. Locke, *An Essay Concerning Human Understanding* , bk. 4, chap. 3, par. 18.

28. I have attempted a brief presentation of this political doctrine on its own in chapter 4 of *An Intellectual History of Liberalism*, trans. Rebecca Balinksi (Princeton, 1994), 39–52.

29. Locke, *An Essay Concerning Human Understanding*, bk. 2, chap. 11, par. 10.

30. Locke, *An Essay Concerning Human Understanding*, bk. 1, chap. 1, par. 7.

31. See in particular the sixth "entretien" of *Les Soirées de Saint-Pétersbourg*.

32. See Diogenes Laertius, *Lives of the Illustrious Philosophers*, "Pyrrho," 9 and 11; and Montaigne, *Essays*, bk. 1, 14, and bk. 2, 12.

33. ". . . [B]odies are not, properly speaking, perceived by the senses or by the faculty of imagination, but only by the intellect . . ." René Descartes, *Meditations on First Philosophy*, Second Meditation, trans. Donald A. Kress (Indianapolis, 1979), 23.

34. Marx writes that Hegel "grasps *labour* as the *essence* of man—as man's essence in the act of proving itself . . ." *Economic and Philsophic Manuscripts of 1844*, in *The Marx-Engels Reader*, ed. Robert C. Tucker (New York, 1972), 90.

35. Locke, *An Essay Concerning Human Understanding*, bk. 2, chap. 21, par. 71.

36. Locke, *An Essay Concerning Human Understanding*, bk. 2, chap. 21, par. 55.

37. See Hobbes, *Leviathan*, chaps. 6 and 11.

38. Locke, *An Essay Concerning Human Understanding*, bk. 2, chap. 21, par. 40 (emphasis added).

39. Hobbes, *Leviathan*, chap. 11.

40. Ovid, *Metamorphoses*, 7.20–21. *The Metamorphoses of Ovid*, trans. Allen Mandelbaum (New York, 1993), 210. See St. Paul, Romans 7:14–15 and Galatians 5:17.

41. Locke says "possibly no other." For him simply to consider it, when there were two other prominent possibilities, was to affirm it. A few pages later, Locke adds that the idea of a will that can will and not will at the same time is "a Contradiction too manifest to be admitted." Locke, *An Essay Concerning Human Understanding*, bk. 2, chap. 21. This is exactly the teaching of St. Paul.

42. Locke, *An Essay Concerning Human Understanding*, bk. 2, chap. 21. See Pascal, *Pensées*, #195 and #233 (Brunschvicg).

43. See Leo Strauss, *Natural Right and History* (Chicago, 1963), 249–51.

44. *Homo oeconomicus* is an ectoplasm dear to all parties. Depending on the situation, it provides an ally or a complacent victim.

45. See David Hume, *A Treatise of Human Nature*, bk. 3, part 2, sec. 3, "Of the rules that determine property," ed. L. A. Selby-Bigge and P. H. Nidditch (Oxford, 1978).

46. David Hume, *Enquiries Concerning Human Understanding and Concerning the Principles of Morals*, par. 259, note 1, ed. L. A. Selby-Bigge and P. H. Nidditch (Oxford, 1975).

47. See Hume, *Enquiries*, par. 145; and Locke, *An Essay Concerning Human Understanding*, bk. 4, chap. 3, par. 18 and section 6 above.

48. See Aristotle, *Politics*, 1254a9 and 1260b37–1261a9. On justice according to Aristotle, see *Nicomachean Ethics*, bk. 5.

49. See Hume, *Enquiries*, par. 13, 14, 49.

50. See Hume, *Enquiries*, par. 50–52.

51. Hume, *Enquiries*, par. 59. See also *Treatise*, bk. 1, chap. 3, sec. 14.

52. See Hume, *Treatise*, bk. 1, part 3, sec. 14.

53. See Hume, *Treatise*, bk. 1, part 3, sec. 14.

54. In fact, the confusion reaches its height when Locke speaks of "[S]uch [secondary] Qualities, which in truth are nothing in the Objects themselves, but Powers to produce various Sensations in us by their primary Qualities." Locke, *An Essay Concerning Human Understanding*, bk. 2, chap. 8, par. 10.

55. See Hume, *Treatise*, bk. 1, part 3, sec. 14.

56. Hume, *Treatise*, bk. 1, part 3, sec.14.

57. Hume thus rejects the distinction between primary and secondary qualities as well as the distinction between cause and occasion. These two distinctions rest on the same confusion between the two notions of power, the confused idea and the clear idea.

58. See Hume, *Treatise*, bk. 3, part 1, sec. 1; and *Enquiries*, par. 132, 138, and 234 to 246.

59. Kant writes: "The notion of substance, for example, if we leave out the sensuous determination of permanence, would mean nothing more than a something which can be cogitated as subject, without the possibility of becoming a predicate to anything else." Immanuel Kant, *Critique of Pure Reason*, trans. J.M.D. Meiklejohn (London, 1934), 122. See also the "Principle of the Permanence of Substance" in the "Analogies of Experience," and the "Paralogism of Substantiality" in the "Paralogisms of Pure Reason."

60. See, for example, in *Critique of Pure Reason*, chap. 2 in the Analytic of Principles, "System of all Principles of the Pure Understanding," especially secs. 2 and 3.

61. See Kant's two Prefaces of 1781 and 1787 to his *Critique of Pure Reason*.

62. See the first antinomy of pure reason in *Critique of Pure Reason*, 260–64.

63. "The question arises of how anything like the world in its unity with Dasein is ontologically possible. Is what way must the world *be*, if Dasein is to be able to exist as Being-in-the-World?" Martin Heidegger, *Being and Time*, 69 c, trans. John Macquarrie (New York, 1962), 415.

CHAPTER V
THE TRIUMPH OF THE WILL

1. See Hobbes, *Leviathan*, chap. 21, and letter to the Marquis of Newcastle "On Liberty and Necessity"; Locke, *An Inquiry Concerning Human Understanding*, bk. 2, chap. 21, paras. 8 to 18; and Spinoza, *Ethics*, bk. 1, appendix; bk. 2, chap. 35, scolia; bk. 2, chap. 48.

2. See Thomas Aquinas, *Summa Theologiae*, Ia, q. 83, a. 2.

3. See Aristotle, *Nicomachean Ethics*, 1111b, 1112b.

4. See Aquinas, *Summa Theologiae*, Ia–IIae, q. 91, a. 2.

5. See Aquinas, *Summa Theologiae*, Ia, q. 83, a. 4.

6. G.W.F. Hegel, *Philosophy of Right*, trans. T. M. Knox (Oxford, 1967), 155–56.

7. Alexis de Tocqueville, *Democracy in America*, trans. G. Lawrence (Garden City, N.Y., 1969), vol. 1, part 2, chap. 10.

8. Tocqueville, *Democracy in America*, vol. 2, part 4, chap. 8.

9. Aristotle, *Politics*, trans. Carnes Lord (Chicago, 1984), 1289b27–1290a7.

10. Aristotle, *Politics*, 1290a13–16.

11. Jean-Jacques Rousseau, *On the Social Contract*, trans. Judith R. Masters (New York, 1978), bk. 1, chap. 6.

12. See Leo Strauss, *The City and Man* (Chicago, 1964), 13–49.

13. Aristotle, *Politics*, 1280a9–11.

14. See Aristotle, *Politics*, 1280a34–35.

15. Aristotle, *Politics*, 1280b12.

16. Montesquieu writes: "Ambition, idleness, meanness in arrogance, the desire to enrich oneself without work, aversion to truth, flattery, treachery, perfidy, the abandonment of all one's engagements, the scorn of the duties of citizens, the fear of the prince's virtue, the expectation of his weaknesses, and more than all that, the perpetual ridicule cast upon virtue, these form, I believe, the character of the greater number of courtiers, as observed in all places and at all times." *The Spirit of the Laws*, bk. 3, chap. 5.

17. Aristotle, *Politics*, 1281a1–10.

18. See Aristotle, *Politics*, 1281a28–30.

19. Aristotle, *Politics*, 1282b22–23.

20. See Aristotle, *Politics*, 1283a3–10.

21. Aristotle, *Politics*, 1283a10–15.

22. See Harry V. Jaffa, "Aristotle," in *History of Political Philosophy*, ed. Leo Strauss and Joseph Cropsey (Chicago, 1972), 110–12.

23. Aristotle, *Politics*, 1283b13–14.

24. Aristotle, *Politics*, 1283b4–5.

25. See Aristotle, *Politics*, 1283a33–34.

26. See Aristotle, *Politics*, 1252b29–30 and 1253a1.

27. See Aristotle, *Politics*, 1282b14–18 and 1284b6.

28. See Hobbes, *Leviathan*, chap. 13, *in princ.*

29. Aristotle, *Politics*, 1288a15–19.

30. See Aristotle, *Politics*, 1284a3–b34.

31. See Plato, *Apology of Socrates*, 21c–22e; and Aristotle, *Metaphysics*, 993a30–b20.

32. See also Plato, *Republic*, 509e–511e.

33. Descartes, *Discourse on the Method*, trans. Donald A. Cress (Indianap 1980), part 4, *in princ.*; see also *Meditations on First Philosophy*, Second Meditation, opening paragraph.

34. Charles Péguy grasps this point very keenly, it seems to me, when concerning Descartes he writes: "And perhaps his greatest invention and novelty and his greatest stroke of genius and strength is to have pursued his thought deliberately as an action." "Note sur M. Bergson et la philosophie bergsonienne," *Oeuvres en prose*, 1909–1914 (Paris, 1961), 1336.

35. See Hegel, *Lectures on the History of Philosophy*, trans. E. S. Haldane and Frances H. Simson (Atlantic Highlands, N.J., 1983), vol. 3, 217; and *Encyclopedia*, paras. 64 and 76.

36. Descartes, *Discourse on the Method*, part 2.

37. Descartes, *Meditations on First Philosophy*, trans. Donald A. Kress (Indianapolis, 1979), Second Meditation.

38. "Souverän ist, wer über den Ausnahmezustand entscheidet." This is the opening sentence of the first edition of Carl Schmitt's *Politische Theologie* (1922).

39. Descartes, *Meditations on First Philosophy*, First Meditation, *in fine*.

40. Descartes, *Meditations on First Philosophy*, Third Meditation. Spinoza will take the idea of God as his sole starting point.

41. To the contrary, the most authoritative theologians emphasized that the existence of God was not evident. See Aquinas, *Summa Theologiae*, Ia, q. 2, a. 1; and *Summa contra Gentiles*, bk. 1, chaps. 10 and 11.

42. See Allan Bloom, "The Education of Democratic Man: *Émile*," in *Daedalus* 107:3 (Summer 1978): 135–53; *Love and Friendship* (New York, 1993), chap. 1, part 1.

43. Karl Marx, *On the Jewish Question*, in *The Marx-Engels Reader*, ed. Robert Tucker (New York, 1972), 43.

44. 42. Marx, *On the Jewish Question*, in *The Marx-Engels Reader*, 31.

45. G. E. Lessing, *The Education of the Human Race*, paras. 80 to 85.

46. See Rousseau, *Émile*, bk. 4. See also *Rousseau juge de Jean-Jacques*, Third Dialogue.

47. This is in sum the sole theme of the second part of *Democracy in America*.

48. 46. Nietzsche, *Thus Spoke Zarathustra*, Prologue, sec. 5. See the commentary of Martin Heidegger in *What Is Called Thinking?*, part 1, secs. 6 to 8.

49. See Plato, *Gorgias*, 503d–505d, 506c–508e; and *Protagoras*, 313a–314b.

CHAPTER VI

THE END OF NATURE

1. See Rousseau, *Social Contract*, bk. 1, chaps. 6 and 8.

2. See Aristotle, *Politics*, 1277b7–32.

3. See Jean Bodin, *Six Books on the Commonwealth*, bk. 6, chap. 4.

4. See Montaigne, *Essays*, bk. 1, chap. 3.

5. See Aristotle, *Politics*, 1287b16ff. and 1292133ff.

6. See Aristotle, *Politics*, 1254a17–1255a2.

7. See Rousseau, *On the Social Contract*, Geneva Manuscript, bk. 2, chap. 4.

8. Friedrich Nietzsche, *Beyond Good and Evil*, trans. Walter Kaufmann (New York, 1966), no. 199.

9. See Immanuel Kant, *On the Proverb: That may be true in theory, but is of no practical use*, concluding corollary, in *Perpetual Peace and Other Essays*, trans. Ted Humphrey (Indianapolis, 1983), 77–83; and *Metaphysical First Principles of the Doctrine of Right*, par. 46 and General Remark A, in *Metaphysics of Morals*, trans. Mary Gregor (Cambridge, 1991), 125–26 and 129–33.

10. Kant, *Critique of Practical Reason*, trans. Lewis White Beck (New York, 1956), 76 and 79.

11. See Kant, *Critique of Practical Reason*, 33.

12. Kant, *Critique of Practical Reason*, 45.

13. See Kant, *Foundations of the Metaphysics of Morals*, trans. Lewis White Beck (Indianapolis, 1959), 39.

14. "Yet by this same nature of ours (if we wish in general so to term that which is innate), as beings endowed with reason and freedom, this happiness is far from being first, nor indeed is it unconditionally an object of our maxims; rather this object is worthiness to be happy, i.e., the agreement of all our maxims with the moral law." Kant, *Religion Within the Limits of Reason Alone*, trans. Theodore M. Greene and Hoyt H. Hudson (New York, 1960), 41–42.

15. See Kant, *Religion Within the Limits of Reason Alone*, 42 and 38.

16. Kant, *Religion Within the Limits of Reason Alone*, 38.

17. See Thomas Aquinas, *Summa Theologiae*, I–II, q. 89, a. 6.

18. Kant, *Religion Within the Limits of Reason Alone*, 52.

19. G.W.F. Hegel, *Phenomenology of the Mind*, VI, C, a and b.

20. See Kant, *Perpetual Peace*, First Supplement.

21. See Hobbes, *Leviathan*, chap. 29.

22. See note 25 of chap. 1.

23. Hobbes, *Leviathan*, chap. 12, *in fine*.

24. Thus the interest his contemporaries took in the course of the French revolution seemed to Kant to provide convincing proof of the "moral disposition" of humanity. And empirical observation supports, or does not contradict, the idea of "indefinite progress." See section 6 of this chapter.

25. See Kant, *Critique of Practical Reason*, part 1, bk. 2, chap. 5.

26. "It is also not to be understood that the assumption of the existence of God is necessary as a ground of all obligation in general (for this rests, as has been fully shown, solely on the autonomy of reason itself)." Kant, *Critique of Practical Reason*, 130.

27. Kant, *Critique of Practical Reason*, 130.

28. "Act as though the maxim of your action were by your will to become a universal law of nature." Kant, *Foundations of the Metaphysics of Morals*, 39.

29. Kant, *Foundations of the Metaphysics of Morals*, 40.

30. Kant, *Foundations of the Metaphysics of Morals*, 41.

31. See Kant, *Metaphysical First Principles of the Doctrine of Virtue*, bk. 1, chap. 2, par. 9, "On Lying," in *The Metaphysics of Morals* 225–27.

32. See Montaigne, *Essays*, bk. 3, chap. 8.

33. See Thomas Aquinas, *Summa Theologiae*, I–II, q. 90, a. 1.

34. See Aquinas, *Summa Theologiae*, I–II, q. 17, a. 1.

35. ". . . good is the first thing that falls under the apprehension of the practical reason, which is directed to action: since every agent acts for an end under the aspect of good. Consequently the first principle in the practical reason is one founded on the notion of good, viz., that good is that which all things seek after. Hence this is the first precept of law, that good is to be done and pursued, and evil is to be avoided. All other precepts of the natural law are based upon this. . . ." Aquinas, *Summa Theologiae*, I–II, q. 94, a. 2, trans. Fathers of the English Dominican Province (New York, 1947).

36. "Moreover, the expression *sub ratione boni* is also ambiguous. For it can mean: we represent something to ourselves as good, if and because we desire (will) it. Or it can mean: we desire something, because we represent it to ourselves as

good. Thus either the desire is the determining ground of the concept of the object as a good or the concept of the good is the determining ground of desire (will). In the first case, *sub ratione boni* would mean: we will someting under the idea of the good; and in the second: we will something in consequence of this idea, which must precede volition as its determining ground." Kant, *Critique of Practical Reason*, 61, note 2.

37. Kant, *Critique of Practical Reason*, 20ff.

38. Friedrich Nietzsche, *The Will to Power*, trans. Walter Kaufmann and R. J. Hollingdale (New York, 1967), Preface, par. 2.

39. Kant, *Critique of Practical Reason*, 76.

40. See Aristotle, *Nicomachean Ethics*, 1123b–1125a17.

41. Aquinas, *Summa Theologiae*, II–II, q. 129, a. 3.

42. See Aquinas, *Summa Theologiae*, II–II, q. 129, a. 6.

43. See John 12:25 and 15:18–19.

44. See Luke 10:21 and 1 Corinthians 1:17–31.

45. See Aquinas, *Summa Theologiae*, II–II, q. 161, a. 1.

46. "I now began to realize that in no wise would you have given such surpassing authority throughout the whole world to that Scripture. . . ." Augustine, *Confessions*, trans. John K. Ryan (Garden City, N.Y., 1960), bk. 6, chap. 5. "[W]hat could be found more striking than this historical record, which has taken possession of the whole world by its towering authority; or what more worthy of belief. . . ?" Augustine, *The City of God*, trans. Henry Bettenson (Hammondsworth, 1972), bk. 10, chap. 32.

47. Matthew 11:29.

48. See Galatians 3:28.

49. See Aquinas, *Summa Theologiae*, I–II, q. 113, a. 10.

50. See Aquinas, *Summa Theologiae*, I–II, q. 110, a. 2.

51. *Naturam expelles furca, tamen usque recurret*. ("You may drive out nature with a pitchfork, yet she will ever hurry back.") Horace, *Epist.* I, 10, 24, in *Satires, Epistles, Ars Poetica*, trans. H. Rushton Fairclough (Cambridge, Mass., 1955), 317.

52. Stéphane Mallarmé, "Hamlet," in *Oeuvres complètes* (Paris, 1945), 300.

53. ". . . no empire followed after the Roman Empire that might have endured and in which the world might have kept its virtue together. . . ." Niccolo Machiavelli, *Discourses on Livy*, bk. 2, Preface, trans. Harvey C. Mansfield and Nathan Tarcov (Chicago, 1996), 124.

Index